Ethiopia
The Challenge of Democracy
from Below

Edited by

Bahru Zewde and Siegfried Pausewang

Nordiska Afrikainstitutet, Uppsala
and
Forum for Social Studies, Addis Ababa

Indexing terms
Democratisation
Governance
Local government
Traditional authority
Peasantry
Land reform
Political power
Ethiopia

Cover photo: Jørn Stjerneklar/PHOENIX

Language checking: Elaine Almén

@ the authors, Nordiska Afrikainstitutet and Forum for Social Studies, 2002

ISBN 91-7106-501-6

Printed in Sweden by Elanders Gotab, Stockholm, 2002

Contents

IV. ALTERNATIVE VOICES

Preface

The Forum for Social Studies (FSS) is an independent, non-profit policy research institution formally established in 1998. It is the first institution in Ethiopia actively engaged in promoting public awareness about the development challenges facing the country and the need for the democratization of public policy making. Its main activities consist of organizing public debates, undertaking policy analysis, conducting research on development and related issues and disseminating widely the findings of such research. FSS is part of the growing body of civil society institutions that, since the fall of the Derg, the military government that ruled the country until 1991, has been actively engaged in grassroots development, advocacy, and public education and consciousness raising. In the short time since it was established, it has published a number of works on rural development, public access to information, the independent press, the environment and natural resource management, food security and poverty reduction.

This book is the result of a collaborative venture, launched in the second half of 1998, between FSS and the Chr. Michelsen Institute with funding from the Norwegian Foreign Ministry. It was the first joint effort for FSS and since then we have had several successful ventures with overseas institutions. At that time, FSS was struggling due to lack of funding and recognition, and the proposal for a collaborative project, which was brought to us by Siegfried Pausewang, seemed to be a vote of confidence in the young organization. The initial agreement was for FSS to commission a number of research undertakings on the broad theme of democratization in Ethiopia and to use the findings of the research as a basis for a public debate involving government officials, civil society groups, the business community, professionals and the media. As it turned out, the workshop, which was held in January 2000, brought together a much wider diversity of papers than originally anticipated, stimulating more critical debate and keen interest. In a way, the book is a collaboration not only between two institutions but between Ethiopian researchers on the one hand and Norwegian students of Ethiopia on the other. It is interesting that while the subjects addressed by many of the researchers are different, the careful reader of the book will not fail to notice an underlying consensus running through all of the chapters. FSS is fortunate to have played an important role in bringing together Norwegian and Ethiopian researchers and providing them an open forum for discussion.

FSS hopes the book will stimulate further research and debate on the democratization process in Ethiopia where, as Bahru has aptly noted in the Introduction, the burden of history lies so heavy and where the basic institutions of democratic order are struggling to emerge. The book will be useful to a wide reading audience, and in Ethiopia in particular, professionals, development practitioners, readers with interest in the emerging civic institutions, and students in institutions of higher education will find it interesting and challenging.

I would like to take this opportunity to thank Siegfried Pausewang who initiated the original collaborative idea, Øyvind Aadland who was instrumental in activating the project when it was flagging, and the Norwegian Foreign Ministry for providing the funds.

Dessalegn Rahmato
Manager, Forum for Social Studies

A Note on Ethiopian Words and Names

The transcription of Ethiopian words and the use of Ethiopian names in an alphabetical list frequently cause misunderstandings. In this book we have agreed on the following general rules:

Following Ethiopian practice and the logic of names, Ethiopian names are not inverted in the references in this book. In an alphabetical list together with European names, Ethiopians thus appear under their first names. Any other order creates confusion for the following three reasons.

— The second name is not a family name, but the first name of the father; often a third name is added, which is the first name of the grandfather.
— Secondly, Ethiopian names frequently consist of two words—such as Haile Mariam or Tekle Haimanot. To list, for example, Gabriel Haile Mariam as Mariam, Gabriel H. makes absolutely no sense. His father was not called Mariam, but Haile Mariam, which means the power of St. Mary.
— Thirdly, women do not change their names when they marry. The second name of a woman, whether she is married or not, is thus always her father's and not her husband's name; addressing her with her husband's name would be meaningless.

The plural form of Ethiopian words has caused some headaches. While some authors use the singular form of Ethiopian words also for the plural, others write the Amharic plural form in the English text. Unfortunately, the reader who is not acquainted with Amharic might take "woredawotch" for a different word not recognising it as the plural form of a "woreda". We decided nevertheless to accept both forms, but not to tolerate an (English) plural-s attached to an Ethiopian word, (several "kebele" or "kebelewotch", but not "kebeles").

Ethiopian words in the texts are transliterated and printed in italics, except for generally used names, geographic and ethnic terms, such as Addis Ababa or Amhara.

Transliteration is, however, rarely consistent. There is no scientific system with exact rules for representation of Amharic sounds in the Latin alphabet. The two or three systems that have been created are frequently not followed in everyday use. Even those scholars who use them are not consistent. Moreover, there is considerable divergence in the spelling, particularly of place names. Some scholars are used to a transliteration which they consider an exact and consistent transcription from an admittedly less consistent Amharic spelling. Some thus insist on writing Shäwa, while others prefer to spell the region Shewa or Shawa; others spell it as Shoa. We have decided in this book to respect the authors' transliteration preferences, and hence have refrained from attempting a consistency which would be artificial in any case.

100 Ethiopian Birr is equivalent to 12 USD (Sept. 2002).

Introduction

Bahru Zewde

As the 1960s dawned, Africa re-entered the world stage resplendent in its colours of independence and loaded with promise and hope. With an array of intellectual leaders of global stature (Kwame Nkrumah of Ghana, Léopold Sedar Senghor of Senegal, Nnamdi Azikiwe of Nigeria, and Julius Nyerere of Tanzania, to name only four of them), the sky appeared to be the limit to the continent's potential for progress and development. Yet, before the decade was out, the promise and hope had been replaced by despondency and gloom. A series of military coups littered the landscape. In many ways, the giant nation Nigeria epitomized both the hope and the gloom. Home of a rich and variegated culture, its very diversity appeared to spell its doom as it was locked in one of the bloodiest civil wars the world has ever known. Thereafter, for something like three decades, military rule of various hues and colours appeared to be its prescribed fate. Elsewhere in Africa, too, dictatorship of one kind or another was the norm rather than the exception. This ranged from the atavistic empire of Bokassa of the Central African Republic, the murderous regime of Idi Amin of Uganda and the proverbially venal order of Mobutu of Zaire to the totalitarian dictatorship of Mengistu Haile Mariam of Ethiopia.

A "wind of change" started blowing on the African continent in the late 1980s and early 1990s. As the Cold War came to an end, most of the authoritarian regimes lost the external props that had sustained them. The East could no longer bail out the dictatorships with "socialist" pretensions. The West no longer saw the need to prop up corrupt and dictatorial regimes as bulwarks of anti-communism. At the same time, a movement from below (whether in the form of urban mass movements or rural guerrilla warfare) rendered dictatorial regimes into untenable propositions. Battered from inside and shunned from outside, these dictatorial regimes collapsed one after another like a row of dominoes (Hyslop, 1999: 1–3). "Democratisation" became the rallying cry that united internal campaigners for political liberalization as well as external donors.

Yet, how exactly that "democratisation" is to be achieved has been the great challenge of the past decade. There is far from consensus on that point. Drawing on Western models, multi-partyism, along with the interlinked institution of parliamentary democracy, has been a generally preferred medium. But, the experience of quite a few countries has revealed that those two institutions do not necessarily guarantee democratic governance. In other words, one-party rule could flourish beneath the façade of multi-party politics and a parliamentary system. Partly in reaction to this, Yoweri Museveni's National Resistance Movement (NRM) in Uganda, which had toppled the dictatorial regime of Obote II, has openly eschewed the hallowed principle of multi-party democracy and opted instead for fostering plurality of views within the Movement (Bazaara 2000: 4–5). This procedure has earned it the label of "movementocracy" from some of its critics.

A slightly more innovative approach to democratisation has been the fostering of civil society organizations and the guaranteeing of human rights. The West has come to make these two developments important conditionalities for financial support as well as for certification of good governance. Partly induced by this external stimulation and partly generated by internal forces, there has been a mushrooming of civil society organizations (CSOs) throughout the continent in the 1990s. The importance attached to these organizations is such that the ECA set up what has come to be known as the African Centre for Civil Society (ACCS) in 1997 with the view to strengthening CSOs (Amoako, 2000: 145). And yet, there is not always agreement on what the components of civil society exactly are in the African context. In general, however, the focus has been on such organizations as trade unions, peasant cooperatives, youth/student organizations, professional associations, the non-government media, NGOs and advocacy groups. These organizations, as distinct from the formal institutions of governance such as parliament and the judiciary, are believed to foster a deepening and broadening of democratic governance through grass-roots participation. One should not, however, adopt a linear vision of CSOs as invariably benign. The anti-democratic potentialities of some CSOs have been evidenced in their buttressing of apartheid in South Africa (Lowe, 1999: 415) and the nefarious role that the media played before and during the 1994 genocide in Rwanda.

Yet another modality for broad-based democratisation has been the revival and adaptation of traditional systems of governance. While the concept of a universal form of African village democracy is probably too idyllic, it is nonetheless true that traditional forms of governance often permitted a greater degree of popular participation than could be said for many of the formal parliamentary democracies of today. Even in chiefly and monarchical systems, they represented a source of authority that competed vigorously and often successfully with modern political forms. Hence the tendency, particularly in southern Africa, to foster a system of what has come to be known as "mixed government", combining the traditional and the modern and including the insertion of constitutional provisions for customary authorities.

In Botswana, for instance, public policies are discussed in traditional public gatherings before they are adopted nationally. The Namibian constitution provides for a national "Council of Traditional Leaders", which is consulted by the president in matters pertaining to control and utilisation of rural land. In South Africa, the ANC in the early 1990s mobilized traditional rulers for constitutional reform through the Congress of Traditional Leaders while its rival, the Inkatha Freedom Party, likewise used the Zulu kingship for its political aims. The interim constitution of 1993 provided for the establishment of "Houses of Traditional Leaders" in the provinces and an advisory "Council of Traditional Leaders" at the national level. One should also note in this regard the recent efforts in Uganda to revive the Baganda monarchy (Sklar, 1999: 115–119).

What these experiments in blending the traditional and modern suggest is an appreciation of both the potentialities and limitations of traditional institutions of governance. Richard Sklar's conclusion in this respect is sober and apposite:

The existence of a multitude of vibrant "second" dimensions of political authority, organised by traditional rulers, their councillors and customary courts, should not be idealised as a continental school for democracy. However, the African bedrock of traditional political identity could prove to be a relatively stable foundation upon which to construct new and experimental governments, including constitutional democracies. Conversely, the second dimensions will surely change in response to the influence of democratic thought and practice in the sovereign states.

One reason why one should not idealize such customary norms is because, more often than not, they tend to marginalize women and minority groups. The roots of female oppression are to be sought as much in custom and tradition as in economics and politics. Even when women's rights are guaranteed legally, the weight of tradition militates against the full exercise of those rights. And society cannot be said to be fully liberated until and unless women are given their fair share of political and economic space.

The African democratisation exercise faces even more daunting challenges in the economic and political sphere. Globalisation, along with its handmaiden SAP, far from solving the continent's problems, has compounded its woes. Only a handful of African countries can boast of an economic record that gives some hope for the future. As if the chronic economic problems from which the continent has suffered are not enough, disease (whether it be in the form of the old enemy, malaria, or the new pandemic, HIV/AIDS) is ravaging the continent and wiping out the most productive sectors of its population. Moreover, conflict has become almost synonymous with the continent. These conflicts might arise from scarcity of resources (as in Somalia and Rwanda) or their plenitude, particularly in the availability of precious metals (as in Sierra Leone or Democratic Republic of the Congo). Ironically, the democratisation process has sometimes tended to aid and abet conflicts rather than to reduce them (as happened in Rwanda before the genocide and in Somalia after the fall of the dictatorial Siad Barre).

Africa thus faces enormous challenges in instituting a viable and meaningful democratic order. True, Africa is not alone in encountering such challenges. Even in the established democracies of the West, the customary norms of governance are being given a jolt from one country to another. Voter apathy engendered by disenchantment with the conventional political alignments has provided a perfect breeding ground for movements of the extreme right. There is no better indication of this trend than the international panic generated by the recent successes of the Popular Front in the first round of the French presidential elections.

In Africa, while there have been encouraging signs of the smooth and popular transfer of power (as in Senegal in 1999 and Ghana in 2001), other transitions have been punctuated by social spasms of considerable cost and tribulation (as in Côte d'Ivoire in 2001). The big question now is whether the new millennium is going to bring something more positive for Africa; or, in World Bank parlance, whether Africa can "claim" the 21st century" (World Bank, 2000). That seems to require not only "Determined Leadership" but also creative, pragmatic and responsible leadership that is ready to adopt the requisite policies to rid the continent of the triple affliction of economic underdevelopment, disease, and conflict. Above all, it requires designing a system that is conducive to listening to the people rather than dictating over them.

When we turn our attention to the geographical focus of this anthology, the general continental observations that we have made above have considerable pertinence. The Ethiopian state has endured considerable vicissitudes since its genesis some two millenia back. At times, it has expanded; at other times, it has contracted. It has changed its loci on a number of occasions. Its component units have also altered with time. But three epochs stand out as formative periods for the evolution of the central political institution: the Aksumite (lasting roughly from the first to the eighth centuries AD), the medieval period (c. 1270–1527) and the modern (1855–1974). All three periods saw the monarchy at the height of its power and the empire enjoying varying degrees of territorial extension. The monarch exercised considerable powers over life and property. This included a good deal of tributary authority over that most vital of properties, land. Contributing to the authoritarian power that the monarchs thus came to enjoy was the absence of a hereditary nobility.

Yet, this power of the monarch should not be overdrawn. As we shall see below, it was tempered by a number of factors. Although a medieval emperor like Zara Ya'eqob (r. 1434–1468) could unleash a veritable reign of terror over his subjects in the name of religious orthodoxy, absolutism, in the strict sense of the word, was a recent phenomenon (Bahru, 1984). Its genesis is to be traced to the greater opportunities that closer interaction with the West provided and the consummate (not to say Machiavellian) skills of Emperor Haile Sellassie (r. 1930–1974). He succeeded where his more charismatic predecessor, Tewodros (r. 1855–1868) had failed, i.e.in establishing a centralized monarchy.

The picture of a centralized monarchy that one often encounters in the literature is thus far from accurate. The prevalent picture—in all the three epochs outlined above—has been more of a decentralized monarchy rather than a centralized one. More often than not, emperors recognized the prerogatives of local strongmen or regional dynasties. In very rare instances did they for instance appoint their own men as provincial governors. Even Tewodros, contrary to his general characterization as a centralizing monarch, often deferred to regional power (as was evidenced in his appointment policy particularly in Tegre and Shawa). His successors, Yohannes and Menilek, pursued what was tantamount to a federal policy. Imperial authority was exercised through the annual collection of tribute rather than by means of direct intervention in local administration.

This picture changed significantly under Haile Sellassie. With the exception of those of Tegray and Wallaga, all provincial governors became imperial appointees. This affected both the components of the classic Ethiopian state, like Gojjam and Wallo, and the newly incorporated but thitherto autonomous entities like Jimma Abba Jiffar. Interrupted by the Italian occupation (1936–1941), this process picked up even greater momentum with the restoration of imperial power in 1941. A tightly centralized system of provincial administration, directly controlled from the Ministry of the Interior in Addis Ababa, was instituted soon after. In spite of some change of nomenclature (such as replacing the title taqlay gazh or governor-general with endarase or representative), the system remained in force until the 1974 Revolution.

Nay, it assumed an even more total dimension under the Derg that came to power riding on the wave of that popular upsurge. Although the somewhat authoritarian designation of taqlay gezat (governorate-general) was replaced by the more benign one of kefla hagar (region), this semantic nuance belied the tighter control that the Derg came to exercise at even the village level, let alone the provincial one. While the urban and rural neighbourhood associations facilitated that control earlier on in the game, the formation of the Workers' Party of Ethiopia (WPE) in 1984, and the mass organizations set up in the name of various sectors of the society (peasants, youth, and women) enhanced it considerably. There emerged in due course two parallel hierarchies, the administrative and the party ones, with the balance of power unmistakably tilted towards the latter. Only towards its demise, in the course of establishing the People's Democratic Republic of Ethiopia (PDRE) in 1987, did the Derg make any concession to regional sentiment by establishing a number of autonomous regions. Even that concession, as Mehret Ayenew's study in this collection shows, was instituted out of an effort (ultimately futile) to contain or placate dissidence—both actual and potential—rather than out of a genuine conviction in devolution.

The picture changed dramatically with the coming to power of the Ethiopian People's Revolutionary Democratic Front (EPRDF) in 1991. The global situation dictated abiding by the canon of democratic governance. Its own long-standing commitment to the principle of national self-determination almost inexorably led the EPRDF to adopt ethnic federalism as the bedrock of that governance. Initiated in 1992 during the tenure of the Transitional Government of Ethiopia (TGE), this creation of autonomous regions based on linguistic affiliation was formalized with the adoption of a new constitution in 1995 and the subsequent establishment of the Federal Democratic Republic of Ethiopia (FDRE). A cardinal element of that constitution has been a contentious article that guaranteed the principle of self-determination of nationalities up to and including secession. These moves were accompanied by measures of political liberalization, of which the guaranteeing of freedom of the press, at any rate at the formal level, has been perhaps the most conspicuous.

However, the tension between the formal and actual, between declaration and implementation, rhetoric and reality, remains a palpable one. While such tension is perceptible in other African countries that have adopted the path of democratization, it is bound to be more pronounced in a country like Ethiopia, where the weight of tradition (the "burden of history") lies so heavy. A number of questions thus present themselves: How much does the regime honour its own hallowed principle of self-determination? Are the voices of the peasants, in whose name above all this second revolution was waged, heard? How much space is civil society allowed in the whole arrangement? How significantly, if at all, has the lot of women changed in reality? How free is the press? And, no less important, how much interest and enthusiasm does it actually generate? In short, what does the democratization process look like at the grass-roots level? What is the view from below?

It is to address such questions that the Forum for Social Studies, in cooperation with the Christian Michelsen Institute, brought together a group of Ethiopian and Norwegian scholars and researchers in a workshop on 24–25 January 2000. A number of papers—some of them commissioned—were presented in that workshop investigating these issues. The papers explored a wide range of topics—from traditional modes of governance to the issue of decentralization, from the generally unrecorded political commentaries of the urban and rural population to the vociferous denunciations of the private media, from peasant participation—or lack of it—in environmental management, elections and land re-distribution to the political space of various segments of civil society. This book is the result of those deliberations.

Although, as outlined above, the classic Ethiopian polity has been characterized by a heavy dosage of authoritarianism, this should not give the impression that the state exercised total control over society. Even within the core, common people enjoyed an appreciable degree of proprietary and judiciary rights. Peasants in much of northern Ethiopia had usufructory right over plots of land that they could claim on the basis of their lineage. This right gave peasants a legal status and, despite their tributary obligations to the state, an independent economic base. Also, the lowest subject could appeal to the sovereign in quest of legal redress. The commoners could also chide and sneer at the big shots, as well as expressing their own predicaments, through jokes and anecdotes that conveniently eliminated accountability by virtue of their anonymity. Rulers are known to have consciously sought out such political commentaries as salutary reminders of their foibles and the vulnerability of the system they had erected. The jokes and the couplets that are treated by Fekade Azeze in this collection thus have a long pedigree.

In the peripheral areas, there was an even higher degree of grassroots participation in governance, or what in contemporary parlance could be characterized as participatory democracy. The most celebrated of this is the Oromo gada system, whereby male members of the community were groomed for positions of political and military leadership. Although that institution has not been able to withstand the stresses and pressures of time, it has not completely disappeared and is portrayed as a model of adapted forms of democracy in contemporary political discourse. An even more resilient system of local governance, known under the generic name of sera, has been prevalent among other Cushitic-speaking peoples of southern Ethiopia and among the Semitic-speaking Gurage. The contributions by Oyvind Aadland, Bahru Zewde and Yacob Arsano investigate the genesis, evolution and contemporary relevance of that system.

While such traditional institutions have been essentially rural-based (though the sera in recent years has had remarkable resonance among the urban Gurage), various segments of civil society have been performing a somewhat similar role in the urban setting. As in the rest of Africa, what exactly constitutes civil society as well as its indigenous and/or exogenous origins has been a matter of some debate in Ethiopia. Dessalegn Rahmato tackles this theoretical issue in the introductory part of his contribution. It is perhaps difficult to dispute the relatively recent expansion of civil society organizations (CSOs). Two factors have played an important role in that process: the greater space that the democratization process has given them and the interest—not necessarily disinterested—that the donor community has shown in encouraging that development.

Nevertheless, it is possible to point to some antecedents of the current CSOs, a number of them tracing their origin to pre-Revolution days. These include the eder (self-help association), the equb (credit association), the ethnic development associations that mushroomed in the last days of the imperial regime, and organizations like trade unions and chambers of commerce as well as some of the professional associations. The imperial regime considered one of those ethnic development associations—the Mecha-Tulama Self-Help Association—such a threat to its security that it resorted to the execution or incarceration of some of its leaders and the subsequent banning of all associations of that genre. The association was briefly revived in the post-1991 climate that has been so conducive to ethnic self-expression, although some of its prominent members again ended up being incarcerated, possibly because of association with the Oromo Liberation Front (OLF). It is worthy of note that, originally, although it had an Oromo origin, the association had a number of non-Oromo, particularly from southern Ethiopia, in its membership.

It is perhaps the advocacy organizations like Ethiopian Women Lawyers' Association (EWLA) and the Ethiopian Human Rights Council (EHRCO) that belong strictly to the post-1991 period. Original Wolde Giorgis gives us a sample of the kind of activities conducted by EWLA while Dessalegn deals with the fate of EHRCO, as well as providing a panoramic view of all the important CSOs and their relations, not infrequently troubled, with the state. Gender discourse in Ethiopia could be said to have barely begun. As such, it is still at the stage where the all-important thing is the liberation of women from legal and social oppression. Nevertheless, there is perceptible progress from imperial times, when women were perceived as objects of philanthropy, and the Derg period, when their primary value became mobilization in furtherance of government and party objectives.

Another relatively new addition to the civil society landscape has been the nongovernmental organizations (NGOs). They had their genesis in the droughts and famines that have captured so much international attention since the early 1970s. Originally, their provenance was essentially foreign. Of late, the indigenous NGOs have attained a level of near parity in number, though there is still a wide gap in the resources they can muster. Over time, too, NGOs have shifted the thrust of their activity from famine relief to development, ranging from the building of infrastructure to environmental protection. Given their legal restriction to famine relief and development, they have perhaps not been as vigorous in promoting the empowerment of the lower orders of society, a situation that has provoked the sharp critique in Kassahun Berhanu's article.

Probably the most visible manifestation of popular participation in post-1991 Ethiopia has been in the sphere of the printed media. Although the FM radio recently introduced has represented a noticeable advance in the dissemination of the views of the common people, it, like all electronic broadcasting, remains a government monopoly. Three periods stand out as moments of relatively greater freedom of the press in the twentieth century history of the country. The first was in the 1920s, when, under the benevolent patronage of the then progressive Ras Tafari Makonnen (the future Emperor Haile Sellassie), a group of intellectuals freely aired their views in favour of change and reform in the columns of the prince's weekly, Berhanena Salam ("Light and Peace"). This free atmosphere did not survive the consolidation of political power by the patron after 1930. Then, in the early years of the Revolution, roughly from February 1974, when the popular upsurge began, to January 1977, when Mengistu's dictatorship was inaugurated, there was an almost uninhibited discussion of national issues, with various individuals and groups advancing their respective recipes for social transformation.

In both periods, the discussion took place within the framework of a government-owned press. What distinguishes the post-1991 period, which is the third period of relatively free expression, is the proliferation of private papers. This, as Shimelis Bonsa's study shows, has not been without its problems. Not only have the owners and editors of the papers been the victims of sustained government harassment under the cover of a restrictive press law, but they themselves have also not shown the highest standards of journalism in the execution of their task. The perfect balance between government tolerance and professional responsibility—two important pre-conditions for the thriving of a free press—has thus remained elusive. The financial viability of most of the papers is also highly problematical. These circumstances have engendered a considerably high attrition rate. But, despite the obvious problems and shortcomings, the private press has contributed significantly to the emergence of a situation far removed and improved from the monolithic picture that had prevailed in the Imperial and Derg eras.

Ultimately, in a country like Ethiopia, the test of a genuine democratization process is how far and how much it has come to involve the peasants, who constitute the overwhelming majority of the population. Are they consulted in matters that affect their livelihood? Or, even better, do the policies and measures of environmental management as well as the production-distribution system emanate from them? Do they have the opportunity to choose their leaders in a truly democratic manner? Or are they just manipulated to cast their votes for the group that happens to be in power? While, as discussed above, rural communities are known to have set up—parallel with elements of the state structure—their own institutions for self-help and the administration of justice, their part in the sphere of national governance has been peripheral at best. The three contributions by Harald Aspen, Svein Ege and Siegfried Pausewang help us to understand what the view is from the lowest level but also from where it really matters in the end, that is the world of the peasant.

What this anthology hopes to project is, therefore, the importance of a grassroots approach to democratization. There may not be much novelty in this approach. But the various contributions have, we hope, succeeded in analyzing in depth the various strands of the argument. While not disputing the value and importance of good leadership, it has to be emphasized that democratic governance can be ensured only when the people whose lives are affected are integrally part of it. The lower orders of society need not be reified and the higher ones completely denigrated. The local need not be fetishized at the expense of the national. But, particularly in a society where values and systems have had a habit of being imposed from above, the view from below represents a salutary corrective. In the end, however, a healthy and dialectical nexus of the two levels is crucial to achieve genuine mass participation, the empowerment of the people in the broad sense of that term and the fostering of good governance.

I

Traditional Systems
of Governance

Systems of Local Governance among the Gurage

The *Yajoka Qicha* and the *Gordanna Sera*

Bahru Zewde

Introduction

The failure of parliamentary democracy in Africa has forced a fresh look at traditional or pre-colonial systems of governance. It is argued that for the continent to emerge out of the vicious cycle of military dictatorship and corrupt civilian regimes, it has to re-examine its traditional political systems, revitalize them and make them pertinent for contemporary application. One person who has argued eloquently and passionately along these lines is Basil Davidson. His earlier exuberance about Africa's achievements dampened by the dismal record of post-Independence Africa in the political as well as the economic fields, he was forced to delve into the continent's pre-colonial past to discover more viable institutions than the ones—including the nation-state—spawned by colonial rule. He sums up the factors that made pre-colonial African states durable in the following words:

> These precolonial societies, or those that endured for centuries and were successful in mastering their historical process, and about which we consequently know a good deal, were centrally concerned in securing and sustaining their legitimacy in the eyes of their peoples. They endured because they were accepted. And they were accepted because their rules of operation were found to be sufficiently reasonable in providing explanation, and sufficiently persuasive in extracting obedience. What this says, in tremendous contrast with times during and after colonialism, is that these communities achieved *an accountability of rulers to ruled and, quite persistently, the other way round as well* (Davidson, 1992:87–88; emphasis added).

Such viable institutions were killed successively by colonialism and the independent African states. Colonial rule destroyed or downgraded these viable pre-colonial institutions which in their own way had provided modes of democratic governance. The post-colonial African political culture has been bedevilled by the twin vices of military dictatorship and clientelism. The solution, Davidson argues, is to be found in the devolution of "executive power to a multiplicity of locally representative bodies" (294). Only then can one have the genuine mass participation that generates the kind of state "that would be able to protect and promote civil society" (295).

In his seminal work, *Citizen and Subject*, Mahmood Mamdani gives a more elaborate analysis of the colonial impact on pre-colonial institutions. No attempt will be made here to discuss in detail this highly influential work. Instead, the focus will be on his treatment of customary law, a subject that is most germane to this paper. Mamdani highlights the manipulation of customary law under colonial rule. The judicial system established had a bipolar character: "customary justice was dispensed to natives by chiefs and commissioners, black and white; modern justice to non-natives by white magistrates" (Mamdani, 1996: 109). Along with the racialization of justice was its tribalization, for there was no one single customary law but as many customary laws—and a corresponding number of Native Authorities—as there were believed to be tribes. Far from restraining the power of chiefs, customary law under colonial rule "consolidated the non-customary power of chiefs in the colonial administration", bringing thitherto autonomous social domains under their domination (110). Thus, the objectives of colonial administration and colonial economy were served under the guise of enforcing custom.

The anti-colonial movement of the post-World War II period was accompanied by the reform of customary law, involving its codification and the professionalization of legal cadres. The reform ranged from the parallel retention of customary and modern courts with integration at the level of the review process to the establishment of a unified court system by abolishing customary courts. What was ultimately achieved, though, was only the deracialization of the legal system (i.e. the abolition of the separate courts for colonial subjects and metropolitan citizens), not its democratization. Only in the radical states like Ghana and Mozambique was the process accompanied by detribalization.[1]

A more meaningful, yet tentative, effort at applying a traditional institution to a contemporary situation is underway in post-genocide Rwanda. With a view to promoting the twin principles of justice and reconciliation—and perhaps daunted by the overwhelming number of Hutu suspects awaiting trial under the manifestly inadequate Rwandan legal system—the RPF regime has been trying to adapt to current conditions the traditional dispute resolution mechanism known as the gacaca. This is an ad hoc assembly of elders that administers sanctions in a redressive rather than retributive manner, the ultimate aim being to reintegrate the offender into the community and thereby maintain social order and harmony. This experiment, noble as it is, has not been without its problems, however, as the recently released OAU-commissioned report on the Rwanda genocide makes clear. Foremost among the concerns expressed are the danger of the system allowing notorious genocidaires to go scot-free and the worry that the tight political control exercised by the current regime is unlikely to encourage the free and uninhibited discussion that is so essential for the operation of such a system (OAU, 2000: 197–199).

In as much as Ethiopia did not experience European colonial rule, the pertinence of the above comparative insights cannot be taken too literally. However, there was an analgous process of interference with customary institutions after the incorporation of the southern parts of Ethiopia into Menilek's empire. Informants generally speak of the introduction of what they call *balabat* rule under Menilek. But they do not go to the extent of drawing a picture of the manipulation of customary law portrayed by Mamdani. Equally challenging is the question of how far those customary institutions can be made workable in the contemporary world. This is a question which even Davidson finds difficult to answer. The hopes that he tends to pin on the radical liberation movements of the 1970s and 1980s do not seem justified by the march of time, either.

The aim of this chapter is to discuss the system of governance developed over the centuries by the Gurage people of south-western Ethiopia. After a brief general introduction into Gurage society, particularly their political system, a detailed description of their customary law is given. Attention will also be focussed on the process of apparent revitalization that these institutions have experienced since 1991. The paper will conclude with the prospects and constraints of this recent phenomenon. Shortage of time has forced a concentration of the discussion on the two manifestations of this customary mode of governance: the *Yajoka Qicha* of the Sabat Bet Gurage and the *Gordanna Sera* of the Kestane. It has not been possible to examine

---

1.   The author is off the mark when he attributes the codification process in Ethiopia to the Derg (132). The Civil Code which he cites was actually promulgated under the Hayla-Sellase regime and has been in force ever since.

the analogous system among the Selte. But the studies that have been made so far suggest that there has existed among the Selte a comparable system, variously known as *YaSelte Sera, Malga Sera,* and *Dambus.*[1] Likewise, the Masqan have had what is known as *YaFaragazañña Sera* and the Dobi *YaSenana Sera.* As a matter of fact, the Faragazañña Sera of the Masqan has had considerable validity among the Kestane, being sometimes referred to as of equal authority as the Gordanna Sera.

Nor is the *sera* institution confined to the Gurage. A chapter in this collection deals with the Kambatta version of the institution. The institution has also been operative in one form or another among the Walayta, the Gamo and the Gofa of present-day North Omo district.[2] Even more interesting is the existence of a kindred institution, known as the *kwor* among the Anyuaa of the Gambella region, providing for graduated scales of punishment for homicide.[3] The term *sera* (as well as the institution) does indeed seem to have pan-Ethiopian significance, although it has come to have the negative connotation of plot or conspiracy in its Amharic rendering. Indeed, it is worthy of note that the equivalent Gamo term *dulata* has in Amharic the meaning of plot or conspiracy! A standard Amharic dictionary suggests, however, a more positive application of the term: *seran khona,* with the meaning of "agreement was concluded between two different communities", "peace and reconciliation came to prevail".[4]

An Overview of Gurage Society

There is no dearth of literature on the Gurage, although history has noticeably lagged behind linguistics. But, studies of the Gurage have generally suffered from the opposite defects of insulation and extrapolation. Either Gurage units have been studied in isolation or a study of one section of the Gurage has been presented as applicable to all. A number of unpublished theses of the Departments of History and Ethiopian Languages and Literature (AAU) fall into the first category. The supreme example of the latter has been William Shack's classic study (1966), which was actually based on a study of the Chaha—or even one clan of it.[5] Likewise, Gebreyesus Hailemariam's *The Guragué and Their Culture* (1991) deals exclusively with the Sabat Bet. The merit of the recent study of the Gurage that has come under the title of *Gogot* is its attempt to point out the commonalities as well as the peculiarities of the various components of the Gurage.

It is largely on the basis of the much developed linguistic studies that the Gurage have generally been classified into three categories: the Western (i.e. Sabat Bet), the

---

1. See Denbaru Alamu, et al, *Gogot. YaGurage Beherasab Tarik, Bahel-na Qwanqwa* (Walqite, 1987 EC), pp. 124–127; Abraham Hussein and Habtamu Wondimu, *BaSelteñña Qwanqwa Tanagari Hezb Ya'Azarenat Barbara Hebratasab Bahel-na Tarik* (Addis Ababa, n.d.), pp. 41–43. The only discordant note struck by the latter work, which deals only with one section of the Selteñña-speaking people, is the fact that, unlike the case among the Sabat Bet Gurage and the Kestane, it locates the emergence of the *sera* after the decline of the centralized administration established by the legendary ancestor of the Selte, Hajj Aleyu, and suggests that it came to be undermined in the mid-19th century with the emergence of strong men who concentrated power in their hands.
2. For an assembly among the Gamo akin to the sera meeting and known as the *dulata,* see Marc Abélés, "In Search of the Monarch: Introduction of the State among the Gamo of Ethiopia," in Donald Crummey and C.C. Stewart, eds., Modes of Production in Africa: The Precolonial Era (Beverly Hills and London, 1981), pp. 51–53.
3. See Bayleyegn Tasew, "An Anyuaa (Anuak) Myth and Its Implication in 'Kwor'", paper presented at the National Workshop of the Ethiopian chapter of OSSREA (February 2000), pp. 10–19.
4. Kasate-Berhan Tasama, *Ya'Amareñña Mazgaba Qalat* (Addis Ababa, 1951 EC), p. 291.
5. An unnecessarily vituperative critique of his work is to be found in Alemayehu Neri, Asat. *YaGurage Bahel-na Yaltyopya Masaratawi Tarik,* Vol. I (Addis Ababa, 1985 EC).

Northern (i.e. Kestane) and the Eastern (the Selte-speaking cluster). In spite of the strong tradition of their common identity, these are mutually unintelligible categories. While there is not much controversy about the components of the Selte-speaking cluster, who exactly constitute the Sabat Bet Gurage has not always been clear. There is particular lack of clarity about the Gumar, who are sometimes subsumed under Chaha, and the Maqorqor, who are occasionally left out, presumably by reason of their small size. The ones that are consistently cited are: Chaha, Ezha, Ennamor/Ennar, Geta, Muhar and Aklil, and Endagañ. Adjacent to the Kestane and with considerable affinity to them are the Dobi and the Masqan.

What unite the Gurage above all are the *ensat* culture, which they share with a number of southwestern peoples, and the tradition of political fragmentation. It is the latter aspect that interests us in this study. This fragmentation bred a good deal of internecine strife and a high incidence of enslavement. But beneath this apparent fragmentation, there was a system of administration which manifested itself at three levels of authority: the village, the clan or territory (*agar* in Kestane parlance), and the region (Sabat Bet, Kestane, or Selte). Informants tend to believe that it is indeed the state of anarchy that had prevailed earlier that forced the Gurage to set this system of governance. The ultimate result of this process was the promulgation of the sets of laws that are the subject matter of this chapter: the *Yajoka Qicha* and the *Gordanna Sera*.

At the core of both Sabat Bet and Kestane socio-political organizations appear to be the clan or agar assemblies. Shack emphasizes the clan basis of Sabat Bet (more strictly Chaha) political organization, writing of a "political community" centred on the clan, a hereditary clan chieftainship (along the senior male line) and a clan council of elders exercising an advisory role to the chief, whose installation and death are marked by elaborate rituals (Shack, 1966: 145–157). The local name for the chief is not given. But, the two titles that are recurrent among both the Sabat Bet and Kestane are *abagaz* and *azmach*. The authors of *Gogot* describe the *abagaz* as a commander chosen for his military exploits whereas the *azmach* was a hereditary political leader of the community (25–27). Fecadu (1986: 42) maintains that, among the Kestane, both *abagaz* and *azmach*, as well as the *negus*, were elected. Kestane informants claim that *azmach* was a title adopted after incorporation into Menilek's empire; formerly, the title negus was used. But the *negus* was not a hereditary ruler but an official elected by what they term the gabbar and confirmed by the *goyta* and the *simbita*, two hereditary titles whose exact import is far from certain at this stage of my investigation.

Among the Kestane, the lowest unit of organization is the *sabuññat*, consisting of households variously estimated at 9–60 (Fecadu, 1986: 36) or 50–100 (informants). Fecadu gave the figure of 233 such *sabuññat* in the whole of Kestaneland, the number in each agar ranging from four to twenty-six. Administered by elected chairmen, the *sabuññat* exercised social and politico-juridical functions. They catered for funerary gifts and services as well as for weddings of first-born sons, ensured equitable use of grazing lands, arranged for oaths of proper conduct—most significantly on the occasion of the Masqal holiday—and adjudicated in cases of dispute. They administered sanctions ranging from assigning a spiralling number of guests to be dined and wined at the culprit's expense (known as *yekka*) to social ostracism (Fecadu, 1986:37). Transposed to the urban setting, the *sabuññat* became the *edir*, an important social institution that has largely been confined to funerary obligations in its new setting.

The agar administration, which in the rural setting was responsible for a population ranging from 1,000 to 6,000, performed the role of the *sabuññat* at a higher level. It administered the communal lands as well as the churches and adjudicated following the rules laid down by the *Gordanna sera*. Its sanctions likewise ranged from the yekka to ostracism. But the most dreaded sanction, according to Fecadu, was the ultimate curse, *yagar yeen yablaha/yablash* (literally meaning "May the eyes of the agar eat you", a form of invoking the total opprobrium of the community) (Fecadu, 1986:39–41). This might very well have been a verbal expression of the act of ostracization.

Yajoka and Gordanna

Origins

The term *Yajoka* is believed to have been derived from the *zegba (Podocarpus)* tree that serves as the venue of the assembly. The term expresses the special feature of the tree, whose branch (*yaj*, hand) is buried in the ground (yoka) only to sprout again. There is no similar clear etymological explanation for the term *Gordanna*, although some tend to associate it with the wooden pillars of a house, an association that is vehemently rejected by other informants.

With regard to the time of its establishment, Kestane informants show remarkable consensus in tracing it back over six hundred years. For Yajoka, a much shorter stretch of time (about three hundred years) is claimed; Shack reduces the span even further when he writes that it was introduced in the first half of the nineteenth century (1966: 92). Another difference in the two systems has to do with the fact that while certain individuals are credited with the establishment of *Yajoka* (Ajamo Mosaco of Ennamor according to one version, four different individuals according to another), there is no such personal association in the case of *Gordanna*. Instead, the Nuranna *agar* of the Kestane are assigned a central place both in the promulgation and on-going interpretation of the *Gordanna Sera*, which is also known as *Yanjari Sera* after the place in Nuranna (Enjari) where the laws were initially agreed upon.

The circumstances for the initiation of both *Yajoka* and *Gordanna* are also somewhat similar. Particularly among the Sabat Bet, the most important factor that is said to have driven them to set up the *Yajoka* was the state of civil war and political anarchy that had prevailed. Among the Kestane, both internal and external factors are adduced: establishing internal harmony among the warring *agars* and strengthening the Kestane's capacity to defend themselves against external aggression (notably from their Hadiya and Maraqo neighbours, as well as subsequently from the Oromo). At the outset, it was the five houses of Gurage (Chaha, Ezha, Ennamor, Geta and Muhar) who entered into the agreement (Worku, 1983 EC: 36); the two others joined later. Likewise among the Kestane, the initial covenant was entered into by fifteen of the twenty-two or so *agar* who now constitute the Kestane community (YaGordanna, 1986 EC: 12). A notable difference between the two systems, however, can be discerned in the role of religion, which appears to be more pronounced in the case of *Yajoka*. Traditional religion, as embodied in the deities *Waq* and *Damwamit*, feature rather prominently in traditions both of the promulgation and administration of *Yajoka*.

Functions and Procedures

The *Yajoka* and *Gordanna* assemblies seem to combine legislative and judiciary functions. Representatives of the constituent units of the Sabat Bet and the Kestane, respectively, were assembled to agree on the fundamental rules governing their community. Periodic meetings were also held to revise the laws when such revisions were deemed necessary. At the same time the assemblies served as courts of final recourse. In both communities, it is this appellate status of the assemblies (known as Gutache among the Kestane) that tends to be emphasized. Individuals who felt dissatisfied with the ruling of their territorial assembly could invoke their right of appeal with set expressions: *Äjoka Yabare* ("Let the *Yajoka* rule on this case") or *Gefacha* ("I appeal"). According to some sources, confirmation (or otherwise) of a lower verdict by the supreme court was mandatory in all cases, irrespective of appeals being made or not.

Both systems developed standard procedures for the conduct of assembly *(shango)* meetings. The assembly had a formal seating arrangement. Shack (1966: 162) gives a somewhat contentious diagram (Alamayahu, 1985 EC: 46–47) with concentric circles and the representative of the traditional deity at the centre. Shimelis (forthcoming) notes a U-shaped seating arrangement among the Kestane. Sessions were customarily opened and closed with blessings. The meeting was led by a respected elder known as *awlañña* (roughly equivalent to chairman) among the Kestane.

Individuals who wanted to express an opinion or present a case stood up as a way of seeking permission to speak. Among the Kestane, it was common for friends and sympathizers of that particular individual to stand up too, to keep him company as it were. When he was recognized and allowed to speak, he commenced his oration with the word *Aterfe/Aterfemuñ* (a manner of seeking permission to speak). Witnesses could be introduced as necessary and asked to give their testimony on oath. Decisions were arrived at by consensus after an exhaustive discussion; voting was unknown. Occasionally, cases would be referred to a smaller group (known as *amseya* among the Sabat Bet), who would discuss the matter in detail and present their recommendations to the assembly. Among the Sabat Bet, there were legal experts known as *Äqicha dana* who would advise an individual as to whether his case had a chance or not.

Rules and Sanctions

One Kestane informant described the *Gordanna Sera* as a combined civil and criminal code. It is a fairly apt characterization and is equally applicable to the *Yajoka Qicha*. The laws dealt with marriage and divorce, homicide, arson, and land use (including the commons and roads)—to name the more prominent ones. Of these, cases of homicide were no doubt the most serious. Three categories were identified, with corresponding levles of penalties that will be discussed further below: pre-meditated murder (*mura dam* among the Sabat Bet and *talmama* among the Kestane); unpremeditated murder (*madara dam* or *sakaba*) and inadvertent homicide (*madara-madara dam* or *sababa*).

Although some Kestane informants allege that, in earlier times, death sentences were passed for homicide cases, this seems to have been rather rare. The prevalent penalty appears to have been payment of compensation to the bereaved, formerly in kind but more recently in cash. This was preceded by visible demonstrations of remorse which sometimes assumed dramatic forms of mortification. One version speaks of clan members of the guilty presenting themselves with a girl harnessed like a horse as a sign of remorse. They would not budge, refusing to eat or drink or go away, even if the aggrieved party disappeared from the scene to avoid reconciliation. According to another version, relatives of the guilty party would tie up the culprit and leave him at the edge of a precipice as an act of total surrender.

The sanctions that were applied for infractions of the law varied with the seriousness of the offence and the compliance or recalcitrance of the guilty. For minor offences among the Kestane, as indicated above, the malefactor was subjected to punitive visitations by a progressively increasing number (2, 4, 6, 8, 10) of "guests" who would expect to be offered a lavish feast. Non-compliance could result in more stringent punitive measures ranging from confiscation of property to ostracizing the culprit. Ostracization has remained the ultimate sanction in Gurage society. In Sabat Bet traditions it is monetary fines that are most often encountered. These fines rise, in the case of homicide for example, according to the degree of intent and inflation. The maximum fine (for pre-meditated murder) has risen from Birr 5,000 in the 1960s to Birr 30,000 currently. An important consideration in fixing the sum has been keeping a balance between the capacity of the relatively affluent urban members of the community and the not so well-endowed rural members as well as between bigger and smaller clans, since payment was a collective clan responsibility.

It is appropriate to point out here the applicability of the above rules and sanctions outside the rural setting. As is well-known, the Gurage have migrated over the years in large numbers and they are now found spread all over the country. But, their links with their homeland have been maintained in a number of ways. Most Gurage, particularly among the Sabat Bet, make the annual visit during the Masqal festivities. Some even have parallel households in their homeland. Moreover, those in cities like Addis Ababa—and this is particularly true among the Kestane—have carried over their agar or clan *(tib)* assemblies with them. Some of these assemblies have been in existence for seventy years or so. Indeed these assemblies had great practical value when it came to mobilizing the population for the construction of the major road systems in the 1960s and 1970s under the auspices of the two parallel organizations—the Alam Gana Walayta Soddo Road Construction Organization and the Gurage Road Construction Organization. It is also common knowledge that the edir that are now such a common feature of urban life are lineal descendants of the Kestane *sabuññat* introduced by migrants, although the latter had broader administrative scope than the edir, which have been confined to mutual self-help in times of death.

Limitations

The system described above, with its mixture of legal force and moral/religious sanction, seems to have operated for centuries with remarkable efficacy. It applied equally to the rich and the poor, the titled and the untitled. Where its overall egalitarian character foundered—as in so many other indigenous democratic systems—was in its exclusion of women and minority groups. Gurage society has traditionally been a strongly male-oriented society and this fact has been reflected in the systems of governance under discussion. There were no women representatives in the assemblies. They were rarely allowed to present their cases themselves. Their social role was largely confined to composing poems in the nature of social commentaries, praising the brave and chiding the cowardly.

It is such restrictions that gave rise to one of the most remarkable Gurage women, Yaqaqe Wardwat. Her defiant struggle against the male-dominated norms of her society has been celebrated in poems and anecdotes. Tradition has it that she led a delegation of women to one of the *Yajoka* assemblies and demanded at the very least to be free to attend meetings and that they should have the right to divorce their husbands. Her eloquent oration has been recorded in the following manner in Gebreyesus (1991:158):

> We women, your sisters, your mothers and your obedient servants for all time, appear before you today to ask for our rights if we, at all, have any! We women are treated as if we are created only for the pleasure of men. You never make us participate in things you are doing or planning. We have no security. If you like us, we are lucky, we live with you, and when you dislike us, we are chased out empty-handed. Therefore, we came here to *Yejoka* today to beg for some rights even if it is not the same rights as for men. It is not to beat our husbands as you do your wives or to scold them. We shall remain obedient to our husbands, continue to wash their feet and cook food for them.

> We are not asking you either to test us in the battlefield at the initial stage. This can come eventually. All we are asking you is to give us some minimum rights, like to be free to come to *Yejoka* and share our views with you concerning all the problems pertaining to "your country" or if we will be allowed to say so, "our country". Second, when we feel repressed, to leave our husbands and go without being tied up by the rigid procedures of divorce, which remain based upon rigid customary laws and traditional beliefs, the *Anq'it*. When you divorce us, you just say go because you are not tied up by *anq'it*. Let us have the same right, although we cannot tell you go from your establishments. But for us to be able to say, "I am going, and goodbye".

The male community—so the tradition continues—was momentarily flabbergasted by this challenge. But, in the end they were able to isolate Wardwat by intimidating her companions. To mollify her, they gave her the right to choose her husband and divorce him whenever she so wished and the option of attending *Yajoka* meetings. The tragic finale of her remarkable story, wherein she is struck dead by a thunderbolt, must have served as a severe warning to all Gurage women to stick to their assigned place.

It was not only women who were excluded from the decision-making process. Marginalized minority groups like the Fuga also suffered from such discrimination. As elsewhere in Ethiopia, their skills as craftsmen (tanners, carpenters, smiths, etc.), far from earning them social respect, led to their ostracization. They were not allowed to mix or intermarry with Gurage. It was thus inconceivable that they would be allowed into *Yajoka* or *Gordanna* meetings. The only concession that was apparently made to them among the Kestane was the dubious task of serving as hangmen in the rare instances when culprits were sentenced to death by hanging as well as disposing of the bodies of dead lepers.[1]

---

1. This is corroborated by a PhD thesis on the Fuga recently completed by Tecle Haimanot Gebre Selassie : "A Historical Survey of the Fuga Low-Caste Occupational Communities of South-Central Ethiopa" (AAU, History: 2000), p. 45.

Changing Perspectives

Two developments have had their impact on the traditional system of governance described above: the incorporation of Gurage society into the larger Ethiopian polity towards the end of the nineteenth century and the Gurage Diaspora which was accelerated by that process. As indicated above, the political system developed by the Gurage, with prerogatives that were earned rather than inherited, could not continue into the twentieth century. The establishment of a centralized court and police system also diminished the power and applicability of the traditional systems of arbitration and maintenance of security. Loyalties came to be divided, particularly in the big cities, as new identities were forged and new affiliations created.

Yet, it is a measure of the vitality of the traditional institutions that, far from disappearing completely, they have managed to survive up to now. Indeed, currently, they seem to be undergoing a vigorous process of revitalization. Ironically, too, it is the urban Gurage who are spearheading this movement of renewal and reinvigoration. We shall see below the constraints of this new development. But suffice here to emphasize that both the *Yajoka Qicha* and the *Gordanna Sera* are far from dead.

The picture that emerges clearly from the literature as well as oral information is that, throughout the previous century, customary courts co-existed with government courts. If anything, the latter sometimes tended to defer to the former. One informant put it dramatically when he said that the task of the government was only to collect taxes. This is a bit exaggerated, for customary courts also lacked the power of passing the death sentence, which they are believed to have exercised in the past; nor did they have a prison system where they could confine the culprit for a determined period of time. It is nonetheless true that if government courts enjoyed legal backing, customary courts exercised moral and ritual sanction. Among the Sabat Bet Gurage, individuals who chose to take their case to government courts were dissuaded from doing so by what is known as *khatarat*. If they proved adamant, it would mean forfeiting their right to a fair hearing in the customary court, if they had to revert to it.

Informants agree that it was in the days of the Derg that the pressures of the state were most acutely felt. The unprecedented control that the state was able to exercise over society through the peasant and neighbourhood associations tended to stifle local initiative. Some informants assert that the customary institutions discussed here were forced to operate in semi-clandestine fashion. Conversely, after 1991, these institutions have witnessed a perceptible revival, particularly among their urban adherents. What amounts to a codification of customary law has been in progress. After an initial attempt to co-ordinate their efforts in this respect, the Sabat Bet and the Kestane seem to have chosen to tackle the matter separately. We shall now see these parallel developments in turn.

After years of investigation and discussion under the auspices of the Gurage Self-Help Development Association, the Sabat Bet published in 1998 the product of their labours under the title of *Ägurage Qicha* (translated as "KITCHA: The Guraghe Customary Law"). The code, which had been reviewed by Gurage experts in various fields (law, education, health, economic development, and administration) not only evaluated and revised as necessary the customary law but also legislated additional rules. Special efforts were apparently made to make it as gender-sensitive as possible. This is particularly evident in the section dealing with marriage, which has provisions for mutual consent of the parties, the woman's right to divorce, and penalties for adultery and kidnapping.

Other innovative aspects of the code include: injunctions against lavish feasts for weddings and mourning; concern at the planting of *chat* and eucalyptus trees at the expense of the indigenous food plant, *ensat*; equation with homicide of the wilful infection of someone with the AIDS virus; banning of smoking during meetings; and measures against alcoholism and *chat*-chewing. The maximum penalty for homicide (*mura* or pre-meditated murder) is set at Birr 30,000. The code further sets down rules for executive bodies such as *azmach* and judges and designates the meeting-places of the various assemblies. Finally, the code invokes the ultimate resort against all who refused to abide by the law: ostracism. On the cultural plane, promotion of the Gurage language is a point that is particularly stressed.

A parallel development, including a concerted effort to preserve their language, has been taking place among the Kestane since 1991. The basic principles of the *Gordanna Shango* were laid down in 1994. The more elaborate code of customary law was approved by the central council in early 2000 and is now being prepared for circulation and implementation. The central objectives of the *Shango* are described as preserving the customary law of the Kestane, suppressing harmful customs while encouraging good ones, and promoting Kestane culture and language. Cultural values particularly singled out for commendation are the traditional method of arbitration and reconciliation in cases of homicide, the *equb* (a sort of credit association), and caring for aged parents. Conversely, traditional practices that invoke opprobrium are kidnapping, the deep nail-cutting of the bride-to-be, wild firing of guns on occasions of mourning and at weddings and the extravagant "return feast" *(mals)* given to the bridal couple after their wedding.

Coming to more contemporary social problems, the code condemns the ostentation that has become the hallmark of urban Kestane weddings, the alien practice of placing wreaths of flowers during funerals and the commemorative mourning on the third day after death *(salest)*. It also imposes strong sanctions on the brewing and selling of the potent local liquor, *katikala*, a scourge of rural Kestane-land. The three tiers of administration—*sabuññat, agar* (or *akababi* for the rural zones), and *Gordanna Shango*—are maintained.

A serious drawback of the code is that almost all the sanctions are in the form of the traditional *yekka* (the involuntary entertaining of guests) rather than the imposition of monetary fines. Thus, depending on the gravity of the offence, a person could be forced to have up to eighty-four "guests" wine and dine at his expense. The ultimate sanction remains ostracism. The obvious limitation of such sanctions is that they have little meaningful social return. The "guests" imposed by *yekka* might have a good time at those forced banquets. But the community hardly gains anything; it would have benefited more if monetary fines had been imposed and the money thus collected used for development.

In the linguistic sphere, the use of the Kestane language in all shango meetings has become mandatory. In addition, the translation of the Bible into Kestane and the compilation of a Kestane-Amharic-English dictionary are in progress. Presiding over these efforts, as well as the revival of the customary institutions of governance, is the Soddo Gordana *shango* headquartered in Addis Ababa but with branches in Kestaneland. The shango has a central council of 115 members, with five representatives from each rural zone and four from each *agar shango* in the capital.

Prospects and Constraints

Gurage customary law has weathered the march of time with remarkable resilience. It has helped to foster and sustain the people's sense of identity. Even more significantly, it has played a non-negligible role in mobilizing them to develop their region. The remarkable progress made in road construction would have been inconceivable without the network put in place by those customary institutions, not to mention the cardinal importance that traditional Gurage society has attached to the honouring of roads and alleys. In the last decade, the general political philosophy of self-determination has given those institutions fresh vigour and impetus. The attempts made to make such institutions as *Yajoka* and *Gordanna* adaptable to contemporary reality by trying to tackle a range of issues from rural development to substance abuse and AIDS are truly impressive. The trend is, on the subjective level at least, for these revitalization efforts to continue.

Yet, one cannot help but observe certain objective constraints in trying to give these traditional institutions contemporary validity. The first constraint is the fundamental one faced by all such traditional institutions in an age of supra-regional affiliation, not to speak of globalization. As perhaps the most mobile people in Ethiopia, the Gurage have exhibited parallel, if not conflicting, loyalties and identities—the regional and the supra-regional. Quite a large proportion of them could be said to have adopted pan-Ethiopian culture and identity. Even if the prevalent atmosphere at the moment appears to encourage regional loyalties and identities, every Gurage must ponder deep in his heart how many more generations it will take before his people are completely assimilated in the dominant culture. The serious attention that is given to the revival and enrichment of the Gurage language is in a way a reflection of this concern.

The second constraint has to do with the predominantly urban character of this revivalist movement. This is most probably because it is the urban Gurage who feel more acutely the prospect of assimilation. Yet, it is only when it is applied in the rural context that such a revitalization effort can be most meaningful with respect to the issue of local governance being discussed here. After all, the institutions being revitalized emanated from Gurageland and it is there that they must run their new course. The paramount concern of the rural Gurage, however, seems to be more economic than cultural.

There is also the question of how far the dominant political order would tolerate the development of truly autonomous local institutions of governance. As so often in life, reality does not always match rhetoric. Guaranteeing full self-determination (up to and including secession) in the constitution is one thing. Preserving political power is another. As in many other parts of the country, there have emerged rival organizations, both claiming to represent the people but one affiliated to the regime and another independent of it. While the former controls the rural political structure, the latter's constituency tends to be more urban than rural. At any rate, its hold on the rural appears to be moral rather than political.

Added to this is the inherently factious nature of Gurage society. Fragmentation has been the dominant theme of Gurage history. In spite of some efforts to remedy this original sin, so to speak, the evolution of a truly pan-Gurage polity is still far from being realized. While district loyalties within the same nationality are not confined to the Gurage (note for instance the case of the Tegre and Amhara), what makes the Gurage case rather unique is the fact that three mutually unintelligible Gurage dialects have co-existed for centuries in an area that is the equivalent at most of an *awraja*. Even within those three categories, clan *(tib)* and district *(agar)* loyalties have competed vigorously with regional loyalties. Among the Sabat Bet, the question of which is the dominant group (Chaha or Ennamor) or the dominant clan (say, within Chaha) has been a constant theme of their history.

The post-1991 period saw the Kestane community rent in two as a section of it claimed to be Oromo (labelled Soddo Jidda) and set up a rival organization to the one originally established to represent the region, the Soddo Gordanna People's Democratic Organization. Consistent with the vicious logic of fission, the discord provoked turbulent divisions within the Soddo Gordanna itself over the issue of reconciliation with the "Soddo Jidda", who in the meantime had shown signs of repentance. In November 2000, an encouraging development was witnessed when the two Gordanna factions finally agreed to bury their differences in an impressive ceremony of reconciliation. It is hoped that this will form the first step towards resolving the Gordanna-Jidda controversy and even forging pan-Gurage unity.

For the revival of the traditional governance systems to be truly meaningful, therefore, three things seem to be of crucial importance. First, the political atmosphere has to be conducive to the development of a truly autonomous Gurage zone rather than one that is centrally directed. Second, the Gurage community has to overcome its inherently factious tradition and start thinking and working along pan-Gurage lines. Third, and perhaps most important, the developmental facets of the revitalized and codified *Yajoka* and *Gordanna* have to be pushed with greater vigour. In short, the economic gap between the relatively affluent urban Gurage and their impoverished rural kin has to be narrowed. Only then can the essentially urban-driven revitalization effort flourish in its structurally pertinent rural context.

Sera: Traditionalism or Living Democratic Values?

A Case Study of the Sidama in Southern Ethiopia

Øyvind Aadland

Introduction

During the last century the Ethiopian central state introduced an administrative set up that was controlled from the center and responsible only to the central Government. When Sidamo was conquered by the armies of king (later Emperor) Menilek II, this system was also introduced in Sidamo. The Ethiopian state did not attempt to integrate, but to dominate the different peoples in its Southern regions. Hence, the Ethiopian state did not build on the local identities but rather competed against them. Even today, the cohesive elements of nationalism are lacking in large parts of the population. Within the Ethiopian political tradition, the term state, or the equivalent in Amharic, mengist, has slightly different connotations from a modern concept of a democratic state: "Imperial authority", sovereignty, divine legitimacy, nation building, and a kind of state-nationalism, but also control and domination.

The process of political centralisation resulted in marginalising the local and indigenous cultures for decades. Some of the indigenous structures continued to exist, but were not very actively involved in the state system either at local or national level. My research in Sidamo shows that the indigenous structures became nostalgic and rather mythological, out of touch with the reality of present day challenges, as a result of being neglected. They were emptied of or reduced in their responsibilities, and not integrated in the official polity for about a century. The political institutions of the Sidama became either rituals without any power, or they were coopted and given entirely new functions in the central state administration.

Sidama people have their concept of sera, which gives them a feeling of identity, a strong moral commitment, and a culturally defined ability to debate conflicts and create consensus. This could be a strong asset for building democracy. But their culture also gives them also a strong sense of status and rank, which excludes large segments of people from this debate, and renders human equality and general participation difficult.

This article tries to identify the tradition and its potential and limits in developing democracy, based on the contextual worldview of the Sidama people. Their traditional communal discourse is confronted with their experience of governance. Are the traditionalists arguing from the basis of a myth? Are they conflating nature and culture, in order to construct a mechanism of consensus, which could eventually establish a social consensus? This consensus is often referred to in Western terms as an element on the way towards "consensus democracy" (Hamer, 1998). Is it a construct, or is it viable in traditional Sidama institutions? I will examine the traditionalists' claims of truth, normative commitment, and sincerity, and the way they use them in argumentative reasoning. Is the concept of truth in Sidama society related to an ancient myth rather than based on objective reality?

The way the Sidama understand their own situation in the political world, their "life experience", has been shaped by a dramatic historical context as well as a tradition of a mythical worldview. The dualism of a state administration with rather negative connotations on the one hand, and a rather mythological administrative tradition on the other hand, is a difficult context for developing a democratic process. If the "life-experience" is interpreted through a mythical worldview, it may restrict critical thinking and a trustworthy communal life, and distract a discourse of real consensus. If cultural traditions have priority, power sharing can be difficult.

We will here analyze whether *sera* can open up for a democratic development, in a rather complex historical situation. We begin with a brief presentation of the political and historical context, followed by an ethnological introduction to the relevant social and administrative structures.

The Land of the Sidama

Sidama is one of the most fertile and most densely populated areas in Ethiopia. With about 2.6 million people,[1] the Sidama make up about four per cent of the total Ethiopian population. The staple food of the Sidama, the enset (false banana) is very drought resistant, (though it has periodically suffered from a virus disease which has caused serious food shortages), and allows under normal conditions a dense population in a relatively small but fertile area.

In addition to a reliable agricultural base, Sidama land also provides valuable resources to the economy. The most important contribution of Sidama is cash crops, mainly coffee but also khat, but Sidama also supplies meat, pepper and fish to the Capital. Especially around Awassa there are recently established small industries which make a considerable contribution to the national economy. The Sidama and their land are thus an important part of the population and of the resource base of Ethiopia.

Sidama-land is located in the south central parts of Ethiopia, to the east and north east of Lake Abaya and to the east and southeast of Lake Awassa. The most characteristic feature of Sidama landscape is the mosaic of clusters of homesteads. The midlands contain a continuing chain of villages, while homesteads in the highlands are a little more scattered. On the open savanna in the lowlands, homesteads are even more scattered. In between the homesteads are patches of farm fields and open land for grazing cattle. Homesteads consist of round huts surrounded by lush gardens of *ensete edulis*, the false banana tree. Coffee plants and a variety of fruit trees, including mangoes, oranges, avocados, peaches, and many others grow in abundance. However, the *ensete* plant dominates the gardens and is the most essential plant for the Sidama.

The lush green gardens give Sidama-land the appearance of a green and fertile land. In the midlands there are small rivers and both hot and cold water springs; the lowlands are more savanna-like with less vegetation. The major rivers, Logita, Genale, and Gombeltu, run to the east, and Gidabo and Bilate run to the west.

Parts of Sidama are located in the Rift Valley, the deep volcanic rift which starts in the Middle East and passes through Eastern Africa down to Mozambique before stretching out into the Indian Ocean. The lowlands to the west, including half of

---

1. The Census of 1994 estimated the Sidama at 2 million. With a growth of 3% annually, the Sidama should pass 2.6 million towards the end of 2002. However, population figures are not very exact estimates and give room for considerable error and controversy.

Lake Abaya and Lake Awassa, are on the floor of the Rift Valley. These lowlands climb the Rift Valley escarpment through the midlands entering the famous East African highland plateau.

The main occupation of the Sidama people has traditionally been farming, and 1,738 square kilometers of Sidama is cultivated land. Conservative unconfirmed numbers indicate that approximately 85 per cent of the total population are farmers. Coffee is the most lucrative cash crop. Khat (*Catha edulis*) is an evergreen shrub, native to tropical East Africa. Khat's dark green leaves are chewed fresh for their stimulating effects. The khat market has become another huge cash crop market in the last few years. But, basically the Sidama cultivate a variety of grains and fruits for household and local consumption. They also depend on dairy products. Sidama land is one of the most fertile areas of Ethiopia, surplus production for cash has been stimulated in recent years by improved transportation facilities and a more liberal market policy.

Awassa, on the shores of Lake Awassa, was established as the capital of Sidama in the sixties, and is today the capital for Region 8, Southern Nations, Nationalities and Peoples' Regional State (SNNPRS). A recent plan to separate Awassa from the SNNPRS and make it a Chartered City, because of its multiethnic population, has been met with strong resistance from the Sidama who fear for their influence in the regional state. Awassa is strategically situated on the doorstep of the northern border towards Oromia, with highway connections to Addis Ababa. It is in the northwest corner of the greater Sidama area. Awassa is an important administrative, educational, and business center, as well as military post. Today, Awassa is a fast growing town with a population of more than 100,000. Some industrial plants have been built in Awassa and today offer employment to a limited number of industrial workers.

Political and Historical Perspective

Sidama people conceive the modern government administrative structure from their historical experience of conquest and subsequent alienation in the past. Therefore, a brief review of the place of Sidama within the modern Ethiopian state is appropriate.

As always, historical reviews allow different perspectives. This review aspires to adopt an ethnographic approach in examining traditional institutions and patterns of political participation.

The author has known Ethiopia for many years. In particular he has collected ethnographic observations and conducted extensive conversations in Sidama during field studies between 1992 and 99.[1] This was a time of yet another political change in Ethiopia. It encouraged a process of ethnification. This process revitalized all that is traditional and specific, including those elements of culture which excluded large population segments from active participation in social life and decision making.

Some observers argue that the cleavages in Ethiopian society are the result of regional identity rather than ethnicity, because the northern administrative structure embraced the entire southern region. This is a contentious issue, as both variables

---

1. Aadland, O. (1994a): (Field Notes). Unpublished raw data. Aadland, O. (1994b): (Structured Interviews). Unpublished raw data. Aadland, O. (1994c): (Tuberculosis Control Program Staff Survey). Unpublished raw data. Aadland, O. (1995): (Field Notes). Unpublished raw data. Aadland, O. (1996): (Field Notes). Unpublished raw data. Aadland, O. (1999): (Field Notes). Unpublished raw data. This chapter also refers in part to an already published political assessment study by Tronvoll and Aadland (1995).

are intertwined, making any analysis apparently difficult. Regionalism can be said to involve the ability of two or more ethnic groups to identify together with a territory. In practical terms, that is the rationale behind the new term, the "Southern Nations".[1]

This classification is probably inadequate, because underlying all regional movements is the persistence of ethnicity. In fact, ethnicity, having been silenced and used in a discriminatory manner throughout an entire century in Ethiopia's recent history, has its positive elements too. Ethnicity provides a group that shares language and cultural values with a sense of common identity. Yet, if ethnicity is captured within a state structure, it may create conflict. If diverse major and minor ethnic groups are defined and administered on the basis of control and domination from the political center, it may produce ethnicity in a negative sense (Tronvoll and Aadland, 1995).

Such negative connotations can be sensed in segments of the southern ethnic groups, among which the Sidama are a major group. Kellas (1991) says that "favorable attitudes are held about the in-group and unfavorable ones about the out-group" (pp. 5–6). Having repeatedly been present in Sidama during the last ten years, the author has experienced that the Sidama people are searching for an independent identity, and harbor skepticism towards any external imposition.

Sidama under the Reign of Emperor Haile Selassie

For the Sidama, the *state* seems to be defined with reference to experiences during the second part of the reign of Emperor Haile Selassie I, when the state attempted to suppress ethnic identity and to implant notions of belonging to an Ethiopian nation.

Central government, *mengist*, was represented through the administrative structure, similar to the former structure of Menelik II. The empire was made up of provinces; each province was subdivided into zones (at that time, *awradja*, and thereafter, counties, *woreda*). As with most non-democratic political entities, an administrator had to demonstrate loyalty to the Emperor, to stay in office. Amharic was the business language, and consequently many of the upper positions were either staffed by people from the ruling ethnic group at the time, the Amhara, or at least by people who were very fluent in both spoken and written Amharic.

The tribute system, *gabar* (a system of feudalism administered at the local level), was probably the most significant contact between the administrative structure and the traditional Sidama people. The *gabar* system was established by Emperor Menelik II to organize a means of support to the military from the local people. After military force conquered the land of the Sidama, the military was remunerated for its efforts both in the conquest and in subsequent administration of the province by—temporary or hereditary—rights to appropriate a portion of the peasants' *(gabar)* produce. This right (comparable to a European fief) was later often transformed into ownership rights. The *gabar* system, as such, was abolished after World War II, but it continued in variations during the reign of Emperor Haile Selassie I. The tribute system was exercised by descendants of the former soldiers and administrators who had retained large allotments of land. The Sidama peasants remained on such land but were heavily taxed (Hamer, 1987).

The *balabat*, one of the lowest ranking government officials, administered land not allocated to Menelik's soldiers. Peasants on such land were likewise taxed; but

---

1. Part of the regional name: Southern Nations, Nationalities and Peoples' Regional State.

they paid tribute directly to the State. It was mostly or most directly at the *balabat* level of administration that traditional and official structures met. According to an informant, the *balabat* was often chosen from among the traditional leaders, for example, a mote, a king of a subtribe. The *balabat* was positioned as both a traditional and an official authority. A *balabat* who was able to mediate between the two and to act as a "cultural broker with the conqueror" (Hamer, 1987) retained his position among the Sidama. But quite a number of *balabat* used their position to obtain land rights and to win favors from the conquerors. Subordinate to the *balabat* was the *qoro* and the *chiqa-shum*. The *chiqa-shum* was in charge of collecting taxes and enforcing orders from the superior officials.

The modern, "westernized" state is an alien concept not only in an Ethiopian context, but more generally in Africa. Under Emperor Haile Selassie, *mengist*, the Ethiopian concept of state, was experienced by people as domination from the center and subjugation under its local representatives who wielded almost absolute power over the local people. The imperial monarchy developed into an absolutist state with a power structure based on feudalism and ethnicity.

Sidama under the Reign of the Derg

The former President Mengestu Haile Mariam (Mengestu) inherited the core problems of Ethiopia as a polity which contained a multitude of centrifugal traditional and ethnic forces and was sustained only by force. This problem still appears to be at the center of forming Ethiopia's political future today. The 17 year long Ethiopian transition during the Derg was orchestrated step by step by the entrepreneur Mengestu and his closest colleagues. Despite its Marxist-Leninist orientation, state formation and nation building continued in a dominant top-down approach. As the first phase of the revolution developed into a power-consolidating phase, it was surprising how policy positions were overwhelmingly adopted from the imperial reign. In fact, the regime was even ready to subvert its own programs if they seemed to jeopardize the basis of the state, the homogenized, inherited Empire of Ethiopia.

Accordingly, nation building, the forging of an all-embracing official consciousness, failed miserably. The legacy of imposition and absolutism wrapped in Marxist rhetoric compelled Ethiopia to remain a militarist state and determined the controlling role of the military in Ethiopian politics and society. Again, modern governance was an alien concept for Ethiopian rulers. The state and government were considered means for the ruler to pursue personal power. The different labels of ideology attached to the different rulers were adapted to specific personal needs. The Imperial reign maintained central power through the introduction of capital and technology, with capital under full control of the nobility, the elite in a feudal system. In this regard Mengestu seemed only to change the persons within the administration. His vast party network completely dominated Ethiopian life down to the lowest urban and rural administrative unit. Mengestu introduced the *kebele* (urban dweller association) and *gebre mehaber* (Peasant Association) as efficient lowest level administrative units and mechanisms of control over the population. In addition, the party representatives and the representatives of its Control Committee maintained intimidating surveillance over the state bureaucracy and the state-controlled enterprises and services.

A state economy has to be evaluated with reference to the state. In some basic characteristics, the economy of Emperor Haile Selassie I and his feudal vassals did not differ much from Mengestu's state economy and his party branches. The economic system under the two previous regimes may have been ideologically different, but there were also striking similarities:

— Both regimes were based on agricultural production to feed the military and the administration.

— There was little success in industrialisation or other economic alternatives.

— Taxation concentrated on extraction of tribute rather than expansion of production.

— Policies were directed not at encouraging initiative and innovation, but at controlling existing capacities.

The government and its representatives were once again not accountable to the Ethiopian people. Both systems rejected in practice the notion that sovereignty resides in the people. However, the Marxist regime manipulated the broad masses. Mengestu constituted his authority on a legal fiction proclaiming that the people had willed the creation of a socialist society. In this society, the Workers Party of Ethiopia (WPE) was the sole architect and Mengestu its sole representative and supreme guide. Mengestu systematically paved his way to absolute power; step by step he imposed his version of a Marxist revolution on the Ethiopian people. Ethnic identities were again suppressed, this time in the name of Ethiopian unity and the "popular masses". Ethiopia was transformed into a military dictatorship held together by control, rather than a democracy.

Sidama under the Reign of the Federal Democratic Republic of Ethiopia

The open, large-scale revolts of the revolution have ceased and the feudal structures of the empire no longer exist. Nor can the former system of land tenure that dominated the Sidama peasantry be recreated. The final land ownership issue is still pending. However, egalitarian principles have been laid down in the new constitution. In that sense, the first phase of the revolution, the dismantling of the old feudal structures, is complete. The pivotal second phase, the redefinition of the Ethiopian state as a democracy, is still in its infancy.

This is the historical frame of reference in which we have to analyze the present situation. We assume that democracy can only be built if it is securely anchored in the political consciousness of the people. This cannot be introduced from the top, but it has to grow from the local level as a democratic culture. Skepticism remains as to whether the politics of the Ethiopian Peoples' Revolutionary Democratic Front (EPRDF) is actually nurturing the spirit of a democratic political culture among the Sidama.

The EPRDF is the driving force in the new government. There seem to be two movements struggling for influence in Sidama, which counteract each other. On the one hand, an external top-down authority is once again being imposed on the people, this time cloaked in the ideological rhetoric of democracy and with external support from the West. "Central" dominance continues directly or more indirectly through satellite parties of the EPRDF. However, within the regime there has occurred a transition, from Amharic to Tigrean domination.

On the other hand, ethnicity has become the most crucial and controversial force in Ethiopian politics of today. The EPRDF maintains the principle of the unconditional right of nations, nationalities, and peoples to self-determination including secession. This principle is stated in the Constitution of the Federal Democratic Republic of Ethiopia of December 1994, article 39.[1] This is thought to allow all ethnic groups to develop their self-awareness, as a precondition for voluntary cooperation in a democratic unity.

There are reasons why the new Ethiopian government had to accept some degree of ethnic autonomy and differentiation after the fall of the Derg, whether they found it politically desirable or not. The major argument that gives sense to an ethnic policy in Ethiopia is found in its history. Many nationalities in Ethiopia, amongst them the Sidama, have a strong feeling of having been suppressed and subjugated through decades of external political domination. When the new regime of the EPRDF came to power in 1991, all resistance against Mengistu was organised in ethnically defined resistance groups. Their cooperation could not be won without promising the ethnic groups self-determination and an equal participation in state affairs.

In the present FDRE Constitution of 1994 the principle of self-determination is included. Thus, the Sidama people are very active in strengthening everything that is Sidama. With the 1975 land reform, the Derg, among other things, tried to solve an ethnically based problem inherited from the former regime. It disowned northern landowners in the south giving the land back to the local peasants. In practical terms, the peasantry was organized in cooperatives administered at the grassroots level through the peasant association *(gebre-mehaber)* and urban dwellers' association *(kebele)*. The land reform abolished the feudal economic system. But Dessalegn Rahmato (1992, p. 43), a prominent scholar on the Ethiopian peasantry, says:

> The national question thus ceased to be, at least to a majority of the rural population concerned, an economic question, but a cultural one, to be resolved by cultural means. I therefore find the ethnic-based politics of the transitional government incomprehensible and dangerous.

Today, as the federal system based on new ethnic regionalization is being implemented, the integrating forces of ethnic freedom appear to lose out against the centrifugal influences of ethnic conflict. The political experiment of adopting multiculturalism as an expression of nationalism; of a nation as a mosaic, constituted of a multitude of ethnic groups, is in danger of falling apart. In light of the historical context, basing nation building on a vision of a multi-ethnic entity, holds the potential for massive conflict as it may also fragment ethnic groups along lines of clan and lineage.

As a reaction to the trauma of domination, the Sidama are experiencing a wave of nostalgia in appraising everything that is Sidama, to such an exclusive extent that it may prevent any attempt at modernization. For an outsider it is very hard to understand what is going on, as the Sidama appear skeptical and very reluctant to expose cultural values to an outsider. From one point of view, modernization and cultural transition seem to take place on a large scale. At the same time, there is a strong trend of resistance against innovation. People are mostly concerned about building on traditional values. The integration of tradition with modern democracy has failed completely. Traditionalists appear to use the revival of Sidama culture as a means to ward off any modern influences, rather than bringing in their cultural heritage to familiarize and improve political life.

The dualism of modernity and traditionalism in the Sidama community is at the core of this problem. The introduction of a modern democratic political administration is difficult at this point in history.

---

1. Quoted after the (unofficial) English translation from the Amharic original of the FDRE Constitution, 1994.

Sidama and the Political Administrative Structure

Today the administrative structure of Ethiopia is divided into nine member states of the Federal Democratic Republic of Ethiopia. Sidama is part of the state of the Southern Nations, Nationalities and Peoples or the Southern Ethiopia Peoples' Administrative Region. This state differs from other states in that it comprises several ethnic groups, while many of the other states are delimited on the basis of settlement patterns, identity, language, and the consent of the people concerned.

Kebele and PA apparatuses need a closer presentation, because they are the administrative units within which practical community services take place.[1] These local units were developed by the Derg regime, to organise the "broad masses". They were a most useful administrative tool for the Derg. The infiltration of political cadres in the local PA and kebele meant that the state could consolidate power by maintaining an impressive network of domination at the village level. The exercise of political power and control through strategic "gatekeepers" developed the PA and the kebele into a stronghold for the Derg. They were organized along bureaucratic and political principles and were imposed on the people in the name of socialism. They literally controlled every village and every human activity in the vast rural areas of Ethiopia. Founded in 1975–76 as representatives of peasants, but recaptured only in 1977, the kebele became functional tools of the government. Higher party officials, without the participation of the local people, decided selection of candidates to administrative posts. The main criteria for the selection of candidates for chairmen were their efficiency in collecting taxes, obeying orders, and organizing peasants to carry out activities *initiated from above*. The skill of a chairman in representing peasant interests or advancing local demands was of minor concern. This bureaucracy pushed aside traditional cultural institutions of local authority, neutralizing the traditional decision-making infrastructure. The regime needed instrumental people in the decisive positions, who could be manipulated and who could manipulate. Implementation was initially very top down; however, local adaptation gained a little more ground as the institution settled down. This was an administrative apparatus in charge of implementing government decisions at the lowest level. Having seen how they forced mothers to "sacrifice" their sons to the war front at gun point, makes a eradicable impression.

Following the downfall of the Derg, the administrative infrastructure of the PA and the *kebele* was weakened. A decentralized autonomy gave room for revitalizing the more culturally appropriate function of elders as an institution less susceptible to manipulation from above. However, during field visits our observations confirmed that the PA and *kebele* apparatus was gradually being re-vitalized in accordance with the old concept. This process became increasingly evident as the central authorities re-introduced a strong system of central control over the formally independent peoples and their local and regional institutions. The experience of growing control at local level is re-weakening the old sense of skepticism towards the kebele structure. The *kebele* are once again monitored and run by political cadres, this time by cadres of the ruling party of the central regime. This raises fundamental questions with regard to identifying the gatekeepers in the Sidama community.

---

1.   References are made to Tronvoll and Aadland (1995) in describing this apparatus.

Ethnological Historical Perspective

The traditional Sidama community is said to have emerged in the sixteenth century about 20 generations ago. Until Emperor Menelik II incorporated Sidama into the Ethiopian Empire, Sidama existed as a tribal unit with several kingdoms. Sidama is defined as an ethnic group or tribe, which is the most inclusive level of social organization. The Sidama inhabit a distinct area as an homogenous ethnic group, today an official administrative division, the Sidama Zone. They speak their own Cushitic Sidama language and are identified by their cultural homogeneity and unifying social organization. The traditional structures have apparently been very well conserved. As Sidama seem to be moving towards an autonomous structure, more or less defined on ethnicity, the Sidama cultural and traditional heritage appears to flourish. Yet the emergence of cultural self-consciousness has also revitalized internal cleavages and ranking. There are three traditional and cultural administrative structures. These reflect the basic social principles in the Sidama social structure which are based on *patrilineage, genealogical purity* and *seniority.* A series of patrilineal segmentary subtribes and subdivisions of the subtribes are stratified into different hierarchical levels, clans, and finally intersected by a system of age-grade (luwa) sets.

Purity

Purity refers to the *anga* concept. Here lies the basis for a superiority and inferiority complex that seems to surface in the Sidama people even today. Those who do not possess *anga*, or who are not of "noble heritage", are potentially victims of social discrimination. Impure groups were in historical times not given land, and had thus little choice but to make a living from professional work as tanners or potters, weavers or blacksmiths. These professions in turn were taken as the source of being unclean. Those who descend from Bushe are said to possess *anga*, while there are some descendants from Maldea who do not possess *anga*. The artisan groups definitely do not possess *anga*, and their impurity is still considered important, in particular for excluding them from participation in decision making and social life. Traditionally the social stratification is based on purity, interwoven with the genealogy. Put in the words of Hamer (1987 p. 24–25):

> This term *(anga)* may be translated literally as "hand", but the idiomatic meaning is to avoid the hand of the impure. Elders receive *anga* when they are promoted to elderhood, after which they may slaughter cattle and in turn eat meat slaughtered only by other elders possessing the trait.... Thus possession of *anga* connotes the authority of elderhood and a sense of superiority over those who lack it... Busheans claim that most Maldeans have lost their anga for two reasons. One explanation is that their continual movement back and forth across the Gidabo and sporadic fighting with the Gugi and Jamjam interfered with gardening and herding. This led the Maldeans to eat all sorts of wild animals in violation of *anga* taboos...

Anga is probably the most difficult and most controversial issue to approach in the Sidama context. One is left solely with oral traditions and sources, in fact, with numerous prolific historic traditions that involve struggles between different kinship groups. Ethnographic findings include that many of the tensions surfacing between different social groups in Sidama are rooted in their patrilineal traditions and their hierarchical clan stratification.

The matter of land control (that is, the sanctuary that Busheans claim to have provided the Maldeans) and the lack of *anga* give rise to claims of superiority of the former over the latter. Though the Maldeans tend to admit this reasoning, they deny that it is important, maintaining that *anga* is useless and simply an excuse for a con-descending attitude on the part of Busheans.

After a man has been circumcised, he undergoes a period of a month's seclusion from segments of the community. During this period there are celebrations and dif-ferent purification ceremonies. The notion of purity is fundamental in becoming a member of the elderhood. At the end of the seclusion period, the man goes to the river to wash and clean himself. Then a final celebration is prepared. The *cimeyye* (plural of *cimessima*) come to perform a cleansing ceremony. A sheep is slaughtered and the hands of the man are washed in blood. Meanwhile, the men say, "May you have a (name of a subtribe) hand". That means *anga*, the "clean hand" which is an exclusive status of the non-artisan subtribes. As a *cimessima*, he can now slaughter, but he has to be very careful not to make his hands unclean. There are certain things he cannot do, in particular he may not shake hands with those in artisan groups. There are certain things that cannot be done at the same time, for example, eating while somebody is whistling. In particular, a *cimessima* has to watch out for the evil eye, *buda*.

Patrilineage

Subtribes *(gosa)* are divided into three levels: first, the *bosallo* (pl. of *bosa*) or clans; second, the *aydde,* agnatic divisions made up of all the descendants of one ancestor about three to five generations in depth, which often constitute an olla, a village; third, the *mine manni,* the nuclear (monogamous or polygamous) family.

The classification of units is extremely difficult in Sidama. The society is so com-plex that different sources disagree on how to evaluate inclusiveness and corporate-ness.

A literature review on the issue from Sidama, as well as a number of informant interviews, indicates as many variations as the number of sources. Even the number of subtribes, *gosa*, is controversial.[1] A certain *gosa* could be considered a fully-fledged subtribe or just a subdivision or clan. But the following nine subtribes are often referred to: *Alatta, Haweela, Qeweena, Saawoola, Fagisa, Garbichcho, Yanase, Malga,* and *Holloo.*

The subtribes are stratified according to the above-described layers into the no-bles, the free-men, the artisan groups and the descendants of slaves. The nobles are the *Yemereccho* (plural). The freemen or cultivators are named the *Wollabiccho,* while the artisans are categorized as the *Hadiccho* (potters) and the *Awaccho* (the tanners and smiths). Hamer (1987) specifies the *Tunticcho* (smiths) as a third cate-gory of artisans. The slaves are no longer called as such, because Emperor Haile Se-lassie abolished slavery in the 1930s. However, their descendants are referred to as *Borojjiccho.*

Cultivators and artisan groups do not interact because of their conceived differ-ence in purity related to the *anga* concept.

Almost every adult Sidama is aware of his/her identity with reference to *gosa* (subtribe), *bosallo* (clan), or maximal lineage, and even the subdivision of the clan, *gare.* And even about other Sidama, this identification is well known and referred to

---

1. During a field study it was observed that a short introduction to social life in Sidama was printed and distrib-uted for use amongst elementary Sidama school children. A controversy on the issue of defining the subtribes ended in the withdrawal of the booklet after printing and distribution.

in many different contexts. The importance of patrilineal tracing was obvious and was generally agreed upon by the informants.[1]

These units constitute the social structures and relationships. The Sidama claim their community to be corporate and non-individualistic. Thus one's identity is defined through one's relationships and place within this social structure. Authorities and gatekeepers are defined at the different levels. Within the smaller agnatic units the roles are defined traditionally, based on age and gender. The patrilineal segmentary subtribes practice varying degrees of inclusiveness and corporateness, depending on the hierarchical stratification level of a clan.

The stratification layers in the Sidama hierarchical structure seem parallel to what Levine (1974, p. 57) observed: "If one were to construct an ideal type of the Pan-Ethiopian stratification pattern, then it would consist of four strata: high-ranking lineages, low-ranking lineages, caste groups, and slaves".

The Traditional Sidama Gerontocracy, and the Socio-Administrative Network

Seniority relates closely to the age cycles of *luwa*. The *luwa* structure has many commonalties with the *gadda*-system of the Oromo, and plays a fundamental role in initiation rites and in maintaining authority roles. The luwa structure was the subject oof a thorough study by Hamer (1976).

There are two terms used to refer to an elder, *gercho,* and *cimessiccho.* The first term refers to the age of a person, a person with gray hair. The other term refers to an elder who has undergone the rite of passage, the initiation into the status of elderhood. The timing of this rite is a function of the luwa age-grade system (Hamer, 1976). The ethnographic field observations of the age-grade sets present much fascinating, legendary material about this social structure and the ceremony of the initiation rite into the status of elderhood.

The *luwa* identity has repeatedly been expressed as a basic traditional Sidama value. The age grade has a 12-year cycle, and each of the five *luwa* generations has its name: *Binancha, Wawasa, Hirbora, Derara* and *Fulasa.* Boys are assigned to one of these age cycle groups, primarily by the age cycle in which each was born. Men of the same *luwa,* age-cycle group, have a very strong bonding. Each age group selects their *gadanna,* leader, who will represent their generation throughout the period of 12 years.

The passage into elderhood, which gives a man the status of *cimessima,* has to take place during the rites of his generation, the *luwa* to which he belongs. A son cannot undergo the initiation ritual, to enter the *cimessima,* which includes circumcision, *berchima,* before his father. He therefore has to wait for the successive *luwa* in order to be initiated.

An elder is expected to live according to the *halale,* the truth concept. Traditionally, this is a moral standard reflecting the truth, by avoidance of any

> ... form of crime, such as stealing, perjury, corruption, injustice, but also a strict adherence to the highest standards of probity, integrity, honesty and truthfulness. Furthermore, an elder is supposed to uphold the mores of the society as they have been transmitted by their forefathers.

---

1. An informant in one of the focus groups brought along an audio tape and played a conversation with his father, who allegedly named 35 generations back to the original founding fathers of the clan, Bushe and Maldea. The oral information of 35 generations back, which may lead back to the 13th century, is probably not reliable, despite the fact that the Sidama have a long oral tradition.

In this respect they are the repository of the tribal heritage which has been passed on from generation to generation. (Vecchiato, 1985, pp. 209–210.)

The daily lives have traditionally been organized around a social network within the *olla*, village or within *mine manni*, the family unit. At the village level the *murricha* (elder) has a leadership role, and in general, the gerontocracy has traditionally dominated the communal network on all levels. Hamer (1970, p. 50) described the Sidama as a "political gerontocracy".

The Sidama people comprise a number of subtribes, *gosa*, which are ruled independently by their own king, actually a supreme judge, the woma. The *woma* of the different subtribes within the Sidama make up the *woma-songo*, the assembly of subtribal kings or judges. In a way, it is the highest traditional authority. There are differentiated lower *songo*, assemblies, which have different areas of authority and responsibility. However, gender and age are limitations to participation. Only the elders, and only the men have a say in these assemblies. The *sera* is defined as the ruling truth, referred to as *halale*. *Halale* proclaimed by the elders is hard to challenge and is often a base for "forced" consensus. As opposed to individualism, decision making in the assemblies is always with one voice, and consensus is valued over the open confrontation of opposing ideas.

The *gare-songo* is at the next level. This is the council of the *mote*, who are the kings of the *gare*, the maximal lineage segment (a sub-division of the subtribe). The *mote* is partly an inherited position, but there may be a choice between the sons of the former *mote*. The *gare-songo* deals with matters closer to daily life than the *woma-songo*. It may, for example, be involved in how to make a disobedient son become obedient to his father. It also deals with matters of loans and serves as a local court and can impose penalties. People who do not pay their penalties in cash, in kind, or in community service obligations may be excommunicated from the community.

Within the smaller agnatic units, such as at the *haracha* level, there are also *songo* (assemblies), headed by the *muriccha*. The *haracha* is made up of a cluster of agnatic units, *olla*, villages, sharing a *sera*. There is a *songo* at the *olla* level, and the head of that assembly is also called a *muriccha*. At both levels, the *haracha* and the *olla*, the *murricha* are primarily in charge of administrating the services related to deaths and funerals. Because of the high authority associated with these indispensable ceremonies in the community, the *murricha* may also be called upon to become involved in other significant community activities. The principle of seniority and communal relationship is still strong at the neighborhood and household level. Observations confirm that the elders still have a very strong influence in the daily life of the ordinary people.[1] Interviews showed that almost 90 per cent of the respondents saw the elders as advisers and having authority at the *haracha* level. In particular, the *murricha* was referred to as an authority.

Gender roles are traditionally defined, but today they are challenged by young educated women.

---

1. Structured interviews of 119 persons during fieldwork in 1995 and 1996.

The *Sera* Concept

In the Sidama community, a web of relations and interrelations has traditionally been ruled by the *sera*. *Sera* is a set of local cultural norms or codes regulating the communal social structure and interaction. Traditionally, *sera* is almost an ethic and moral codex. It may be seen as an unwritten law, but it constitutes at the same time the morality and the conscience of the individual and the community. *Sera* also provides social security to the members. It provides the community with a procedure of decision making through consensus. It obliges the individual to accommodate to the majority, to seek harmony and consensus rather than an individual opinion and personalized justice. The *sera* mainly relates to domestic communal life. It works traditionally at the basis of commonality and consent, rather than individualism. *Sera* also rules over the social collaboration that is sought from every member *(serancho)*, for example, when a house is built or a funeral is held. It regulates the contributions and obligations within the communal fellowship.

The *sera* also ascribes financial or social punishment inflicted on a member for not fulfilling the obligations of the community. When sentenced according to *sera*, it is said that the *sera* is applied, *sera* worrani.

The traditional Sidama community with its *sera* has an indigenous positive caring attitude towards suffering members. If a person is genuinely suffering and not able to fulfill his social obligations, other members of the community will traditionally take care of those responsibilities. This is i.e. practiced in case of long term illness. It is a tradition that relatives, friends, and neighbors present gifts, *gumata*, of food, milk, honey, meat, or even money to a suffering person to make him or her recover. This is also practiced towards a person who has been circumcised recently or a woman who has recently given birth. In general, good food is considered essential when caring for a patient. Thus, an activity performed collectively with other members of the *olla* is referred to as *serunni losate*, to work the *sera*. A member of a unit comprised by a *sera* has to obey the codex of the law. The *sera* law or rule is advanced with reference to the social communal life particularly on the domestic level.

However, today there is an individualistic tendency which ignores the traditional obligations and social classification. Individualism puts constraints on certain marginal groups of the community. These groups seem to receive less attention e.g. in the case of illness.[1] Reports from the professional health care institutions state that local caring for suffering people is often neglected, and there is a tendency for women to be most vulnerable in this regard. The status of the *sera* concept in Sidama today seems to be challenged by a weakening of corporate thinking.[2]

---

1. Oral statement from the former Medical Director at Yirgalem Hospital, as well as observations during fieldwork both in the hospital and during visits to the countryside.
2. When following up the observations with structured interviews on present values in the Sidama community, none of the respondents mentioned sera to be a primary value. Only 14/119 (11.8%) mentioned sera to be the second most important value, while likewise 14/119 (11.8%) mentioned it to be the third most important value. Given that sera has traditionally played a fundamental role in communal life and was mentioned during conversations to be one of the basic values, these responses seem to indicate a rather low percentage of respondents who exclusively consider sera one of the basic values.

Concluding Remarks

In Sidama, neither did the state initiate democratic rural administrative institutions nor have local and indigenous forms of self-administration led to popular participation in local government. The Sidama seem to live in two worlds that are difficult to unite. They experience repression from a modern communal administration that demands rational political decisions. They retreat into a social context in which their "life-experience" is determined through a traditional mythical worldview. This dualism restricts constructive criticism and a trustworthy involvement in political life, and distracts from a discourse of real participation. In concrete terms, if a person cannot be trusted, because he is an artisan, a political argument is wasted and democratic decision impossible. If cultural traditions predecide, how can power be shared? And if the value of an argument depends on the *anga* of the man who formulates it, how can democracy be developed?

Thus we are faced with a pluralistic revival of Sidama. Traditions are revived with an underlying intention to uphold the mores of the society as they have been transmitted by the forefathers, reflecting truth, *halaale*. Dealing with domestic issues at family level, this structure may still seem adequate. But as heterogeneity grows, the gap between the "life experience" and the "mythical worldview" grows. The complexity of reality demands more complex knowledge than the truth of halaale, the true way of life, which is exclusively decided and transmitted by elders.

For historical reasons, it may be understandable that the Sidama defend themselves with a mythical worldview against what they conceive as cultural and political domination from outside. Any ideas of modern rationality are excluded by reference to traditional qualities of *halaale* and *sera*. As long as the Sidama feel it important to rebuild their self-image by insisting on their *anga*, their superiority over those who possess less purity and are born lower, they cannot open up for democratic discourse. They have reason to use the tradition as an alibi against rational thought. But once they are sufficiently self-assured to open up for debate on different aspects of this same tradition, they may be able to appreciate its more democratic and inclusive qualities.

Some intellectuals may have understood the dilemma inherent in *sera* traditions. But so far, if they try to push the Sidama into the direction of opening their world view to more rational application, they are frozen out and silenced by the majority who insist on preserving the purity of their tradition, and who feel threatened by an open discourse.

Neither does the administrative structure today offer any assistance to potential reformers. Demanding loyalty and obedience to orders from above does not allow much room for a rational adaptation of traditional interests. And where elections to *kebele* and *woreda* positions are pre-determined by internal party decisions, there is little room for rational adaptation of the elected songo to modern democratic practice.

The structure of *sera* has a good potential for enabling democratic decision making. But it cannot be employed as long as the criteria for decisions are restricted to those who possess *anga* on account of birth and patrilineal descent, excluding all others, such as artisans, or women.

A reform of these criteria is not possible as long as they are sanctioned by the mythos of an ancient world view. And this mythos will not open up for a reform, allowing wider participation, before the local state institutions allow the Sidama a chance to express their views freely, and to represent their interests effectively within political processes on a local and regional level.

For the sake of simplicity, two major philosophical paradigms can be used to illustrate the contrast between the fact oriented and the mythological worldview in Sidama. The criterion for what is real or has meaning is what exists in fact. A rational world view is structured with the help of symbols which are a representation of reality. All rational thought involves the manipulation of abstract symbols which are given meaning only via conventional correspondence with things in the external world (Lakoff, 1987).

But it is argued that meaning is in people, not in words, objects, or things. People actively create meanings in response to their environment. Nothing has absolute meaning. Therefore, different individuals will interpret events differently, even more so when they come from different environments and cultures (Ogden and Richards, 1946). But also, people will interpret events differently if they live in different environments. The underpinnings, the worldview, the understanding of reality, are shaped by everyday experience. However, it seems that the Sidama voluntarily retreat into a traditional view, more influenced by the mechanisms of imagination, such as metaphor, mental imagery, and emotions.

Rational communication in polity and communal life is endangered by the fact that the "life experiences" of the Sidama are confronted with past experiences and a nostalgic tradition of a mythical worldview. "Beneath symbolic systems, beneath ideas about sacredness and purity and religious duty, we need to see the realities of power: who has it, who uses it, in what ways, to what ends" (Keesing, 1981:299).

Unfortunately the reestablishment of control from above revitalised their trauma of being subjugated, depressed and dominated. This in turn revitalised traditions, without a critical view on hierarchy, rank and *anga*—at the expense of the democratic potentiality of *sera* which is unable to overcome the anti-democratic practice of discrimination against those who are less "pure".

The feeling of being controlled from above also reinforces a mythical world view which employs the revival of tradition not in a constructive way, but as a means of defence against the demands of central authority, control and domination. It does not integrate tradition into democracy to create a modern, yet culturally adapted democratic political consciousness—but it "purifies" and mystifies tradition to ward off or at least to reduce all influences from the "modern" ideologies of the central state. In this mythical world view, no concept of modern democracy, however beneficial it might be, can penetrate the protective shield of "purity", seniority, lineage and heritage.

Thus, one may conclude that tradition indeed has a potential to familiarize and adapt democracy, but as long as democracy is curtailed in practice by control from above, this potential is checked and immobilized by the superiority of the "pure" over their less fortunate brethren not to mention their control over women.

However, another notion emerges from this article's focus. It attempts to examine claims of truth, normative commitment and sincerity, embedded in argumentative reasoning. It must also ask: Whose reasoning?

The diffusion of an innovation into the Sidama community depends on how the people relate to each other. Lewis (1970) summarizes the main features of the caste system which defines the hierarchical structure of social life: "(1) endogamy; (2) restriction of commonality; (3) status hierarchy; (4) concepts of pollution; (5) association with a traditional occupation; and (6) caste membership ascribed by birth" (pp. 182–183).

A crucial question in this context is whether "sera" has the potential to absorb the reasoning of all Sidama people, to also include the *hadichio*, the potters, the women, and the descendants of slaves. As we see it, as long as suppression and control from above restrict the Sidama to cultivating their traditions and watching over their purity, this is unlikely. But if they were allowed a chance to develop a more modern and adapted self-awareness, they would easily open up their world-view to new realities, and their community to more inclusive democratic participation.

Seera: A Traditional Institution of Kambata[1]

Yacob Arsano

Introduction

Kambata is located in the southern region of Ethiopia, and consists of three main *woreda* (districts) with a population of about half a million. A sizable portion of the population lives outside Kambata, including in resettlement areas.[2] The livelihood of the population is based mainly on mixed farming while off-farm labor, commerce and craftsmanship are supplementary activities. A growing number of the younger generation has entered the career employment structure as school teachers, health workers, etc. *Enset* constitutes the staple crop, supplemented by a variety of cereal and root crops. Livestock, comprising cattle, small ruminants and equines, are raised on a small scale.

The Kambata community has a long history and consists of more than one hundred and twenty tribes. It is believed that almost all the tribes migrated to the region at different times, a process that lasted until the end of the 19th century. The settlement has been accompanied by the intermingling of tribes.

The biggest traditional unit of territorial organization of Kambata is *kokata* while the smallest is *heera.* There is also an intermediate level known as *gotcho.* The leaders of secular institutions are recruited in the process of socialization from among non-hereditary candidates. *Kokata* is an assembly-like structure covering the territories of several gotcho and heera. *Kokata, gotcho* and *heera* are not strictly hierarchical although they are functionally symbiotic. Their modus operandi is more of a cooperative as opposed to a command relationship. *Seera* is the totality of code of conduct operational throughout Kambata. It is an unwritten body of rules and procedures binding on the community members with regard to all patterns of relationships.

After the incorporation of Kambata into the Ethiopian empire in the late 19th century, the imperial regime destroyed some of the traditional institutions and modified others with a view to using them as entry points for administrative control. The institutions of *woma, gotchi-dana* and *muricho* were modified to *balabata, sanghidana* and *chikashooma. Heera* and its adjunct structures, however, survived the state intervention mainly because they were less political as their main function was self-help and community welfare. The 1974 Revolution abolished the *balabat* and *chikashum* institutions and replaced them by peasant associations. The public functions of *heera* were then reduced to rudimentary activities, mainly related to funerals.

---

1. In spite of the different transcription, the seera treated in this chapter is analogous to the sera discussed by Bahru Zewde and Øyvind Aadland.
2. Pushed by overpopulation and poverty, large groups of Kambata peasants have resettled in Wondo Tikka, Wondo Kosha, Arsi, Metekel, Teddelle and Gambella over the past thirty years or so. Similarly, there is a large exodus of young men and women to Maana, Libido, Wonji, Matahara, Awassa, Shashamana, Bilate, Arba Minch, Amibara, Babaka, Wushwish, Finchaha, Alaba and Ziway for work on seasonal and permanent basis.

After the overthrow of the Derg the new EPRDF regime was not immediately able to ensure the necessary level of peace and security at community level. This circumstance contributed to the rejuvenation of the *seera* and the reemergence of kokata. Presently, not only are their structures pervasive throughout *Kambata* but their functions have also become increasingly binding.

This essay is mainly based on interviews conducted during the summer of 1999. Personal experience of the author and field notes from his trips to Kambata in 1994, 1996 and 2000 are utilized as supplementary data. The categories of persons interviewed during the 1999 summer included: community elders, teachers, youth, women, members of the police, judges, merchants and religious leaders, ranging in age from 40 to 90 years. The interviews were conducted in Hangatcha, Katcha-Biira and Kadida-Gamela *woreda*.[1]

Settlement Pattern of Kambata

The original site of Kambata settlement is believed to be at Mount Hambaricho, the most important mountain in Kambata. Most informants agree that the first settlers of Mount Hambaricho were people who might have migrated from present day Sidama and Gedeo. Mount Hambaricho is described as having a flat top and gentle slopes. Informants assert that the mountain was covered with forest which served as the habitat for a variety of wild animals. It is believed that the mountain provided an attraction to the first migrants, who had initially intended to stop over for a while and hunt and gather food. Then they apparently decided to settle down for good.

The term "Kambata" originated from the expression *"kambat"* which according to oral tradition means "this is the place", i.e. an "ideal" place where the first migrants wanted to settle. The term *"kambat"* has essentially the same meaning even today. How and when the expression *"kambat"* was transformed to Kambata could not be determined. However, one may speculate that the suffix "a" might have been added to form the noun, because most singular names of masculine gender in the Kambata language end with an "a", as in *manna, laga, saa, saanna, Buulaa*, or with an 'o', as in *Hambaricho, Digibamo, Daato*.

According to Kambata oral tradition the first settlers comprised seven houses which are believed to have evolved eventually into the original seven tribes of Kambata which settled on Mount Hambaricho: Ebejena, Efeghena, Fuga, Goroma, Hiniera, Saga and Tazo. All informants agree on the story of seven nucleus tribes. But there is no consensus on the list of tribes. While Ebejena, Efegena, Fuga, Hiniera, and Tazo are accepted by all informants as five of the seven founding tribes, Goroma and Sagaa are replaced by any two of Baza, Gadenna, Oyyeta, Gulba and Hessesee in the recollection of other informants.[2]

Nor is there clarity on the nature of the human population prior to the migration described above. Some informants maintain that hunters and gatherers had lived and worked on and around Mount Hambaricho. They further assert that the *Fuga* community might be taken as one of the indigenous inhabitants. They explain that although *Fuga* are included in the list of the seven founding tribes of Kambata, they

---

1. I wish to express my great appreciation to my research assistant, Ato Dawit Seyoum, who conducted the interviews in the three woreda of Kambata on the basis of a semi-structured questionnaire.
2. The problem has already been indicated by Tesfaye Habiso, "Kambatanna Hadiyya Yeastedader Akababinna Yebiherasabotch Tarik BeEthiopia Yetarik Gatsita", monograph in Amharic, Addis Ababa (1983 E.C.), p. 58.

might not have necessarily have migrated from outside like the rest of the other tribes.

According to the standard version of the story, the seven tribes settled together in a small area of Mount Hambaricho and roamed the entire mountain hunting and gathering. They needed to stick together for mutual protection and collaborative hunting. The need to work together ultimately took a permanent character of inter-tribal solidarity which, in turn, gave rise to a formal council type organization. Informants unanimously attribute the origin of the present *kokata* to this process. The inter-tribal council ensured internal harmony and unity against outside intruders. As the new settlement provided abundant resources for their livelihood, it seemed there was no longer internal conflict arising from competition for essential resources. Instead, the community's main concern now became protecting the small colony of settlers from outside intruders as well as from wild animals.

The inter-tribal council established the *seera* (code of conduct), which obliged everyone to respect the rules and mores of the seven tribes. One of the rules set from the very beginning was that every settler had to place seven bundles of straw on the outer apex of his thatched conical house (locally known as *tukul*). The council and the members of the tribes were to enforce the tradition on all newcomers. The tradition is observed even today by every Kambata who puts up a *tukul*, without being conscious of its origin or the circumstances of its emergence. However, the conduct signifies the symbolic authority of the founding fathers and the stability of that tradition.[1]

Worthy of mention here is the phallic symbol of the outer apex of the Kambata *tukul*. The 'old fashioned' thatched *tukul* in Kambata have the phallic curving on their outer top to this day.[2] None of the informants, however, could explain the origin and the symbolic significance of this detail. In other traditions the phallus symbolizes fertility, present or desired. It can be presumed that the original colonists of Kambata were few in number and would have desired to multiply by leaps and bounds.

The original settlers adopted hoe cultivation and livestock raising only gradually. This may be attributed to the influence and contribution of the immigrants who trickled in during the subsequent decades and centuries. It is claimed that two of the seven tribes, namely Fuga and Sagaa, chose to remain hunters and gatherers and that they adopted the trades of pottery and tanning. The two tribes also maintained the old belief system known as *Fandannan* for a much longer period than the other five tribes, who seem to have been more receptive of change with respect to work and beliefs brought in by new settlers.

As more settlers trickled to the hilly land of Kambata from neighboring Enarya and Damot,[3] presumably during the 11th and 12th centuries, they settled on and around Hambaricho, intermingling with the members of the seven tribes. Their settlement sites were given to them by the council of the seven tribes. Informants explain that various factors pushed the newcomers from their original locations. Some came to escape famine, slavery or persecution. Others came in search of hunting ad-

1.   The number 7 is sacrosanct in Kambata tradition: the seven houses of Hambaricho, the seven founding fathers of Kambata, the seven lineages of a tribe, etc.

2.   I have witnessed this during my trips to Kambata in 1994, 1996 and most recently in July 2000. Elsewhere in Ethiopia, there exist many traces of phallic structures. Two prominent examples would be the phallic points of the stele of Axum and the phallic shape of the cylindrical stone popularly attributed to Ahmed Gragn of the sixteenth century. 'Gragn's stones' can be found in several southern regions of Ethiopia, including Kambata, Wolayta, Kafa and Gamo.

3.   Other settlers from nearby Enaria and Damot might have included: Zaato, Weshesha Hessesse, Baza, Enara, Ganza and Damota.

ventures. Still others came with invading bands for opportunistic gains of some sort including conquest, plunder or resettlement.

Many informants mentioned that a good number of new settlers came to Kambata during the reigns of Zarako (Zara Yacob) and Amde Tsion in the 14th and 15th centuries, respectively. Orthodox Christians and religious teachers were among those who came and settled in Kambata during that time. It was said that Emperor Zara Yacob was particularly keen to expand the frontiers of Christianity, and for that reason he encouraged settlers from the north (Gondar, Bulga, Menz, Beta Amara, Angot, Gayint, Agaw Midr, Tigray, Jirru). That might be one reason for describing Kambata as one of the Christian outposts in the south. For instance, Lapiso Dilebo (1982:168) writes that Kambata, located south of Guragae and west of Bilate River, was an integral part of the medieval Ethiopian state.

Another wave of settlers came to Kambata from the south, east and west during the 16th and 17th centuries. Informants explain that the numbers were massive and the process was probably precipitated by Ahmed Gragn's Jihad and the Oromo wars of conquest. Ulrich Braukämper observes that "Kambata served as a refuge for political refugees and economically threatened groups from northern and southern Ethiopia", and that "the immigrants... often became the founders of new clans, whose numbers rose in the course of time..." (Braukämper, 1983: 296). Thus, Kambata received immigrants from Arsi, Bale, Gimma, Wolayta, Borana, Alaba, Gamo, Sidama, Kafa, Ziway, Gurage, Enariya, Gadab, Dawaro, Hararge, Guji, Bonga, Tambaro. All of these presently constitute an integral part of Kambata community while keeping their place of origin as their tribal names. Each tribal entity is a corporate group with an independent structure based on patriarchal lineage.[1]

Seera

As indicated above, *seera* refers to the code of conduct practiced and internalized among the Kambata. Relations between individuals, tribes and territorial units are regulated by *seera*. It is alternatively known as Marietta, which means commitment to the truth. *Seera* is a broadly conceived normative realm within which individuals and groups are expected to behave. The territorial or tribal councilors function according to their respective *seera*. Love affairs, marriage and family relations, peer group associations, work and entertainment parties, games and sports, hunting bands, etc. are all bound by *seera* relevant to the specific activity. Child care, socialization of the young, circumcision, initiation and rites of passage are handled as *seera* requires. *Seera* prescribes the way farmers relate to the environment, young to old, women to men. For instance, a farmer must not cut down a tree on his land without planting one or two young trees in advance as replacement. Young persons must give precedence to older ones as a sign of respect to older generations, because the older generation is believed to possess experience, knowledge, wisdom, grace and power. In addition, elderly persons are believed to have the power to award or punish, to bless or curse the younger ones, depending on what they deserve.

Sera is not a codified body of rules but it is several sets of norms. Hence, during the execution of *seera* reference cannot be made to specific articles. There are no particular experts specializing in *seera*. Sanctions are not formalized but influenced by

---

1. See Norman J. Singer, "Some Notes on the Origins of the Cambata of Southern Shewa", Paper for Discussion at the Conference on Ethiopian Origins, 28 and 29 June, 1977, Centre for African Studies, School of Oriental and African Studies, University of London.)

circumstances as the elders see fit. The entire exercise of the implementation of *seera* is creative, consultative and compromise-oriented. *Seera* administration aims at pacification, conciliation, correction and reintegration. It is the community elders who are in charge of *seera* administration. Elders are generally expected to have wisdom, patience and broad views about justice and peace. They are expected to restore and maintain balanced relationships in the community.

However, elderly persons who lack experience and have not demonstrated the necessary caliber to handle sanctions may not be chosen for *seera* administration. Younger persons with intensive experience and reputation may be chosen instead. Although it is widely believed that women's judgement is impartial and clear-cut they are not preferred for the formal handling of *seera*. Women are often consulted in the house by their husbands, sons, relatives or neighbors who are entrusted with handling the administration of *seera*. During the deliberation the elders may take a recess of a few days or even weeks. The time gap is often needed for consultation, additional fact-finding and opinion gathering about the case at hand. Women's opinion is of special value during this time. It is often solicited through family connections and neighborhood networks.

The Arena of *Seera*

Seera is administered in different arenas. The most important ones are the: (1) *heera* arena, (2) tribal arena, (3) *gotcho* arena and (4) *kokota* arena.

Heera arena: violations of *seera* by individuals in their relations with other members or groups within heera are first handled by heera elders. If the cases are not so important they are pushed downwards to relevant adjunct organizations. If the cases are very important to the extent of affecting other heera or the community at large they will be brought to the kokata arena. If the case concerns family or tribal matters it will be dealt with at the proper levels of the tribal arena. The *gotcho* arena is no longer functional because the gotcho as a territorial unit has been abolished since the Ethiopian Revolution of 1974.

Sanctions under the Kambata *seera* range from mild to punitive measures. But all sanctions take a form of conflict settlement, unlike in state courts, where sheer equity is the objective. Elements of precedence and future implication influence any particular proceeding of *seera*. Mild sanctions take the form of reparation to the aggrieved party. In addition, a material contribution is further requisitioned for ritual performance as a sign of the formal end of the conflict. More stringent sanctions are imposed in the form of ostracizing the offending party and excluding him and his family from the social, economic and political life of the community. Once a decision is taken to this effect all members of the community join in effecting the sanction. In the case of a member of the community failing to comply with applying this ultimate sanction, he/she will be liable to the same sanction. The rigor of this procedure has been somewhat compromised in as much as parties opt to go for a civil legal procedure.

Traditional Institutions under Kambata *Seera*

Over the centuries, the number of tribes in Kambata has grown by leaps and bounds, i.e. more than 17 fold the original seven.[1] Each incoming group settled down on available space, intermingling with previously settled communities. As the population increased and immigration continued, the settlement extended to the foothills of Mount Hambaricho and to the far-flung plains. The initial council form of organization of the seven tribes was further transformed through the participation of the newcomers. Each incoming group, irrespective of its origin and language, adopted *Kizoma*. *Kizoma* is a way of life characterized by permanent settlement, self-restraint, cooperation and solidarity with other fellow inhabitants. The informants explain that every settling tribe melted in *Kizoma*, the effect of which can easily be observed even today. *Kizoma* remained as the integral feature of Pax Kambata, maintained through the system of multiple strands of organizations which include: *kokata, gotcho, gogata*, and *ilammo*.

Kokata

Kokata is the general assembly of all Kambata including the *Woma* and the representatives of territorial units known as gotcho. It is a deliberative assembly where *Seera* (rules) were laid down and sanctions given through lallaba (oratory). A series of orations on political, military, security and social affairs of the community are made by representatives of territorial and tribal units. *Lallaba* is a system of relay speech. A speaker calls upon the next speaker of his choice for particular attention and then proceeds to make his points. The next speaker will be the one whose attention was drawn by the previous speaker. All speakers do the same thing until the issue at hand is exhausted or put off to another meeting. *Lallaba* continues until a decision is taken by consensus. The decision of the *kokata* is binding and respected because it is believed that the eyes and the spirit of Kambata are behind it as a hidden force. There is a belief that the *gada* (grace) and the *ayana* (blessing) of Kambata are in it. Defiance or breach of a *kokata* decision is believed to attract the "black" eyes and unpronounced curse of Kambata on those who go against it.

Gotcho

Gotcho is a territorial organization of Kambata. When the initial settlement of Kambata expanded, radiating out from Mount Hambaricho, territorial sub-division was necessary in order to keep the peace of Kambata and the style of *Kizoma* internally and to protect the community from external dangers. Thus, the territory was divided into thirty assymetrical units known as gotcho. The literal meaning of *gotcho* is 'gate'. All thirty territorial units have their *gotcho* (gates) at Mount Hambaricho. Hambaricho is the cradle of Kambata and the mythical source of gada (grace) and ayana (blessings). The most powerful spirit known as *Abba-maganancho* (grand spirit) resides at Hambaricho in the person of *Abba-mancho* (the man with Abba, i.e., the man with grand spirit). Although the spirit *Abba* belongs to one tribe it has been accepted by all other tribes, in addition to their respective tribal spirits. The greatness of *Abba* (the grand spirit) is associated with the grandness of Hambaricho.

The *kokata* assemblies were held near Hambaricho. For cultural, historical, spiritual and political reasons Hambaricho is the epicentre of Kambata. Every year in the month of September, during the festivity of *Meskel*, young men of Kambata from

---

1. The total list of tribes of Kambata, including the original seven, as furnished by informants in August 1999 consisted of 122. Tesfaye Habiso's report claims that the total number is 160: see note 2 above, p. 77. Desta Lorenso, "Yekambata Hebretasab Balaejotchinna Sinekalachew", B.A. thesis (AAU., 1982), puts the total number of the tribes of Kambata at 130.

all thirty territorial units make a ritual trip to Hambaricho. On their way there and back they perform *gifaata* songs and chants in honor of the unity of Kambata and the greatness of the *Abba-mancho* (grand spirit). The converging place for the young men is at the shrine of the grand spirit. They go back to their respective places with symbolic branches of the homa tree from the shrine of *Abba-mancho*. On their return, they are received with enthusiasm and songs of praise by those who have not gone to Hambaricho.

Hambaricho is shared by all members of Kambata, as all thirty territorial units touch on it. The territorial units had their traditional leaders known as *gotchi-danna*. They were permanent members of *kokata*. They sit in council together with *woma*, clan heads, and other notables of the community. Historically they were selected by the territorial communities. When the *woma* became increasingly influential they became his appointees. After the incorporation of Kambata into Menilek's empire in the early 1890's, the *gotchi-danna* were transformed into *sanga-koro*. They were made responsible to the new authority with the main function of tax-collecting and assisting with the administration of the *gotcho*.

Muricho

Gotcho have sections and sectional leaders traditionally appointed by gotchi-yaa (the assembly of *gotcho*). This was the *muricho*. The yaa selected its *muricho* and presented him to *kokata* and *woma*. The *muricho*, a non-hereditary appointment, election to which was highly competitive. The office rotated every few years among energetic personalities. The minimum criterion is that the candidate for *muricho* must be good at *lallaba* (oratory). In the oral society of Kambata it was and still is expected that the leader should be articulate in presenting his community's case and debating with others. *Muricho* was expected to be the advocate of his people. Although he naturally belonged to one of the tribes he was expected to be impartial to all tribes within his jurisdiction. He functioned as judge and administrator. His activities were checked horizontally by the community elders including his own tribesmen and vertically by the *gotchi dana* and *woma*. The institution of muricho was transformed to chikashum after the incorporation and was abolished by the Revolution.

Gogota

Gogota was a traditional army consisting of males between 18 and 50 years of age. Every family, community and tribe trained its young men in socialization and physical development. Young men were expected to prove that they were physically developed and duly initiated to manhood. From childhood onwards men were engaged in competitive sports including a traditional ball game (*torbo*), athletics, varieties of free wrestling, horse racing, swimming and hunting. The pivotal moment of physical development is immediately following circumcision which usually takes place at the age of 18 to 20. Circumcision is a group performance which takes place during the month of *Kakumie* (Pagume), which comes at the end of the rainy season. The season is chosen for two reasons: (1) *Kakumie* is believed to be the blessed month of the year and; (2) it is followed by the Meskel festival (towards the end of September) and the harvest season. Those circumcised in the same season are known as *misso*. They are well fed not only to heal the circumcision wound on the genital skin but also to build the body to be fit enough for the tough physical competitions during the subsequent season.

The physical competition of free wrestling known as gammisha first takes place between those circumcised in the same neighborhood. Then the competition moves to *heera, gotcho* and *inter-gotcho* levels. Furthermore, the circumcised go hunting for trophies also on a competitive basis. Every circumcised young man officially passes to manhood through this process. Without this rite of passage no male can be a member of *gogota* or be accepted for any post of leadership and responsibility. Secondly, the circumcised are given honorific names commensurate with their individual performances in wrestling, hunting or other sports. They are called upon to serve in the *gogota* only in time of war. *Gogota* was not a standing army, and often war does not happen for generations. But the cultural infrastructure of *gogota* has been kept alive through the rituals and performances of circumcision. The political *gogota*, i.e. the military institution of Kambata, was destroyed at the time of incorporation. The cultural *gogota* still continues in certain forms.

Ilamo

Ilamo is a collective membership of a tribal group often of patriarchal lineage. Day-to-day activities and community functions take place in inter-tribal settings and on a territorial basis. But matters that particularly concern the members of a tribe are dealt with by the *ilamo* (tribal) council. There are several activities specifically handled within the bounds of *seera*, including marriage, inheritance and blood settlement.

The council ensures that marriage is strictly exogamous. No person of the tribe marries internally from his/her paternal line. On the maternal line, marriage is permissible after seven generations have elapsed. In exceptional situations, however, permission can be obtained from the tribal council for arranging marriage if the blood relationship is more than four generations. In traditional marriage arrangement the consent and mutual selection of the spouses are respected. However, elders see to it that marital age for the female is not below seventeen and for the male not less than twenty. They make sure that there is an acceptable level of tribal compatibility between the potential couple.

All matters of inheritance among the members of a tribe are settled by the tribal council. If one of the parties or all involved are not satisfied with the decision of the tribal council at all levels, they may wish to take the case to the kokata, or even to a civil court. Blood-related matters are of top importance within a tribal set-up. Blood is sacrosanct because it is considered as the living link with the ancestors. Elders and the tribal council take a great deal of care so that the blood of their members will not be spilt, and that their members do not spill the blood of others.

When an outsider is killed at the hands of a tribesman, the council organizes negotiations with the tribal council of the killed person for a peace settlement. The council coordinates material contributions towards *guma* (blood settlement).[1] When their own member is killed by an outsider the council takes the responsibility for peace negotiations and *guma* settlement on behalf of the bereaved family. The tribal council gives special attention to maintaining peace in the community in accordance with the requirements of *seera*, peace and *kizoma*.

---

1. *Guma* is a traditional peace settlement with rituals and ceremonies of reconciliation, especially in blood-related matters.

Overall tribal affairs are coordinated by the *woshaaba*, who is appointed by the tribal council for life. His functions are not limited territorially as tribes in Kambata are not settled territorially. He is the coordinator of his tribal affairs and represents the tribe in external relations where and when that is required. He is closely assisted by lineage heads and counseled by elders consisting of the most experienced, knowledgeable and influential personalities of the tribe. The *woshaaba*'s function is not limited within Kambata. He attends to the concerns even of tribal members residing in the neighboring territories of Alaba, Wolayta, Hadiya, or elsewhere in the country.

Heera

Heera is the smallest unit of territorial organization and it is comprised of dozens of rural households. One *heera* comprises two to four hundred households, depending on the density of population of a specific location. Everybody is born into a *heera* and dies from a *heera*, hence, membership is not optional. Even guests and dependants are cared for by the *seera* of *heera*, as long as they do not violate the *seera* during their temporary stay. *Heera* is the strongest and the most resilient organization of Kambata. When most of the traditional institutions were submerged under the dominance of the national state structures, *heera* survived and has become the repository of *seera*. Hence, in as much as every person in Kambata is a member of a *heera*, he/she remains the embodiment of *seera* at the lowest level of community organization.

Heera is the basic institution that binds together all households irrespective of their tribe, religion, level of wealth and education, political or social function, caste or class. It is a self-help organization led by an elected *danna* (head) and councilors. Informants assert that the genesis of the *heera* institution is the necessity for overcoming bad times through collaborative endeavour. Presently the functions of *heera* have grown to include local funeral services, community protection and crime control, public works, local conflict management and community welfare. Neighboring *heera* have a long tradition of collaborating in crime control, public works and conflict management.

The functions of *heera* have been partially taken over by *kebele* (peasant associations) and there is competition between the two organizations. However, the kebele has never been able to take over the essential functions of *heera*. Although the kebele is a politically constituted state structure, *heera* enjoys legitimacy and the trust of the community. While many of the public affair functions are more or less controlled by the *kebele*, the most important functions of community welfare and social service continue to remain in the domain of *heera*.

Under the auspices of *heera* several subordinate associations do exist to provide a large range of community level services under both voluntary and non-voluntary arrangements. These associations can be gender-specific or mixed. The most prominent ones include saving associations, mutual help associations and several social entertainment and cultural performance associations. *Heera* is territorially further sub-divided into several functional neighborhood units, each having its own elected head and council.

Woma

Woma is a territorial chief, a concept more or less denoting "king". Its origin is not clearly determined. Most informants attribute its emergence to the time that followed the upheaval wrought by the two consecutive conquests of Ahmed Gragn and the Oromo in the 16th century. That difficult period is described in Kambata as *dawdigalaa*, which means total chaos. The chaos disrupted the normal functioning of *seera*. Many informants expound, with a touch of speculation, that the *kokata* felt the need for restrengthening the *seera* with a coordinating leadership. They trace this to the oral tradition which holds that a 'hunger' contest was arranged for clan representatives. The rule of the game was that the contenders were to go on a total fasting competition for as many days as their physical stamina could sustain. The one who would fast for the greatest number of days would be appointed as paramount chief of the country and the leader of *kokata*. Leaving aside the stories of tricks and twists around the rules of the hunger contest, the one who ate last was acclaimed the paramount *woma* of Kambata.

Ever since then and until the Revolution, the institution of *woma* was maintained through hereditary succession in the male line. Every time the *woma* died, *kokata* sat in council and selected a successor from among the sons of the deceased *woma*. Then the *kokata* formally conferred the office on the new chief through a special *giffata* (ceremonial chanting) known as *hebboyyata*.

The *woma* often entered into conflict with the community interest whenever he attempted to control the economic and political powers of Kambata. Informants assert that several conflicts took place between the *woma* and the populace. Land was the main issue of the conflict. The *woma* was often tempted to take the best lands and the most strategic heights for his entourage and allies. This contradicted the perception of the community that land belonged to those who had settled and worked on it. As the *woma* and his men entered into the realm of ruling they went on requisitioning food grains, livestock and labor power from the community. The populace resisted the actions of the emerging rulers who, in the eyes of the people of Kambata, breached the seera and defied the spirit of solidarity. The last war between the people and the *woma* took place at the time when Emperor Menelik's forces were advancing to reincorporate Kambata. The divided forces of Kambata were defeated without any meaningful resistance. Many informants assert that the conquest by Menelik was a welcome opportunity to the opponents of the *woma*, as he was captured and killed together with his advisors. The institution itself was abolished and replaced by *balabat*, a new institution which functioned as a link between the new regime and the local community. Several clan heads and notables from the thirty territorial units were appointed as *sanga-koro*. Kambata then was ruled by officers appointed from outside by the Ethiopian Emperor.

Seera as an Institution of Kambata Solidarity

Internally, the Kambata tribes find themselves bound by a web of numerous associations. Most tribes have members settled in different *gotcho* and *heera* intermingling with several other tribesmen and women. In political and cultural activities one tribe cannot do without the other. This association is further reinforced by continuous marriage arrangements between exogamous tribes. A member of one tribe finds himself as a cousin, in-law or uncle of someone from another tribe. Hence, the *seera* of inter-tribal cooperation is inherently deep and interwoven. Overall solidarity and day-to-day cooperation are reinforced through the web of inter-tribal relationships.

Externally, the Kambata have established long-standing relationships with the neighbouring communities such as Hadiyya, Wolayita, Alaba, Gurage, Donga or Tambaro.[1] Such alliance is characterized by marriage, mixed settlements, economic interaction and cultural ties. There are no days during the week that the Kambata do not interact and transact with their neighbouring communities. The weekly and biweekly markets are the most regular venue for such interactions and transactions. For instance Alaba and Kambata meet at Kulieto (in Alaba) or at Durame and Dambaoya (in Kambata). The Kambata and Wolayita meet at Araka and Himbetcho (in Wolayita) or at Shinshicho and Hadaro (in Kambata). Kambata and Hadiyya meet at Wachemo and Jajura (in Hadiyya) or at Doyogana and Hadaro (in Kambata). Similarly Kambata and Tambaro meet at Mudula (in Tambaro) or Hadaro (in Kambata). There are numerous other situations and venues of inter-community interactions. Weddings, funerals or peace settlement meetings also offer opportunities for interactions with the neighbouring communities.

Such interactions are supported by a traditional and long-standing system of protecting the property and lives of the members of the neighboring communities. Not only are economic relations facilitated through the interactions but exchange of ideas and values also takes place on a continuous basis. The communities respect and deal with one another with special care and sensitivity. The base-line of the mutual code of conduct is governed by the respective seera traditions of these neighbouring communities. Although there is no formal institution that is in charge of managing inter-community collaboration, the elders of the communities take upon themselves the responsibility of overseeing the conduct of the relationships on an ad hoc basis. Several examples can be cited about inter-community co-operation and alliance. In this way conflicts are prevented from taking place or from worsening once they do occur.

Seera under the Three Regimes

Following the re-incorporation of Kambata in the 1890's, the new authority destroyed some of the institutions and transformed others. *Gogota* was one of those institutions destroyed. *Woma* was transformed to *balabat*, *gotcho* to *sanghi-danomma*, *gotchi-danna* to *sanga-koro*, and *muricho* to *chikashum*. The transformed structures were absorbed by the new political system, which superimposed itself on the community and its institutions. The *heera* institution, by and large, remained intact. So too did the *seera* and subsidiary organizations. Similarly, the tribal and lineage organizations continued functioning in keeping with *ilammo seera* until the end of the era of Emperor Haile Selassie I. With the revolution and the subsequent change of political regime, those traditional institutions which were modified to serve the "ancien regime" and its institutions were abolished. *Balabat, sanga koro* and *chickashum* were totally abolished, and their political functions were replaced by *kebele* associations organized at neighbourhood, zonal and woreda levels. Part of the functions of the *heera* was taken over by peasant associations. *Heera* and most of its subsidiary organizations continued functioning in competition with the politically powerful *kebele* associations whose territorial jurisdiction often overlapped with that of

---

1. Tambaro and Donga had separate kingdoms but their languages are the same as that of Kambata. The Alaba language is a slight dialect of Kambatigna.

heera. Tribal institutions were effectively weakened under the Derg regime because they were viewed both by the state and some radical members of the local community as primordial and inimical to modernity and socialism. They further believed that the traditional associations would hinder the universal solidarity of oppressed peoples.

During the last years of the Derg regime, there prevailed a growing security problem in problem in Kambata, as was the case in many other places in Ethiopia. The civil war was intensifying in the north. National resources and the attention of the political authorities were geared to the war effort. The peasants were requisitioned in kind and in cash to support the costs of the war. Young men were conscripted into the army. Those who escaped conscription went into hiding and roamed the countryside as outlaws. The *kebele* and local government structures entered into conflict with the community because of their involvement in the forced conscription and the burden of grain requisitioning on farmers.

On the other hand, the local administrative, security and justice organs were unable to function normally or to provide protection for public safety. Crime was on the rise as a function of the fast increasing security, economic and political problems. Roads, market places, villages and even private compounds were unsafe. There was no public authority around to attend to those problems. It was at that juncture that the *kokata* started to re-emerge out of the clear necessity of containing the crisis, and salvaging the community from plunging into total anarchy.

When the Derg regime was finally overthrown there was a total absence of political authority. The *kokata* elders resorted to informal and formal meetings in the interest of revitalizing the traditional institution of *seera*. The *heera* institution was reactivated and tribal solidarity reinforced. Several months elapsed before the new regime's first cadres and security forces were put in place to fill up the local political structures. There was an additional time of limbo until the inexperienced "core" members and fighters knew how to handle the political, security and administrative affairs. It was in this process that *kokata* and *heera* re-emerged to the forefront of community affairs.

During 1991–1995 demobilized soldiers and highway robbers roamed across Kambata and Hadiyya country. The government security structure was not then adequately in place. The life and property of the members of both communities were in serious danger. It was the locally initiated inter-community conferences and ad hoc council meetings that stopped the conflict from expanding. Subsequently, the ad hoc councils managed to identify the culprits and their tribes and *heera*. Then the tribal councils and heera structures managed to stamp out the crime. *Seera* re-emerged as communities clung to it in a situation where there was no functioning structure of the formal state in Kambata. The internal and external alliance systems have been used with a good degree of keenness and efficiency to prevent and manage conflict within Kambata as well as with its neighboring communities.

Furthermore, the *kokata* actively participated in the "peace and stability" program of EPRDF and maintained a bridge between the community and the new regime. The revitalized *kokata* has gained recognition both from the political authorities and the community at large. Presently the kokata is a recognized traditional structure organized in all three *woreda*[1] of Kambata and its functions are coordinated at community, tribal and *heera* levels.

---

1. *Kokata* is known by the same name in Hangatcha woreda, but is called *gogota* and reda in *Katchabiira* and Kadida Gamella woredas, respectively.

Concluding Remarks

Seera and the traditional institutions of Kambata have survived remarkably well: (1) the influence of the numerically overwhelming influx of populations from all directions; (2) the rise of and usurpation of power by the *woma* institution; (3) incorporation into the Ethiopian state administration; (4) mass conversion to Islam or various forms of Christianity; (5) the rise and radical changes of "socialism"; and (6) the political and security crisis caused by the absence of state authority during the spring of 1991. When need arose, the seera revived to ensure the well-being of the community as well as to protect its members from disarray and shame. When it regained its power, collective responsibility and intra-community solidarity once again became the modus operandi. For individuals the revival of the seera became a source of personal pride and honor. It became an opportunity to share the duties and responsibilities of maintaining peace and managing internal conflicts as well as those with the communities bordering on Kambata.

External forces and influences have always penetrated Kambata but without permanently obliterating or substantially modifying the traditional institutions. On the contrary, the intruding forces were absorbed into or modified by the customs and institutions of Kambata. This can only be attributed to the strength and deep-rooted nature of the *seera* and its influence.

The pivotal institutions like kokata, heera and seera have proven resilient. They appear to have provided the Kambata with peace and stable unity based on: (1) the alliance and unity of the tribes; (2) intermingled settlement of the population; (3) maintenance of the territorial principle of political or economic organization; and (4) observance of the *seera*.

Presently, notwithstanding the pressures from the state structures, seera is not only pervasive but also morally authoritative throughout the community. Moreover, it has come to enjoy recognition and limited legitimacy from the local state structures. In matters of public safety and crime control, the traditional sector has passed the test of time under the successive regimes and overarching political systems of Ethiopia. The relationship between the state and seera can, thus, be characterized as one between the indomitable voice from below and the pervasive power from above.

Glossary of key terms

Abba: grand, grand spirit.
Abaa-mancho/abba-sharecho: a person possessed by grand spirit.
Ayyana: good luck, fortune.
Bunny-heera: small heera, inner heera.
Danna: judge, local leader.
Fandannano: traditional religion with spectacular ritual performances.
Ghifaata: traditional chant in praise of leaders, country, people or spirits.
Gogata: traditional army comprising of young men mobilized in time of war.
Gada: blessing, grace, source of good feelings.
Gazenna: commander of gogata, leader of hunting band.
Gotcho: gate, any one of the thirty units of Kambata with a gate at the Hambaricho mountain.
Gotchi-danna: leader or head of one of the thirty territorial units of Kambata.
Gotchi-dannoma: administrative institution of the territorial units (gotchos).
Gotchi-yaa: the general assembly of gotcho (territorial unit).
Guma: peace settlement with regard to conflict involving blood (killing).

Hambaricho: the grand mountain of Kambata, the cradle of the Kambata and their institutions.

Hebboyyata: a special song for conferring a new woma.

Heera: the basic territorial organization of Kambata.

Heera-danna: leader or head of heera.

Heera-muricho: heera-danna, leader or head of heera.

Heera-Seera: norms, rules of heera.

Ilamo: blood-related tribe.

Ilami-yaa: assembly of tribe.

Keghia: blood, human blood.

Keghi-seera: norms, rules pertaining to blood (life)-related matters.

Kizoma: the Kambata way of life, outlook of peace and unity.

Kokata: overall cultural, political, economic institution of the Kambata.

Lallaba: Oratory, eloquence.

Maganancho: man of god, the man in whom god dwells, spiritual head of a tribe.

Menti-Seera: rules pertaining to women, women associations.

Menti-gezima: women's work-related self-help association.

Misso: peer group circumcised and initiated in the same season.

Muricho: leader of a section of a gotcho, leader of heera.

Sanga: mature bull or horse, big bull, big horse (literally castrated).

Seera: rules, general code of conduct, totality of norms.

Sangi-danna: the head of a territorial unit, gotchi-danna, (traditional office).

Sangakoro: officer of a territorial unit; modified office of gotchi-danna after the incorporation.

Woma: King, paramount chief.

Worjami-seera: rules of sanction involving fines with bull.

Woshaaba: head, leader of a tribe.

Wozino-seera: rules pertaining to compensation, emancipation.

II

The Peasant and
the Management of
Power and Resources

Models of Democracy— Perceptions of Power

Government and Peasantry in Ethiopia[1]

Harald Aspen

Introduction: Transition to Democracy?

The distance between the Ethiopian central government and its peasant subjects has long been great and characterised by a deep power imbalance. For centuries the emperors were sanctified by divine status, until the Revolution of 1974 removed for good any reference to divinity in relation to government. Instead, the Därg regime imported an ideological screen for its brutal oppression, leaving the peasants in their seemingly perpetual role of suppliers of the fruits of their toil to an encompassing and insatiable state. Although an important driving force behind the revolution was the predicament of the rural poor, other forces pushed it through and took power in 1974. The peasantry never became sufficiently organised or politically articulated to pose a real threat to the political and economic order.

With the fall of the Mengistu regime in May 1991, a historic opportunity seemed to present itself to the Ethiopian people. The long military resistance against the government forces was rewarded with victory, just at the time of the breakdown of communism and the end of the Cold War. The victorious forces of EPRDF, backed by international support and acclaim, turned out to have left the TPLF Marxist stand in favour of democratisation and reconciliation.

This paper is principally based on my report on the 1995 national and regional elections in Ethiopia (Aspen, 1995). A grant from NORAD enabled me to conduct brief fieldwork in Mafud *wäräda*, Northern Shäwa, with the purpose of writing a report from these elections, from a specific local point of view. With a research permit from the National Electoral Board of Ethiopia I spent two intensive weeks in the field, observing the local preparations for the imminent elections. I also visited several election sites on the election day, 7 May 1995. I had very good contacts in the Mafud district, after several longer and shorter periods of fieldwork there since 1989. Long term personal relationships, dating back to 1989, with former *Därg* officials as well as with the cadres and local leaders of the new political establishment gave me very good access to the work and opinions behind the official scene. Since 1989 I had also my own house in the rural area, about two hours walk from the town of Däbrä Sina, which I also used during this fieldwork. This also gave me the opportunity of getting direct access to the everyday life of my neighbours at the time of the historic multi-party elections.

1. Acknowledgements: this is a revised version of a paper presented at the workshop on "Globalisation and Localization: The Quest for Local Development Alternatives" organised by the Institute of Development Research, Addis Ababa University and the Norwegian Institute for Urban and Regional Research, 12–14 March 1996 in Sodore, Ethiopia. I am grateful for comments from the workshop participants and from Bahru Zewde, Svein Ege, Robert Gillespie and Siegfried Pausewang.

On this basis, the present paper deals with local perceptions of democracy in general and of the elections in particular. The paper may serve as a critical assessment of the extent of agreement between the government's models of democracy and the peasants' perceptions of it. Readers who want a more comprehensive account and documentation of the election process in Mafud may refer to my report (Aspen, 1995).

The End of Marxism and the Därg

When the Mengistu regime fell in May 1991, and the Transitional Government took over, the stated political model was no longer Marxism but multi-party democracy (although TPLF prior to their victory had announced that they represented purer Marxism than the regime they fought against, Marxism was not in their vocabulary after they took power as the leading member of the EPRDF).[1] The Marxist slogans that were spread all over the country during the Därg period almost always seemed strange and external to the local communities they appeared in. This was particularly apparent in the house of a former *baladära* (representative of the landowner, whose responsibility used to be to control and supervise the estate in the owner's absence) of one of the few big pre-revolution landowners (a one-time Governor of Harär) in the area in which I worked in 1989. Now the *baladära* was an old man living with his equally old wife, both of them childless, and dependent on a *tägazh* (sharecropping tenant) for the cultivation of their land. The old man received us in the upper room of a two-storied house (a witness of past greatness), of which the lower room was used as a kitchen. His wife, bent by hard work and old age, served us the local beer (*t'äla*). The old man, eagerly and without attempting to hide his longing for the 'old days', told about the agricultural inventions his old landlord initiated in the area, such as forcing our host to plant coffee and the strange orange trees instead of the popular *gésho* (a bush used like hops in brewing). It was therefore surprising, and totally misplaced, to read the slogans in English(!) and Amharic on the black walls inside his house. The two English inscriptions read "Marxism-Leninism is our guid (guide)" and We shall build PDRE". When I asked if he himself had written these things on the wall, he told us that this was done by the campaigners[2]—this was their work—and he did not seem to be very interested in that topic.[3] The meaning of the phrases, or the reason for this activity carried out by the campaigners, seemed to be of no relevance to him. They were the signs of external agents, representing external powers. We shall see later in this paper how the new concept of "democracy" was conceived in the Ethiopian rural setting.

The Marxist state was a distant but influential and uncontrollable factor in the peasants' lives. Many of them got the opportunity (or rather were forced) to attend "seminars" arranged by the authorities—usually the regional (*wäräda* or *awraja*) Peasant Association (PA) or Ministry of Agriculture (MoA). The topics ranged from the value of cattle hides for export to lessons in Marxist ideology. I recall the chairman of the control committee in the PA where I conducted my fieldwork, when he returned from a two-day seminar in At'ayé. Tired, but happy he summarised the experience with the following: "We drank and slept. In the morning, we woke up,

---

1. TPLF—Tigre Peoples' Liberation Front. EPRDF—Ethiopian Peoples' Revolutionary Democratic Front.
2. This observation was made in January 1989. The campaign had taken place "the year before" according to our informant, most probably in connection with the proclamation of the PDRE in September 1987.
3. This passage was originally printed in Aspen, 1994:91, footnote 46.

switched on the (electric) light and drank more". The unusual luxury of electric light seems to have been the most important and memorable benefit he had from the seminar.

It was probably the Därg that introduced the word *säminar* to the Amharic language. A parallel was even found in spirit cults where *weqabi* spirits summoned their followers for seminars, with the purpose of teaching them correct behaviour at spirit sessions (Aspen, 1994:216). Marxist ideology did trickle down to the peasantry, through seminar attendance, visiting MoA and higher-level PA officials, and other state agents. Some households, although they were few, could afford a transistor radio and the necessary batteries and were able to follow the propaganda transmissions, including the endless speeches by President Mengistu, and these were also sources of information about the state ideology. Some of it was cherished by the poor peasants, and most of them were particularly positive to the social revolution that followed the Revolution and the Land Reform. The various sources of information did not however always coincide with the lived experience and the real encounters with the state and its representatives—rather, experience was usually contradictory to the slogans.

In October 1989, for example, an old man complained to me that he could not understand what had happened to the PA committee, which was supposed to act on behalf of the state. "The state is for the poor", he said, "but now the 15 men (in the committee) bury me". In 1989 there were several cases in the PA resulting from conflicting interpretations of rules and regulations regarding land; individual peasants felt they were manipulated by the local PA leaders, while these in turn were under pressure from higher-level organs of the PA structure. The PA leaders were under constant threat from above of punishment for "disobeying the correct centralism" and were sometimes fined or imprisoned (Aspen, 1989). One informant believed that the problems the local population experienced in relation to local representatives of the state could be explained by the central government's lack of knowledge. The afforestation programme, which was carried out as Food-For-Work (FFW) programmes, dispossessed peasants of their grazing lands, and they obtained no rights in the trees that were produced on the enclosures. The informant claimed that he did not know "the secrets" behind the afforestation programme—"they ordered us to go there and plant trees and they gave us wheat—we don't know for whom we did it. As a consequence of this, poor people with little land have to plough steep hills. The state doesn't know about people's problems", he said.[1]

Marxism failed as a model for mass mobilisation and participation in Ethiopia like elsewhere. The slogans remained foreign artefacts without obvious links to peoples' daily lives and problems. Marxism belonged to, and was associated with, a powerful and dictatorial State. Marxist ideology and organisation probably also contributed to making the State into a factor that was matched only by Nature and God in unpredictability and power—although such a perception was not new to the Ethiopian peasants after centuries of "Divine Rule" by dictatorial Emperors. It is also important to remember that peasants in Northern Shäwa would not naturally place the responsibility for the wrongs and ills they experienced during the Därg regime on its purported ideological basis; rather, they would firmly place the responsibility with the regime itself and its officers. But despite the Peasant Association structure, which was purportedly created for mass mobilisation and which in form and content could have ensured a certain representativeness and transparency, the

---

1. Fieldwork in Northern Shäwa, February 1991.

peasants had no means of making the structures or the individuals that were responsible for the misery accountable for it. The accountability went only in the wrong direction, from the bottom to the top. Neither, in effect, was there support in the system for any transparency or representativeness to the benefit of the peasant subjects of the state.

The New Ideology

After a period of virtual occupation by the victorious forces after May 1991, the preparations began to establish a democratically elected government, based on a new Constitution for the country. The EPRDF-based Transitional Government had two enormously difficult tasks to achieve: to keep control over the country and to prepare the ground for democracy. Two rounds of elections preceded the first regional and national elections that were based on a democratic constitution, in May 1995: a round of local elections in 1992 and the elections in 1994 to a Constitutional Assembly. Both rounds of elections were reported by Norwegian observers to be unsatisfactory as genuine instruments in the democratisation process.[1] The present paper is mainly based on observations I made during the May 1995 elections (see Aspen, 1995).[2] I shall focus in this paper on local perceptions of democracy in general and of the elections in particular, questioning if the government's models of democracy agree with the peasantry's perceptions of it. Rephrased into a more general question, the problem appears to have many similarities with those related to the former period in Ethiopian history, when Marxism, not Democracy, was the alleged ideological guiding star of the powerholders, namely: what happens to a "universal" ideology when it becomes localised?

Addressing this question, I shall not dwell on the (in itself) critical question whether the post-Därg Ethiopian Government actually and sincerely wanted to introduce democracy as the leading principle for state governance—or whether the elections, the new Constitution (Transitional Government of Ethiopia 1994) and the court trials of the Därg officers were only components of a smoke-screen for some sort of a hidden agenda which would turn out not to include democracy and the observation of human rights in the very end. I shall not pursue this question (raised by internal opposition groups), simply because it will involve too much unqualified speculation to be fruitful. I shall rather deal with the elements that could be observed and that were claimed by the government to be parts of a democratisation plan, and how these elements were received and understood by the peasants in Northern Shäwa.

Global Models of Democracy

"Democracy" has become the "new orthodoxy" of development thinking, and yoked with human rights, viewed as the necessary basis for development.[3] One may

---

1. The Norwegian observer group to the local and regional elections 21 June 1992 concluded that "the elections did not in any meaningful way represent the free and fair will of the Ethiopian people in a democratic manner" (Norwegian Institute of Human Rights, Human Rights Report No.1, August 1992, p. 14). The report from the Norwegian observer group to the June 1994 elections (Pausewang, 1994b), states in the executive summary that "it is doubtful whether this election can add legitimacy to the constitution which is to be endorsed" (p. 1).
2. See also Tronvoll and Aadland (1995) and Poluha (1995).
3. Cf. Andreassen 1995:542 and Hawthorn (1993:330–332).

rightly question the reasons for this new interest (and investment!) from the North for democracy in the South (cf. Poluha, 1993 for a thought-provoking essay on this subject in relation to Ethiopia, and to Sweden). What matters in the present context is the concept of democracy as it was understood by the Ethiopian peasantry under EPRDF rule. It will nevertheless be useful for an objective analysis to agree upon some key elements that characterise democracy. I have found a comprehensive paper by Geoffry Hawthorn (1993) to be clarifying and useful for my purpose. "Minimally", he states, must a democracy consist of "a regular competition for power, the rules of which are agreed in advance and the outcome of which is at least formally decided by those over whom the power is to be exercised" (p. 331). More fundamentally, we could add, must the people be able, and have a legitimate right, to get rid of the powerholders by peaceful means. Several questions naturally arise, such as "who constitute 'the people'?",[1] and what instruments do they command to exercise this right? Three aspects, already mentioned, are central for the democratic political process, namely accountability, transparency, and representativeness.

The Ethiopian answer, mainly to the latter, but also with reference to the other two, became ethnically and regionally based representation. This risks the dangers both of encouraging differences (a kind of 'multi-Mobutuism')[2] and of excluding other bases for political formation and action from the legitimate stage of national politics. It seems that the transitional government, with its origin in regional movements for independence, had no choice but to grant the same rights to other regions that they had struggled for themselves: local and regional (or "national") independence. Pausewang points to the parallel to the previous government, and its reliance on fulfilling its revolutionary slogan land to the tiller: "In 1974 the key to legitimacy for the new government lay in solving the land question. In 1991 no new government could hope to win legitimacy without solving the nationality issue. A solution was found in the charter[3] which provided for a federal state, promising wide local and regional autonomy" (Pausewang, 1994a:219). The elections of 1995 showed however that although there were very many political parties, almost all "nationality"-based, the EPRDF umbrella re-united them into one ruling party.

The Question of Ethnicity

The question of "nationalities" is of little relevance for a local population which regards itself to be mono-ethnic, as is generally the case for Amhara peasants in the escarpment of Northern Shäwa. For the majority of them, ethnicity or nationality is not a natural or operational basis for their relations with the state. Although the southern populations in many respects probably have fared worse than the northerners due to the "Amharisation" which followed the conquest of the south, this does not change the fundamental character of the relations between the peasants of the north and the state: it is a relationship between the centre of power and a poverty-stricken population that periodically suffers from famine, and chronically from lack of social, economic and political power. The question is, are there any signs in

---

1. Poluha (1993:4) points to the fact that the Greek translation of *democracy* reads "government by the people"—but "the people" in Athens around 400 B.C. only included free, male citizens; women and slaves were excluded from decision-making.
2. Mobutu's encouragement of difference produced more than 200 political parties by the beginning of 1992, creating a situation which the Zairians called "multi-Mobutuism" (Hawthorn, 1993:341).
3. The Transitional Charter which was adopted on 22 July 1991 as an interim Constitution and basis for the Transitional Government of Ethiopia (TGE).

the present process of political change that indicate a change in this situation? Is there a feeling of being empowered, improved and reckoned with in the peasant population?

Elections, Democracy and the Cadre System

A major instrument applied by the government for sensitizing the rural population in democratic thought and action, including the electoral procedures, seemed to be the cadre system which was mushrooming all over the country. A group of 12 "peasant cadres" were elected from each *qäbälé*[1] and formed a committee which was in addition to the formal PA executive committee. The peasant cadres reported to the *wäräda* (district) party cadres (ANDM/EPRDF[2] leaders) with whom they interacted in regular meetings. There was a considerable overlap in cadre and PA committee membership, and at higher levels, the border between government administrative structures and the party became increasingly blurred. For the layman, there was hardly any difference between party and government officials; both categories merged into one as representatives of the state or government *(mängest)*.

The "peasant cadres", as well as the PA committee members, were recruited from a narrow section of the local communities, because very many were *a priori* excluded from election or assignment. Any official position under the Därg, and any accusation or suspicion of "banditry" *(sheftägna*—a term that included both criminal activities and government opposition) or corruption were reasons for exclusion from post-Därg elections. The result was an overweight of young men in leading and controlling positions, while older members of the society—the traditional leaders—were conspicuously absent from the formal political stage. The inherent generational conflict was further increased by interest conflicts between the generations: while the elders usually controlled some land they considered as their own, many youngsters depended on their parents for access to land. The still unsettled question (in 1995) about land regulations and the rumours about a new land redistribution were fuel to the flames of a potentially blazing fire in many people's minds.[3]

Most of the cadres were however probably not in this position because of their own will or interest (although some might have seen their chance or followed their conviction that they did represent the interest of the people by serving as cadres). There seemed to be a certain amount of enforcement when peasants were recruited as cadres—the orders came from above that each PA should elect a group of 12 cadres, and this quota was "delivered" by a PA committee which was used to obeying orders and minimising conflict with the government. The position as a cadre meant a delicate balance between local and central legitimacy—maintaining one's relations to neighbours, friends and work-group partners and showing one's party leaders a certain amount of willingness to fulfill one's duties as a cadre.

The difficulties in maintaining this balance stemmed from the character of the task. Much of the cadres' work had the character of controlling fellow peasants and the PA committee members, and they were supposed to report any irregularities. Cadres spent their time advising other peasants and committee members on how to avoid being reported, by conforming with central rules and regulations. In connec-

---

1. *Qäbälé* is the lowest administrative unit and is administered by a Peasant Association (PA).
2. ANDM—Amhara National Democratic Movement, a member organisation of EPRDF.
3. This has changed since this paper was written. A land redistribution was carried out in the Amhara region in 1997. For an interesting and detailed study of this process, see Ege (1997).

tion with the elections in 1995, they were to teach about the political platform of the party, the electoral procedures, and the best candidates to elect. A similar role seemed to be taken by the PA executive committees. For both kinds of officials, the memory of the previous regime and its top-down flow of orders was recent and illuminated the present situation—the parallels were vivid and clear. The parallels were of course not unnoticed, or left uncommented, by the peasants. Some peasants dryly summarised the change in regime—and the basically unchanged power balance between state and peasant society—by commenting that "under Mengistu, the enemies of the state were 'anti-revolutionary'. Today they are 'anti-democratic'".[1]

Local Perceptions of Democracy and Elections: Popular Passive Resistance or Political Passivity?

Addressing the question of "local perceptions of democracy" in this context opens up a whole range of pitfalls for the investigator. Informants' statements cannot normally be taken at their face value, and especially not in a culture, like that of the Amhara, where rhetoric is a valued art of statements with double meanings ("wax and gold"), and in a political situation which people have experienced to be far from democratic. The informants may represent other pitfalls too, in pretending to hold opinions or convictions, in withholding information or controlling it by other means, and in paying lip-service to one opinion or another. The researcher also certainly influences the validity of his or her findings. In his search for "perceptions", is he *a priori* looking for misapprehensions, misunderstandings or other forms of "false consciousness" due to lack of information, instruction or intellectual capacity? May "local perceptions" be equivalent to "local experience", knowledge and judgement? I have tried to be aware of these pitfalls, both those represented by my informants and myself. I tried to establish the latter kind of "perceptions", which acknowledge the political capability and intellectual independency in mind and opinion of the local peasantry of Northern Shäwa. I believe the peasants understand the issues of democratisation, participation, representativeness, and political power much better than their literal statements sometimes indicate. For example, an old peasant in Mafud remarked that *democracy means one who does not like the system*. This should not be taken as his definition of democracy, but rather as his comment on the prospects for democracy in the country, paired with an understatement (and understanding) of the core democratic right of expressing opposition to the current power-holders.

The institution of elections was in focus during my fieldwork in Northern Shäwa in April and May 1995, when for the first time in Ethiopian history, the Ethiopians were called to participate in a nation-wide election open for multi-party competition and endorsed by the new, democratic Constitution. The election machinery worked excellently—ballot boxes, registration forms, colour-coded seals to close the boxes, and other necessary equipment arrived in time to the most distant constituencies. If democracy were fulfilled with technical implementation of elections, Ethiopia could have been a model for the rest of the world. The act of casting the vote however, and the information and competition basis this act rests on, are more important than election logistics. In both these respects, the May 1995 elections were generally less than good. Several reports show that both the pre-election campaign and the election

---

1. Fieldwork in Northern Shäwa, 1995.

day were characterised by compulsion, threats, and unfavourable treatment of non-EPRDF candidates.[1] None of the reports attempts to assess whether the various infringements of the Electoral Law (Transitional Government of Ethiopia 1995) that were observed were intended and desired by the central authorities or not; such questions go beyond the scope of these reports and would probably only amount to speculation. It is, however, fairly well documented that in some constituencies, local PA and electoral committees were given orders by peasant cadres—themselves receiving orders from district *(wäräda)* party officials—about candidates that should be voted for and "information" about the harmful consequences other results would have (see, e.g. Aspen 1995). Punishment for not registering as voters and for not participating in the elections was also a widespread rumour which was substantiated by peasant cadres and PA leaders. Political rhetoric was mixed with lower-level threats about penalties and loss of land rights. It might have passed just for that had it occurred in a genuine multi-party contest for power. In the situation as it was then, the rhetoric was taken as messages from the current powerholders—whom no-one doubted would also hold power after the elections. One should keep in mind that the recent history of the Mengistu regime was constantly the frame of reference in which the EPRDF actions were interpreted. In addition, prior to the elections, particularly in 1994, Northern Shäwa experienced a series of violent clashes between opposition parties and EPRDF which resulted in the eradication of open, organised opposition. A peasant cadre expressed himself in the following manner:

> We don't know the other (non-EPRDF) candidates, but I believe (that EPRDF told us) not to vote for them because they are not from this party, so they are probably opposition candidates. So if they are elected they will not work for the government, since the government is from this party.
> The election will not reflect the interest of the people, the candidates are only running for power. We do this only because we are ordered to do it, not because of our willingness or interest to do it. People also say that there have been elections so many times but we don't see any change in government or any improvement or anything that reflects the interest of the people and therefore people say this is useless. (Aspen, 1995:24).

Another peasant cadre, when he prepared himself to call people on the election day, expressed his feelings in this way:

> This is to force people to vote for these persons, we fear that if we don't vote for them we will be harassed. The cadres are also forced to force the people. We were told that if these persons are not elected, EPRDF will not be in power any more and that we may face a very dangerous and difficult time if EPRDF is no longer in power. (Aspen, 1995:41).

In this light, the seeming passivity of the voters may become easier to understand, not as political apathy or lack of interest but as an expression of a political stand. The process of registration and voting was so closely connected with compulsion and lack of alternatives that even non-participation was judged to be a foolish and risky political expression. A common argument was that since the election would change nothing, to register and vote would do no further harm. On the other hand, to boycott the elections would also make no changes except to result in increased personal exposure and risk. Political articulation therefore had to be done in more subtle forms, and the major message it carried can be read as "we do not believe we have the power to decide what we want". Hence, the statement quoted below, by an old man who had just cast his vote together with his wife, can be interpreted either as a call for better training in electoral procedures, or, alternatively, as a bitter joke

---

1. Cf. Aspen (1995), Poluha (1995) and Tronvoll and Aadland (1995).

about the futility of it. For him, it did not matter on what grounds he made his decision, since there was no possibility open for him to influence the outcome of the election in a direction he desired. He simply stated that:

> It was a bit difficult to understand the symbols. The electoral board asked me if I preferred the sickle or the basket, and I chose the latter because it conains enjära (bread) (Aspen 1995: 32).[1]

Conclusion

How can democracy work in Ethiopia, and what forms should it take? What are the interests of the peasants, and do they match those of the national government? These are questions that should be asked, even if answers are difficult to find.

People know what they need and what they want. While their needs are often physically felt, their wants are harder to express. Their needs are related to survival and procreation for their own and the following generations. Although the poorest housewife in a distant rural community may turn out to have borne all her children in Addis Ababa hospitals, or even to receive occasional letters from a son, residing as a university student in the United States, national politics are distant events that do not seem to have much relevance for the rural poor—as long as they lack the means of voicing their interest in the national political game. One extraordinarily intelligent and widely respected peasant in Mafud explained to me that:

> Peasants are not strong and they do not work together. We need the educated and urban people to take action and the lead because they know more about politics and these things. People know what they want—what is to be and what not and what they want and what they don't want. But they don't get acceptance for their views, so it is better to keep quiet. Instead of getting killed, to die, because of one's views and outlook, it is better to wait until God brings us changes. (Aspen, 1995:14.)

What can the state offer the illiterate masses of African peasants? Basil Davidson seems bitter on behalf of the Africans, rejecting the African post-colonial nation-state as a positive force for progress: "The state was not liberating and protective of its citizens, no matter what its propaganda claimed: on the contrary, its gross effect was constricting and exploitative, or else it simply failed to operate in any social sense at all" (1992:290).

At present in Ethiopia, the most rational peasant strategy in their encounters with the state has not changed fundamentally—it is still to minimise the contact with the state by obeying only the inescapable demands it imposes on the peasantry, and otherwise to ignore it. This applies not only to the common peasants but also to the local-level state and party representatives, the PA officials and the peasant cadres.

As long as the peasants have no confidence in the state and it has seemingly nothing to offer them, materially or potentially, the question of democratisation becomes hopelessly unreal, even irrelevant. Many writers tend to see potentials for democracy in Africa to be limited to the local level. Funeral associations, rotating savings clubs, neighbourhood workgroups and similar structures all entail a high degree of general participation in decision processes as well as in implementation of their programmes. In a way this points to a situation of hope but also of irony. The irony stems from the fact that it is the inefficient and exploitative state that has sustained these local initiatives and associations, as Hawthorn also points out (1993:344). De-

---

1. Fekade (1998, and this volume) demonstrates how peasant oral poetry is a rich source for artistic and dramatised expressions of feelings of powerlessness and discontent.

ciding, or rather being forced, to "exit" from the state, the peasants have to rely on their own forces, initiatives, and resources.

During the Mengistu period, the PA committees and the traditional ad hoc "elder councils" operated side by side and sometimes overlapped each other. But the PA would have the last say in cases that could be brought to higher levels of state administration or PA structure. "Elders" *(shemagelewoch)* were chosen by both parties in a conflict, thus assuring that their representatives were competent, respected and able to make sound judgements. The PA committees only met to discuss cases related to their administrative responsibilities. The elders met to discuss matters that mattered and which were of general interest to people, leaning on long local traditions for local-level decision-making (although not necessarily democratic in all respects). The saving clubs (equb) elected their secretaries, voted for their own rules and regulations, and kept rosters of members and books of accounts as well as protocols from the meetings. So did also the funeral associations *(eder)*.[1] Matters that were discussed by the PA committees also mattered for people. But both the PA leaders and the members knew they had no influence over the instruments they had at hand for decision-making. Neither did they control the rules of the game. Those above them were always looking over their shoulders. The local experiences of participation, accountability, transparency and representativeness could not be transferred to the sphere of formal politics. The government was not interested in real grassroots political initiatives.

Geoffry Hawthorn concludes his assessment of prospects for democracy in sub-Saharan Africa rather pessimistically. He states that "if the hope for a democracy lies anywhere, it is in those associations which the successive architects of 'the modern state' in Africa, pre-colonial, colonial and post-colonial, have all dismissed as primordial, parochical and divisive". And he adds, "the shape of such a democracy is obscure" (Hawthorn 1993:345). We can easily agree with him in that. As long as the state is a distant power which cannot accommodate mechanisms of peaceful change, it will continue to represent nothing but power, whatever models it claims to implement.

Abbreviations used in the text

ANDM	Amhara National Democratic Movement
EPRDF	Ethiopian People's Revolutionary Democratic Front
FFW	Food-For-Work
MoA	Ministry of Agriculture
PA	Peasant Association
PDRE	People's Democratic Republic of Ethiopia
TGE	Transitional Government of Ethiopia
TPLF	Tigre People's Liberation Front

---

1. These local institutions are treated in Aspen (1993).

Peasant Participation in Land Reform
The Amhara Land Redistribution of 1997

Svein Ege

In early 1997, land redistribution was implemented in the southern half of the Amhara region.[1] Officially it was a correction of past injustice and affected only land illegally taken by misuse of power and land exceeding a certain ceiling. In fact it was a very dramatic redistribution that ruined many households, uprooted the existing land tenure system without replacing it with a well-defined new system, and created a new state-peasant relationship.

Research papers dealing with the land redistribution appeared almost immediately after the reform. Teferi Abate wrote two conference papers based on fieldwork in two *qäbälé* in South Wälo (Teferi, 1997a, 1997b). Of these, the report presented in the workshop of the Land Tenure Project (1997b) provides the more precise description of the land redistribution. Yigremew Adal wrote a conference paper and published an article, mainly focusing on policy issues and the general patterns of the land redistribution, but with some specific material from two *qäbälé* in West Gojam (Yigremew, 1997a, 1997b). The former served as a draft for the latter, but contains some additional peasant complaints about the legality of the reform and therefore remains a useful source. I wrote a report on how the peasants in the Yefat area of North Shäwa experienced the reform as it unfolded (Ege, 1997). Taken together these studies provide a sufficiently clear picture of some main features of the land redistribution, notably the general rules and the mode of implementation, while we still know very little about the results of the reform, be it the effects on social equity, agricultural production, resource conservation or state-peasant relations.

All these studies were written immediately after the land redistribution, and each author had little information about what was going on outside his own area of fieldwork. These studies can be characterised as glimpses into the land redistribution,[2] supplemented with attempts to make sense of the alarming and rather confusing picture that emerged. All the three authors noted that it was a very sensitive subject, and all stressed the surprisingly great difference between the official version about the land redistribution and the findings in the field.

The three authors approached the subject from different backgrounds, with different methodologies and concerns. Most notably, Yigremew and Teferi primarily dealt with the axis from Baher Dar to the *qäbälé* officials. They depended heavily on the information of the local officials. I dealt with the axis from the *qäbälé* officials to the peasants and relied almost exclusively on information from the peasants. The studies of Yigremew are particularly valuable for the presentation and analysis of the rules of the land redistribution, and his points echo typical peasant complaints all over the Amhara region. The studies of Teferi are characterised by the fact that the author was actually present in the field during the land redistribution, and they con-

---

1. It was explicitly limited to the areas where the EPRDF had not implemented land redistribution before the fall of the Därg. In practice, even some of these areas were excluded, for unknown reasons.
2. They appear as glimpses even more so because all the three authors found it difficult to get full access to the required information.

tain some marvellous accounts of meetings and concrete cases. My study depicts the unfolding land redistribution process, seen through the eyes of the peasants. It brings out the shock, fear and local conflicts created by the land redistribution. The three studies are quite different in their approach, but if we try to see through them, it is easy to see that they refer to the same underlying society and the same experience in state-peasant interaction. The authors stress different aspects of the story, but we are telling basically the same story.

After these initial reports new research results have strengthened the general picture already established and added some new perspectives. Teferi covered the land redistribution in his Ph.D. thesis (2000). His account leans heavily on the former paper (1997b), but with an improved description of the setting. Yigremew added two papers, one comparing the impact of the land redistribution in two communities in West Gojam (2000) and another focusing on female-headed households in general, with some data on how they fared during the land redistribution (2001). Getie Gelaye described the general land redistribution process, somewhat imprecisely, and presented a number of interesting poems composed to express complaints or support for the redistribution in East Gojam (1999). These reports present new material but otherwise add little to our understanding of the land redistribution. Their main role is to significantly increase our confidence in the first batch of reports.

The land redistribution took place over a large and varied region and consequently one might expect considerable variation in the land redistribution itself. There was variation, but not in the way one might expect. Except for the fact that land redistribution was called off in most of Wälo, there is no apparent regional variation in the picture painted by the available studies of the redistribution process. [1] The rules were the same, the administrative style was the same, and the results, to the extent that we know them, were also remarkably similar. All the authors point out, however, that there was considerable local variation in results. There was little variation in the aggregate data for the various zones, but two neighbouring qäbälé could show remarkably large variation. The pattern of this variation has not yet been explored, but it seems that the main explanatory variable is ecological factors.

The current article leans heavily on the previous studies but seeks to add to them in several ways.[2] First of all, it describes the overall process in more concise terms to put the focus clearly on the important aspects. Secondly, it concentrates on state-peasant interaction seen from the point of view of the peasants, specifically how they were informed about the planned reform and how they were able to influence the outcome, with quite surprising results. Thirdly, it presents material from Kasayé Agär, a lowland *qäbälé* in the Yefat area, and thus expands the regional basis of our knowledge.[3] Fourthly, it is not just an empirical account, but seeks to contribute to a theoretical discussion of peasant politics and state-peasant relations, not by explicit theoretical analysis, but by the concepts used and the way the account is organised. The story told has its primary reference to Kasayé Agär and can be read as an empirical account of the redistribution there, but it has in many ways the status of 'model' story of the land redistribution, and to some extent of wider state-peasant

---

1. It is a paradox that land redistribution, so dear to the ruling party, was implemented in only a few *qäbälé* in Wälo, arguably the main basis of the Amhara National Democratic Movement. Land redistribution was launched in 157 *qäbälé*, but carried to its end in only 9 (Teferi 2000: 217).
2. It is in practice impossible to fully cross-reference to the previous works, and they are mentioned only when specific points are made.
3. Currently the district is named T'arma Bär, but both the name and the borders have changed several times during the last decade. Kasayé Agär is located in the lowlands below the area that served as primary reference for Ege 1997.

interaction. Finally, although the general picture of the land redistribution is the same as established by earlier studies, much of the specific analysis goes against common views, e.g. about peasant attitudes to land redistribution, the role of corruption, and the status of the *birokrasi* in the local community.

A Bird's Eye View of the Land Redistribution

The basic feature of the redistribution was its peculiar class analysis, which stigmatised the officials of the preceding regimes as oppressors, but ironically enough lumped the current officials together with the oppressed peasants, without further criteria needed. The term *birokrasi* was used to refer to the quite numerous peasants who had served in various local offices under the Därg, while persons who had been officials or significant landowners before the revolution were referred to as 'feudal remnants'. Both groups were treated in the same way, and in the following they are therefore treated together under the *birokrasi* label.[1]

The *birokrasi* were systematically discriminated against by the official rules of the land redistribution. Other peasants were allowed to keep up to 12 *t'emad* of land, while the *birokrasi* were allowed only 4 *t'emad* (1 hectare),[2] in both cases independent of household size. Thus, theoretically an 'oppressed' household of one person could keep 12 *t'emad*, while a *birokrasi* household of twelve or more members could only keep 4 *t'emad*, i.e. a theoretical range of inequality of about 1:40, in favour of the 'oppressed'.[3] Fortunately, the actual range of inequality was usually less, partly due to household processes and partly due to a local sense of justice that made the local officials bend the rules to prevent the more extreme cases.

These discriminatory rules constitute the 1997 Amhara land redistribution in a nutshell. There were many other problems, ranging from specific rules to more general issues of land tenure policy. But the discrimination based on political criteria completely overshadowed all other problems, at least in the short run. The political overtones also set the style of implementation, and this style clearly demonstrates that the harsh treatment of the *birokrasi* was not based on demands from below, but on orders from above. Almost without exception, peasant action softened the attack on the *birokrasi*, while the actions of the state sharpened the attack.

From the point of view of peasant participation in the land redistribution, the process can be divided into three phases:

1) Launching the redistribution.
2) Registering households and land holdings (enumeration committee).
3) Measuring, confiscating and distributing land (redistribution committee).

These phases were characterised by quite distinct state-peasant patterns of interaction. In the first phase, the peasants participated mainly as spectators. The second phase took place in a 'secret room'. Only in the third phase, discussed below under the heading 'the political scene', did the peasants have any influence on the outcome of the redistribution, and then only in a quite perverted form.

---

1. In general there were few 'feudal remnants', and in Kasayé Agär there were none. For more details on the class analysis, see especially Yigremew (1997b: 67).
2. This is the official conversion, but local reality is much more varied.
3. The theoretical range of inequality is here defined as the degree of inequality per person produced by the rules under realistic worst case assumptions.

Launching the Redistribution

The first phase, announcing the land redistribution and electing the committee, took place in the public room but without any opportunity for the peasants to influence the direction of the reform. They listened to the official message, but without any chance to change it. They elected the committee members, but were limited to the candidates approved from above.

According to the official version, the land redistribution was the result of demands from below: "The issue of land redistribution was raised in every meeting, and the government only responded to the popular demand."[1] None of the studies of the land redistribution have identified such a demand. It seems that there was no active demand for land redistribution, but of course, if the government ordered land redistribution, the youngsters, together with all who believed they had less land or lower quality land than the average, could be expected to favour it.[2] Above all, when the government announced a new deal, each individual would have to move into position for the ensuing struggle—or be prepared to lose.

Land redistribution was on the agenda of the ruling party, and it had been simmering ever since the fall of the Därg. At various times there were rumours of an impending redistribution, such as in 1994, linked to the debate on the constitution. But nothing materialised. In Yefat the peasants felt great uncertainty, and some persons who said they would like to buy land, deferred their decision until there was a clearer government policy. The evaluation of the situation seems to have varied locally, and to judge by the frequency and type of land sales, it seems that the peasants in the lowlands felt more secure than those on the upper part of the Yefat escarpment. In Kasayé Agär, one visitor commented that the peasants were "used to selling land just like oxen or goats" (N4507; also N4794).[3] Contracts of land sales or mortgages in Kasayé Agär during the years 1993–96, often involving several thousand Birr, show that in this area land was sold, not just mortgaged (*wäläd agäd* or *kontrat*), as the agreement usually claimed.[4] Many of those who bought land were land-poor youngsters, which indicates that buying land had become a method for primary household accumulation. The able youngsters were taking matters into their own hands rather than waiting for land redistribution. The acts of the Kasayé Agär peasants indicated a feeling of increased predictability—that their future depended basically on their own decisions, on hard work and careful household management. The 1997 land reform changed all that.

In October 1996 it was announced on the radio that there would be land redistribution, and the news spread immediately all over the countryside. Nothing was said about the type of land redistribution to be implemented, but the peasants clearly expected it to be an updating of the existing land tenure system, an equal distribution of land based on household size, to correct the inequalities that had developed over the years. This had great legitimacy. First of all, there were exaggerated expec-

---

1. This is a paraphrase of statements reproduced by countless informants, from zone officials to common peasants. It came as a surprise to me, since I had never heard of such demands in qäbälé meetings. But peasant cadres called to the district for training, were "taught" that there would be land redistribution.
2. Getie has argued that landless youngsters and female-headed households supported land redistribution when it was launched (1999: 176). This is based on post-redistribution information and is therefore heavily influenced by the fact that these two groups were the major winners. It does not provide reliable information on pre-redistribution attitudes. In my previous study, I found a surprisingly positive attitude to the prospects of land redistribution among the peasantry at large (1997: 21). The key point is that the peasants did not expect the type of land redistribution that followed.
3. See note on references to fieldwork data at the end of this paper.
4. Ege, private archive, FA 2.00: 1036: D7154, D7174.

tations about the possible results of redistribution: "Most people thought that they would get more land, not that they would lose land (N4499)". This might partly be due to official propaganda, which would certainly stress that poor peasants would gain land and be rather vague on the source of land, which would necessarily have to be other peasants, most of them quite poor. Furthermore, equality by itself had great legitimacy. One informant summed up the attitude of those who lost land: "We liked that the government ordered the redistribution. God does not like that we eat while others are starving." He supported land redistribution, but certainly not the kind of redistribution that took place (N4806).[1]

In December there were meetings to launch the redistribution and elect the members of the enumeration committee.[2] Informants varied somewhat in their evaluation of these elections. Some described them as free, apart from the obvious fact that the former Därg officials were excluded, others told in some detail about manipulations. This probably reflects the position and political awareness of the informant rather than the nature of the elections themselves. In fact, the mode of elections was very open to manipulation by the administration. In principle the people nominated candidates, but in some cases nominations were openly made by the *qäbälé* leaders. The candidates were elected unless there were specific complaints against them, and the elector (*asmärach'*), normally a representative of the district administration, decided whether the reason for opposing the candidate was sufficient. The elector could also reject candidates supported by the people, specifically those "contaminated" (*neke-ki*) by the Därg. Sometimes there were not more candidates than the posts to be filled.

The important moment in the elections was not the voting, even when there was a formal vote, but the nomination, where the administration could veto undesirable candidates and push its own candidates (Ege, 1997: 37–39). Sometimes this deteriorated into heated arguments between the elector and the people, but in general the people seem to have resigned and accepted. Furthermore, most people feared to be elected, partly due to the time required, partly because they felt incompetent for such responsibility, and partly because they knew well that they would be criticised and slandered. Therefore, when the peasant cadres and militiamen, mixing with the assembled people, nominated their candidates, they had a fairly easy game.

Those elected to this first committee were referred to as enumerators (*qot'ari-woch*), about twenty in each *qäbälé*.[3] Their task was simply to register the households and their land, with separate forms and registration procedures for the poor, middle, rich, *birokrasi*, and feudal remnants. In the meetings that launched the redistribution, there had been propaganda against the *birokrasi*, and the thrust against them was underlined by the strange registration procedure, with classes without any roots in local understanding of society. But at this stage neither the peasants at large, nor the enumerators, and perhaps not even the district officials, knew the precise rules. At this stage even the term *birokrasi* was still largely undefined, a strange, foreign word of the political propaganda. The most important part of the work of the enumerators was to stick this label to concrete persons in accordance with the directives from above (cf. Teferi, 1997b: 8).

---

1. This is a quite typical statement by *birokrasi* after the redistribution. It may be somewhat tongue-in-cheek, since they had already lost and could contrast their own support for a fair redistribution with the injustice to which they themselves had been exposed.
2. The timing of the redistribution seems to have varied slightly between the regions, perhaps due to lack of manpower. In Wälo the elections were held in late January 1997 (Teferi 1997b: 4).
3. *Qäbälé* here refers to the old unit, not the enlarged qäbälé established shortly before the land redistribution.

The Secret Room

After the enumerators returned to their own *qäbälé,* they were sitting in an office or another suitable house, surrounded by guards. Nobody could approach them, and they could not leave. People were surprised, scared, and confused. The militiamen were sent to collect food from all the inhabitants of the *qäbälé.* If the person forced to contribute was a *birokrasi,* he had to taste the food, to check that it was not poisoned. This was clearly by orders from above, not to check for poison, but to strengthen the impression of class struggle. It was practised in all the *qäbälé* where information is available, but later, as soon as control was relaxed, the members of the distribution committee happily accepted the invitations of the *birokrasi.* This was even more remarkable since it was precisely at this stage that the *birokrasi* would have a reason to take revenge, i.e. after they knew that they would be attacked (N4497).

According to the district envoys, the enumerators were kept apart from other people so that they could not take bribes. But this measure did of course not remove the influence of kinship, friendship and enmity that the enumerators brought with them into the secret room. The enumerators themselves believed that they were kept apart to guard the political secrets for a few days, but in fact they did not know many secrets. Both these explanations capture some of the purpose, which was probably to isolate the enumerators and create a 'pressure cooker' effect as a method of breaking local resistance. None of them could feel safe, neither from the attacks of the district envoy, nor from being exposed by other enumerators. Most safe were those who appeared most committed and who could thus play the political card. In any case, since their work was used in quite unexpected ways, they were helpless victims rather than local policy-makers.

The registration was based on the knowledge and the social relations of the enumerators. There were frequent conflicts between them, but there is also reason to believe that there were some quick alliances formed. The registration depended very much on the knowledge of those enumerators who were neighbours of the person to be registered. If the enumerators of the hamlet in question agreed, there was a fair chance that their estimate was accepted. It gave them enormous power to decide on the future of a household. However, the enumerators did not know the consequences of their acts, and therefore it was essentially blindfolded power.

The district envoy used conflicts between the enumerators systematically, and the enumerators were encouraged to expose each other in the regular evaluation sessions. The evaluation sessions were used to break the community spirit and turn the enumerators into instruments of the party. But the evaluations were also a political weapon open to misuse by the powerful enumerators against their weaker colleagues, especially since the judge was the district envoy, an outsider without proper competence on local affairs. He could not be expected to see through the current episode into the underlying web of local conflicts, even if he tried. Furthermore, he had a completely different agenda and might not care too much about how peasants settled their scores.

There was a great push to increase the estimates for the holdings of the *birokrasi.* The initial registration was crosschecked by new teams,[1] and as far as my informa-

---

1. This was done in all the Yefat *qäbälé* for which there is information, with the exception of Doqaqit. But note how my source from Kasayé Agär attributed it to the act of one specific official, a typical feature of these accounts, which tend to explain acts in terms of local conflict and intrigue, rather than in terms of government orders. The same pattern is also very noticeable in the evidence presented by Getie (1999: 191–195).

tion goes, this invariably resulted in increased estimates. In Kasayé Agär, after the enumerators had been sitting together for some days, it was rumoured that there were errors in the registration, and an official described as the "land registration cadre", not a member of the registration committee, is said to have reported this to the district envoy. Teams, composed of enumerators from other hamlets, were sent to check the estimates, apparently with a clear understanding that their task was to increase the estimates. For example, the land of Gashaw Mogäs was initially registered as 10 *t'emad*, although it was known to produce 100 quintals of grain, probably in a bumper harvest. The estimate for this land was later increased to 25 *t'emad* (N4498, N4520).

Another standard procedure was to pick one of the enumerators to serve as a scapegoat. In Kasayé Agär this lot apparently fell on Tayé Wändemu, not an enumerator, but a militiaman who served as a guard for the enumerators. His father, Wändemu Märsha, was a *birokrasi*, whose land was initially registered as 6 *t'emad*. During the later rounds of crosschecking it was increased to 10 *t'emad*. Tayé protested and said that the land of his father was only 4 *t'emad*. The enumerators complained that Tayé interfered in their work, and he was put under arrest for two days. The land was registered as 10 *t'emad*, and for some time Tayé was a good example of the official whose work was influenced by nepotism—and of the strong measures taken against such misuse of power (N4498). The irony was that when the land of Wändemu was later measured, it was only 4 *t'emad*. Truth had changed from a reasonably objective entity to whatever was politically convenient. Peasants are quick to learn such lessons and shape their acts accordingly. This created a situation where it was highly problematic to follow the official rules. They had little legitimacy, but at the same time they were the only existing rules. Much of the administrative irregularities must be attributed to this situation. Rather than trying to implement rules perceived to be fair and equal, everybody had to struggle in a chaotic situation to protect the interests of himself and his friends.

After the households had been registered, the people were called to a meeting for all of Mafud *qäbälé*, of which Kasayé Agär was one of the three sub-*qäbälé*. This took place about 23 January 1997 (15 Tear 1989 EC). The main purpose was to report the results of the registration, and it was potentially one of the most critical moments of the redistribution. The meeting was led by the district envoy. He explained that the land of the *birokrasi*, the feudal remnants and the rich would be decreased, but he did not explain the rules to be applied. He himself probably did not yet know them.

The results of the registration were reported, and the exaggerated figures on the holdings of the *birokrasi* certainly confirmed the official understanding of the need for land redistribution (Ege, 1997: 102). The district envoy told the assembly that everybody was entitled to land, with the exception of the *birokrasi* and feudal remnants. The account of the meeting in Mafud is not very detailed, and it only mentions one case of a *birokrasi* who tried to protest. Sisay Wäldé asked why they were called *birokrasi*, insulted and discriminated against. "We did not want to be elected, but we were elected by the people." The district envoy said that this was an improper question, "that the *birokrasi* have been oppressing the people until now, but now the poor are given rights, therefore the land of the *birokrasi* will be taken, and you have no right to talk" (N4500). There is every reason to believe that the meeting followed the common pattern of these meetings, where some *birokrasi* tried to protest against the exaggerated estimates of their holdings, that they had been elected to office against their will, and that the people could judge them (see Teferi, 1997b: 11–14; Ege, 1997: 52–54).

These were strong challenges to the official policy. The *birokrasi* had a good case, both in their description of their past relations to the community and in their protests against the biased estimates of their holdings. Furthermore, they were, with few exceptions, highly respected members of the community.[1] Many of them were also capable politicians, and they could match anybody in an open discussion in front of the people, their own constituency. The role of the district envoys was difficult. They will have known that the official analysis was problematic, and they will have known that it would be difficult to defend the analysis and the results of the registration. If, on the other hand, they really believed in the policy and their own arguments, this would have been an excellent opportunity to expose the *birokrasi*, let them talk, and then defeat them by the evidence amassed about their land grabbing and maladministration. Since the district envoys also claimed that there was overwhelming popular support for the redistribution, the task should not have been too difficult. The solution routinely adopted, to silence the *birokrasi* by threats of being arrested, even killed, indicates that the district envoys had a weak case, and they knew it.

In addition to the exaggerated estimates of the land of the *birokrasi*, there was also an observable tendency that much of their land was registered as fertile, while the land of the poor was registered as infertile. The impression at this stage was that the biased registration would serve as a direct basis for the actual redistribution of land, but that the rules themselves would be based on formal equality. It is somewhat surprising that this was not done, since it could have served the basic political purpose of crippling the *birokrasi*, not with more social justice, but with fewer irrelevant negative effects. Furthermore, it would also have covered up discrimination much better than the crude discrimination actually applied.

Some of the *birokrasi* protested that the estimates of their holdings were exaggerated, but the district envoy replied that he could not do anything, since the estimates had been made by representatives elected by the people. This was of course true, but he did not say that he had twisted the arms of the enumerators to make them give the desired estimates. He let the enumerators take the blame for a policy that they would have been extremely unlikely to invent themselves, or even support if there was any alternative. Regimented participation had become a weapon against local protests, putting the captured *qäbälé* officials as a shield between the state and the peasants, sometimes at a high price for the persons involved.

Towards the end of the meeting, the "landless youngsters" we represented, with their name, age and existing land. Most of them were registered without any land, clearly a result of the political situation rather than the basic socio-economic conditions. In principle, any peasant child had land rights, and a peasant son of twenty would be likely to plough his own land (*gulma*), sub-divided from the holding of his father, and covered by the tax of his father. But in a situation of land redistribution, to register the land of a son as belonging to the son would have the predictable result that this land would be lost to the father. To register him as landless, on the other hand, was to put a claim on the land fund of the community, i.e. on the land to be

---

1. When I did fieldwork under the Därg, I always treated peasant officials with caution. It was only after the fall of the Därg, when people could criticise them freely, that I came to understand their solid position in the community. In fact, if there had been free elections under the new government, the peasants would have taken the chance to get rid of a few unpopular leaders but re-elected most of their former leaders. The new administration knew this, and felt extremely frustrated. Arguably, the strong attack on the *birokrasi* was due to their popularity, not to general resentment against them.

confiscated. Therefore, many of the *birokrasi* whose children had been registered with their own land, protested that their children did not have land, in the hope that they would get land during the redistribution. The district envoy again replied that the registration had been made by the representatives of the people, and that he therefore could not do anything. "He did not give much response"(N4501).

The peasants came to this meeting to get to know what the enumerators had been doing secretly and what the plans were for the redistribution. When they left, they had unwittingly confirmed the results of the registration, despite the many errors in the records. These meetings were officially considered as public confirmation of the results, although it is doubtful that the peasants who participated in the meetings regarded them in this way. Furthermore, even if they had intentionally voted to confirm the specific registration results, it would be misuse of power, since votes do not change facts. There were later cases where everybody agreed that the holding was much smaller than the registered figure, but the figure could not be corrected since it had been confirmed by the people. The registers became official documents, and they could not later be changed, officially at least.

The meeting may have served a political purpose, to demonstrate that the *birokrasi* really had a lot of land. It certainly did not serve as an adequate check of the registration made, neither the classification into classes, nor the land estimates. The complaints of the *birokrasi* could be empirically checked, and one would tend to feel that there was an urgent need for an appeal system at this stage, to address the grievances and correct any mistakes committed during the registration. The absence of such an appeal system, and the later refusal of the administration to hear any appeals, was one of the factors that undermined the legitimacy of the redistribution in the eyes of the peasants.

There was also a need to clarify the rules of the redistribution so that everybody could make their choices with full knowledge of the consequences, rather than letting luck rule. There were many cases where seemingly innocent facts, like the way a household was registered, had dramatic impact on their post-redistribution economy, in ways completely unpredictable both for the household members themselves and for those who had made the registration. If an old woman, her son and his wife were registered as one household, they had the rights of one household, but if they happened to be registered as two households, they had the rights of two households and could hold twice as much land. If the joint household was registered as *birokrasi*, but this applied only to one of the households when they were registered separately, the difference was 1:4 (for a specific complaint, see Teferi, 1997b: 14). The margins between winning and losing were very narrow, unclear, and highly manipulable. In other words, the scene was set for secret deals.

Also in this meeting, the arguments were between the district envoy and peasants who felt they were unjustly treated, rather than between the peasants themselves. The district envoy was basically there to accomplish his orders, as efficiently as possible. Not only the work of the enumerators, but also his own work was subject to evaluation, and any deviation from the directives made him vulnerable to attack, and possibly to loss of his salaried position. His career depended, as far as we can judge, on unquestioning loyalty and efficient implementation of the orders from above. But it is interesting to note that he refused to address the questions raised by the *birokrasi* about the *gulma* land of their children. He did not try to find out what was true, neither did he take the chance to strengthen the attack on the *birokrasi*, which in some cases he could have done very easily, simply by accepting their claims that their children did not have *gulma*.[1] Instead he washed his hands of the matter and let chance and peasant politics rule. There are no convincing signs in the practical acts of the district envoys of the class struggle they were preaching. They simply implemented administrative orders.

Enumeration of households and their resources took place completely within the secret room. This phase shaped the basic outcome of the land redistribution. It is therefore remarkable that peasant accounts about the land redistribution are so weak on this phase. The explanation is probably that this phase was driven by government directives, on which the peasants and their representatives had no influence. Furthermore, the point of injustice was sensitive, and the peasants may have regarded it as so obvious that it should not have needed any further explanation. There is an impression that the peasants, including the current officials, expected observers to understand such an obvious point even when they said that the land redistribution was good. Thus a *birokrasi* might thank both God and the government before he turned to his complaints. The atmosphere was quite tense—under the smiles. It seemed as if even those who claimed to support the land redistribution might provide a contrary opinion, as soon as they felt safe.[2]

Another reason for the weak coverage of the first phase was of course that the important decisions were made in secret rooms, and outsiders in principle knew nothing about the arguments used, or even if there were any arguments at all. The registration of household members and land was a secret. The method made registration quick, but it was neither transparent, nor democratic, and it produced some most arbitrary results. In fact, even on its own political terms the land redistribution suffered from a remarkably weak design and did not necessarily target those who had misused their power under the Därg.

The Political Scene

In the third phase, a new committee was elected to measure the land to be confiscated and to distribute this land by lottery. These officials were referred to as 'distributors' (*dälday*). Most of them had also served as enumerators, but a few of the enumerators were dismissed. The distribution committee officially took over the registers of the enumerators and started to transfer the data to new forms, to calculate the amount to confiscate from or add to each household, based on the directives from the regional government. When the data had been transferred to the new forms, the distributors started to measure the land with the rope.

First, however there was a pause in the land redistribution at the local level. After the work of the enumerators had been reported to the people, the leading officials in the districts and zones assembled in Baher Dar, the regional capital, to receive further orders. These orders were passed down the administrative system, first by meetings at the level of the zones and districts on 28–29 January (20–21 T'er), and then at the *qäbälé* level on 31 January and 1 February (Kefefel Plan: 38).[3] According to

---

1. The *birokrasi*, like other peasants did this in order to put the claim of their children on the public land fund rather than on the family holding. For other peasants it worked as planned, but for the *birokrasi*, who were in any case to lose land, it typically meant that the total household was left with only 4 *t'emad*, instead of saving some extra land in the name of a child or two.
2. The peasant officials often expressed the official stand publicly. I have tried to check up persons who seemed to be ardent supporters of the land redistribution, but none of these have supported the discrimination of the *birokrasi* when interviewed more closely in private.
3. These dates seem to have been observed in the Yefat area, but in Wälo the land redistribution apparently took place later.

the orders of the regional government, the directives were to be read and explained to the people. It is well documented that this was actually done, although perhaps not in general assembly meetings. But the official discrimination of a part of the population was so shocking that these directives were talked about in a lowered voice. Therefore, although strictly speaking ill informed, one of the distributors captured the atmosphere well when he later stated that "some of the *däldays* were telling this secretly"(N4503).

This phase of the distribution was characterised by new patterns of interaction between the peasants and the local land distribution committee. When the distributors started to go out into the field to measure the land, they became accessible and the process opened up somewhat. In this phase some peasants were able to modify the outcome of the redistribution, in a few cases by having their appeals accepted officially, but more typically by secret arrangements. Peasant accounts of the land redistribution deal overwhelmingly with this phase, probably because it was visible, it made for good stories, and it was not so dangerous to talk about.

Formally, the distributors did not have any contact with the *birokrasi*, but when the distributors started to go out into the field to measure the land, the system rapidly cracked. From the accounts in various *qäbälé*, it appears that they were initially afraid to accept invitations, and in general they stuck more strictly to the rules for the first few days. They were testing the borders, however. A typical pattern was that they first accepted an invitation under a tree, formally arranged by a non-*birokrasi*, perhaps even a committee member, but with food and drink provided by a *birokrasi* relative. When nothing happened, others followed suit, and in the end they might even be eating in the house of a *birokrasi*.

At this stage the secret room opened up, it changed into a political scene and peasant participation started in earnest. What happened was certainly not visible to everybody, and many peasants seem to have kept deliberately apart, with a sickening feeling about what they heard and saw. But the rules were now clear, the distributors were accessible, although only informally, and many of the *birokrasi* had to enter the political scene whether they wanted to or not. The alternative was ruin.

The great majority of people remained rather passive and did not challenge their role as spectators. This was a design element of the redistribution. During the enumeration, when very little was known about what would happen, everybody was waiting; after the rules became known, only the *birokrasi*, a few feudal remnants, and a very few "rich" peasants feared they would lose land and had reason to protest. Those who felt safe could cease to worry about the redistribution. The design made the population rather passive, and their participation was basically reduced to a sigh of relief. It was a strange class struggle.

The main actors on the political scene in Kasayé Agär were some ten *birokrasi* and a handful of the leading distributors. The majority of the *birokrasi* remained passive and limited their efforts to asking the distributors to measure their land favourably. This was important enough, since measuring land in the field is a much less exact undertaking than what is normally believed. In most cases their requests were granted, and if some of the distributors refused, it was typically regarded as an act of revenge. Some of the distributors also systematically refrained from holding the rope, so that they would not have to bear the blame.

It is likely that those *birokrasi* who intervened most vigorously fulfilled a set of criteria: they risked losing a lot of land; they were not among those unlucky whose land was measured during the first few days when strict supervision allowed for no appeals to the compassion of the distributors; they had some pretext that they sought to put forward; there was no better path open to them; and they had the courage to try their luck. Some of them failed, but most of them succeeded to some degree. Sometimes the request was resisted by some of the distributors due to a private conflict with the *birokrasi* in question. Sometimes it was rejected simply because the *birokrasi* did not approach them with enough humility. Two cases illustrate the extremes.

During the redistribution, some people were relaxing and drinking liquor in a local 'bar', the house of a single woman who lived from producing liquor. Among those present were two distributors and one of the *birokrasi*, Kätäma Yefra. Kätäma was high on liquor and complained that the distributors had not registered the land properly. "Good administration and everything was during our time. Now the herdsboys have been elected." Kätäma insulted one of the distributors present, Nägash, his neighbour, since he had heard from one of the other distributors, also a neighbour, that Nägash was the one who had reported the exaggerated estimate. Nägash was infuriated, and he said he would report Kätäma, and started to list those present as his witnesses. The matter changed from a peasant quarrel to a matter with serious political overtones. Those present tried to calm things down and asked Nägash to excuse Kätäma, since he was drunk. But Nägash argued that although Kätäma was drunk, he meant what he had said. Finally he accepted reconciliation, but he was still furious and Kätäma had to pay dearly for this episode (N4528).

Nägash told the other distributors how they had been insulted by Kätäma, and when they measured his land, he was treated very harshly. According to one of the distributors, he did not even get the 4 *t'emad* to which he was legally entitled. Furthermore, a son of Kätäma had been registered with 2 *t'emad* of his own land, but he only got very infertile land. It is quite possible that this was the land he actually held as *gulma*, since the strong young sons were often given the most difficult parts of the family holding, while the parents kept the more fertile land nearest the house for themselves, a quite rational allocation of land in relation to physical strength. In any case, under the redistribution it often happened that the *gulma* was moved to the more fertile parts of the holding, a secret move at the discretion of the distributors. But Kätäma had lost the goodwill of the distributors, and although he came every day and invited some of the distributors to the bar, he did not succeed. Nägash and the team leader seemed to enjoy the situation:

> They accepted others, but not him. For others they would even take back land registered for the lottery to give it as *gulma*. But in the case of (Kätäma), in the evening they were drinking his liquor and said yes, but the next day they again refused. (N4528: 69)

My informant also believed that some money was paid, and success was tantalisingly near, but the opposition of even a single person was enough to block such a case. With a more humble approach, and a good invitation to show both humility and friendship, Kätäma could very well have received about twice the amount of the land that his household actually got.

Other *birokrasi* played their cards more wisely. One of them was Kätäma's son, Akalu. He evaded any conflict with the distributors, treated them with the courtesy due to power-holders, and pushed his case gently but steadily. He also wisely divided up his requests into appropriate portions, none of them too big to swallow. He scored victory after victory. He seems to have had a very clear strategy, working systematically to create a favourable climate so that his requests for *gulma* for his children would be granted.

(Akalu) did not say anything when we measured the land, and he even told us to measure it as we thought best. He was the *birokrasi* in Kasayé Agär who did not bother the distributors. Others were arguing that here is steep land (aräh), here is a waterway, stones, can you measure a little higher etc. When we measured his land, we gave him about half a unit (lek) extra, and he even protested that we should not give it to him. He accepted the land happily and offered all the distributors honey.

The land of Akalu had initially been registered as 33 *t'emad*, and the distributors had expected to find 29 *t'emad* of surplus land.[1] When they measured it, the size fell to 17 *t'emad*. The son of Akalu appealed that he had 3 *t'emad* of gulma. This was not true, and there were some arguments among the distributors, but in the end the friends of the son carried the day. Another son also got 2 *t'emad* of gulma, and thus the amount of land confiscated fell to only 8 *t'emad*. The household was left with nine sizeable *t'emad*, rather than the four small *t'emad* left to Kätäma, his father (N4525).

The other *birokrasi* who sought to influence the committee fell between these two extremes. With a good case, a fair pretext and a friendly atmosphere, the family would be granted some extra land, typically in the form of gulma for an adult child, even when this child was known not to exist. But it was by no means an automatic process, a shadow law secretly agreed upon locally to compensate for the obvious discrimination of the *birokrasi* ordered from above. The discrimination against the *birokrasi* had little legitimacy among the distributors, as evidenced by their willingness to grant the requests of the *birokrasi* for land to their children. On the other hand, the official discrimination of the *birokrasi* put them at the mercy of the distributors. If any of them had some score to settle, this was the time to act. Therefore, rather than a shadow law equal for all community members, the outcome depended on personal relations, relations which could be improved or destroyed by the approach of the *birokrasi*.

By far the most efficient way to claim extra land for a *birokrasi* was to argue that some of the land belonged to his children.[2] Consequently the outcome for a *birokrasi* household depended both on his social relations and on the composition of his household. A *birokrasi* with many young children did not have any pretext to save any of his land, but a *birokrasi* with many adult sons could save much of his land in their names, and if the children were married but had not yet built up an independent land holding, the redistribution could even be a great opportunity. It was irrelevant whether any of these people had actually misused their power. There is even reason to believe that in such a chaotic situation as the 1997 land redistribution, the unscrupulous *birokrasi* fared better than the honest ones, certainly a design weakness of the reform on its own terms.

The distributors operated in very muddy waters. The rules were seemingly detailed and clear, but they were not robust. Minor variations in the application of the rules led to great variation in the results. The rules produced some unexpected winners, including *birokrasi* households, but they also produced some great losers, households who got so little land that they were not viable any more. This may not have been the aim of the redistribution, but it was certainly implemented with full knowledge of the consequences, which puts the claim that the redistribution was to give land to the poor into a strange light. The redistribution reduced poverty for

---

1. Surplus (*terf*) referred to the land exceeding 4 *t'emad* for the *birokrasi*, 12 *t'emad* for others.
2. *Birokrasi* were mostly men. Widows of *birokrasi* were treated in the same way, and in some I the leading executives of the Women's Association were labelled as *birokrasi*.

some, but it also created poverty for others, and the administration did not seem to care.

There were also a number of grey zones when the rules of the redistribution were confronted with rural realities. The distributors therefore took on the role of politicians, making key decisions, although in a chaotic way. There was rarely, or perhaps never, any discussion among them on how to apply the rules. Rather this took the form of a decision on a concrete case, where the outcome was heavily influenced by feelings of friendship and hatred. Later this decision set a precedence that others could refer to.

The distributors held absolute power during the redistribution. If they agreed, they could have anybody arrested, and in many cases they even held the fate of leading qäbälé officials and their families in their hands, although they knew that after the redistribution the roles would be reversed.[1] It was certainly painful, and perhaps also dangerous, for the distributors to apply the strict rules to a relative, a neighbour, or a respected person. And kinship and friendship could be extended by small-scale corruption. The typical form of rural corruption, inviting the officials for a good meal, was very common in Kasayé Agär, and there were also an exceptionally high number of cases of money bribes. But it is important that all the cases of corruption (including invitations) reported to me, actually reduced the social injustice of the land redistribution, they did not increase it.[2]

In some *qäbälé* the distributors flagrantly misused their power, with the outstanding example of Armanya. Protests against such acts were risky. The *birokrasi*, the experienced politicians of the area, were of course excluded from protesting, and also others who protested were most likely to end up in jail themselves. It was simply for the distributors to claim that a recalcitrant person had a secret gun, order his arrest, and send him to the district police station with this report. When he was released, after the distribution, the economy of his household might have been crippled. Opposition against the distributors rarely paid.

The absence of any real appeal system opened up for flagrant injustice, even injustice not legitimated by the rules of the redistribution. The secrecy, the strong political overtones, the widespread use of repression in the official implementation of the redistribution gave all the cards to the most ruthless local actors, which supports the points made by Poluha (1994) on the effect of local publicity, that transparency and the opportunity to make information public are vital resources for the peasants to control their leaders, arguably much more important than elections.

The peasant accounts of the land redistribution stressed the secret deals, corruption, misdeeds against individual households, and not the least, land-grabbing by the distributors and their friends, even exaggerating these elements. In Kasayé Agär land-grabbing was in fact exceptionally common, affecting an estimated 10 per cent of the land distributed.[3] One of the reasons for land-grabbing may have been that the distribution did not significantly benefit those it claimed to benefit, the poor peasants. In Kasayé Agär, ordinary peasant households, including the poor, would

---

1. This situation, where officials are ranked on several independent scales and the superior in one context is the inferior in another context, is typical of the political setup under the EPRDF, the Därg and probably even before, in intricate systems of checks and balances.
2. Social injustice is here defined with reference to the average land holding per person. Getie argued that land was given only to those who could bribe the officials, but this is actually contradicted by his description of the groups that supported the redistribution, landless youngsters and female-headed households (1999: 192 vs. 184–85).
3. In real terms the amount of land taken by irregular practices was quite modest. There were many officials who gained, but no official gained much, and many gained less than they would have done if land had been distributed equally according to household size.

usually have more than 4 *t'emad*. Those who had less would typically be very young, or divorced women, or a few paupers who preferred to live on the community, perhaps with some petty work at the church.[1] Many of the 'households' with less than 4 *t'emad* were not households at all, but members of other households, such as a daughter who had given birth without marrying and who continued to live in the house of her father.

In fact, few of the households locally regarded as poor qualified for land, since they already had too much land. "It was mostly people who did not have land before, like single women (*sétägna adari*),[2] women who gave birth to illegitimate children (*diqala wälaj*) and also youngsters, who got land in the lottery." (N4557). This apparently came as a shock to the community. Just before the lottery, an appeal committee had been elected, but after the lottery those elected refused to work:

> The appeal committee said they would not work together with the distributors, since the land had been given to single women, idlers (*bozäné*) and youngsters, while it should have been given to peasants. How could you give it to the drunkards? We will not come and participate in your work. *Bozäné* are people who have sold their land and left, or who have sold the land and are just roaming around. The reason why the appeal committee said this was that the single women and drunkards had land before, but some of them had sold it, and some of them had left it fallow. Now they will sell or exchange the land again, and therefore they should not get more land (N4557).

The appeal committee was told to stick to the tasks assigned to it and not interfere in political issues. They were forced to accept their role on pain of being arrested. In any case the existence of an appeal committee was in practice a formality only. It had a very limited mandate (the *birokrasi* could not appeal), it existed only for a few weeks, and it settled few or no appeals.

The distributors supposedly represented the poor peasants, and they were typically young. But according to the official registers, only five of the eighteen distributors got land in the lottery. This shows that even in this carefully selected group few peasant households qualified for getting land.[3] From the peasant perspective, it was a land reform for the lumpen, in sharp conflict with the dominant industrious peasant (*gobäz gäbäré*) ideology.

This was an aspect of the redistribution criticised quite liberally. Certainly, those distributors who had a small holding, too small for their household size, and who felt that they had been promised land, must have been very disappointed by the redistribution, which took unexpected directions both in the way the land was confiscated and in the way it was distributed. They did not need much of a pretext in order to make the other distributors agree to give them land, and in Kasayé Agär it seems that towards the end of the redistribution, no pretext was needed at all. They just shared the small spoils, as a compensation for the time spent, and as a fruit of office.

---

1. There were cases when very poor persons actually refused to take the land assigned to them, since that would reduce the legitimacy of their begging and they feared that their economy would suffer. Sometimes their land was returned to the *qäbälé*, and sometimes it was taken over by an enterprising relative, typically an official.
2. *Sétägna adari* is often translated as 'prostitute'. In the countryside this is a connotation rather than the denotation of the term. *Sétägna adari* may refer to any female-headed household, but typically to an unmarried woman who operates her own household and has children with one or more men. They are not open access prostitutes, and they do not sell sexual services. They have lovers, not customers. *Sétägna adari* is a term that it is more or less impossible to translate, but 'prostitute' is certainly misleading.
3. In view of their recruitment, one would expect more or less all of them to suffer from land shortage. It is therefore surprising to find that so few of them qualified for the lottery, especially since they had the easiest access to the lottery: their own holdings were likely to be given lower estimates than similar holdings of other peasants, and they were in a strong position to influence how their own households were registered.

Legitimacy

Officials at the district level vigorously defended the land redistribution, whether out of conviction or as a function of their office. But there was certainly a problem of legitimacy at lower levels. Many members of the redistribution committees found it difficult to defend the redistribution, not land redistribution as such, but the discriminatory rules applied, and even the work of their own committee. Thus, one of the members of the redistribution committee in Kasayé Agär described it in the following way:

> The redistribution was by kinship, money and liquor. The smart (*näqa yaläw*) people had served in office under the Därg, and therefore those who remained did not know or understand anything, and therefore nothing could be done. If the *birokrasi* made an accusation, they were not heard, since it had been ordered that they had no right to speak. (N4524)

This informant believed that many of the Därg officials had a lot of land, and he seems to have favoured redistribution. But although he served on the committee himself, and was thus among the most powerful local persons during this period, he felt frustrated by the direction of the redistribution, due to the discriminatory criteria for land confiscation, the lack of precision in targeting the poor, and the great role played by peasant politics.

In general one would expect peasant opinion to be divided over such an issue as land redistribution, basically on the pattern that the winners would be positive and the losers negative. In the case of the Amhara land redistribution, however, more or less nobody claimed that the redistribution implemented was completely fair, and those few individuals who supported the discrimination of the *birokrasi* did so precisely because it was unfair, an act of revenge. The majority of peasants expressed support for redistribution, but when they were interviewed carefully, it turned out, with few exceptions, that they supported redistribution based on equality, not based on what they regarded as artificial class criteria.

The style of the Amhara land redistribution was very much that of a revolutionary process, an approach inherited from the liberation struggle. It was based on some form of mass mobilisation, of participation manipulated to break local resistance. Revolutionary land reforms typically aim both at improving the economy of the poor peasants and building support for the political movement in charge of the reform. The Amhara land redistribution failed on both counts. In the economic field it disturbed the land tenure system and created serious tenure insecurity. In the political field, it apparently aimed to break the influence of the *birokrasi* and build a support basis for the current regime. It partially succeeded in the former, but utterly failed in the latter. In both the economic and the political field it is a liability for the current government that will be hard, but not impossible, to overcome.

Fieldwork Data

My fieldwork notes are referred to by the number they have in the database (preceded by "N". This protects the anonymity of the informant but provides precise source identification for future researchers.

All names of Yefat peasants used in this article are pseudonyms. A list of the correct names is found in N5021.

No Environmental Protection without Local Democracy?

Why Peasants Distrust Their Agricultural Advisers

Siegfried Pausewang

Peasants see the threat of environmental degradation as soon as its impact becomes visible. They search for remedies, and they seek assistance from experts who can give them help in checking the deterioration in the fertility and productivity of their land. Yet, in some situations, peasants choose not to turn for help to those who are close by and are specifically trained in environmental conservation measures.

Ethiopian peasants are no exception to this rule. They see deepening erosion gullies cutting into their grazing land, and feel the decline of fertility on their fields. Yet, it appears that most of them do not ask for professional advice from the agricultural advisers or "development agents", who are easily to be reached almost everywhere in the rural areas. As this chapter will show, they appear to prefer to look for other alternatives. They seek help from international or national NGOs, or they try to find adjustments which allow them to make a living as best they can in spite of growing signs of environmental degradation. Such disregard of a service offered to peasants all over the country asks for an explanation.

A Mis-Directed But Good Request

In 1997–98 a group of teachers going to rural areas in different parts of Ethiopia to teach people about human rights and democracy was approached several times with a request to give instruction on environmental protection. The teachers belong to a small programme called *ENWEYAY*—"Let's Discuss"—which engages people in a debate on the principles and practice of democracy in their own everyday life. Debate, rather than lecturing, was the central methodological approach of this programme.

The teachers are not agricultural extension agents and have no training in ecology. But they passed on the peasants' request for teaching on ecology to the office in Addis Ababa, asking for a teaching kit on the environment. The office immediately raised the question: Why do peasants ask us for knowledge on environmental protection, and not those experts from the Ministry of Agriculture, who have the technical knowledge demanded, and who are accessible almost everywhere in the country? It is common knowledge that the Ministry of Agriculture is the only ministry in Ethiopia which can reach almost every corner of the country through its "development agents". Would it not be better to pass on the request to the Ministry of Agriculture, as the agency with the technical and personnel resources as well as the administrative responsibility for environmental protection measures?

In fact, the teachers of ENWEYAY started working on a teaching kit on the environment. They gave one of their colleagues, who had a training as an agricultural extension agent, the task to translate her knowledge on the environment into a pedagogically sound set of questions which could be illustrated for a flip chart to be used for stimulating peasant discussions. She worked for some time on questions like:

What is a healthy environment? Which threats are there to our environment? What is your experience about degradation of your environment? What can be done to prevent negative effects and to preserve the fertility of your fields? How can conservation measures be implemented on your fields?

The first attempt was more or less in line with the "Guidelines on Soil Conservation" from the ministry (Ministry of Agriculture, 1995), translating them into pictures and questions for a debate with peasants. At this point we asked whether peasants really had asked our teachers for this kind of technical knowledge. If so, the request would rightly have to be transferred to the Ministry. However, we suspected that peasants did not want to go to the Ministry, that it was an entirely different set of issues they aimed at. They had requested environmental teaching from those teachers whom they had experienced in open and tolerant debates on democracy.

Even a cursory look at the experience of peasants with the extension agents of the Ministry of Agriculture during the last 20 years gave sufficient reason to understand peasant suspiciousness towards these agents. The extension service had been systematically expanded in the early years of the Mengistu regime, combining the personnel and the services of the Ministry of Agriculture with those of Haile Selassie's Ministry of Community Development (which was discontinued). Except for some nomadic people, the regime could through its line of command reach practically all peasants at very short notice.

The development agents were central in administering the land reform of 1975, together with the students in the "*Zemecha*" campaign (Pausewang, 1983:101). Already in 1977 the service changed its character, and by 1985 it was obvious that the extension department of the Ministry of Agriculture had become the line of command through which the government reached the entire rural population with its orders and its control. The "Development Agents" had to explain to peasants any new restriction imposed on them. They had to implement the system of forced sales quota to the Grain Board. As the only state agents in place, they had to ensure the collection of taxes and contributions, and they had to bear the responsibility for implementing the immensely unpopularresettlement and villagisation programmes (Mulugeta et al., 1987). All this made the agents extremely unpopular among peasants.

But did the bad reputation last so long that peasants even seven years after the fall of the Mengistu regime would avoid asking them for assistance? Or were there new experiences which tended to revive peasants' distrust towards the agents of the Ministry of Agriculture?

A Qualitative Study

We decided to conduct a limited number of group discussions and individual interviews among peasants, to find out more about possible reasons.[1] Lack of funds for extended research or a survey among peasants limited the number of people to be interviewed.[2] But collecting experience on the record of extension agents with the

---

1. In the same regions from where we received the request—mainly in Southern Region and in Shoa, Oromia. There may be regional differences which are not reflected in this report.
2. About 25 group discussions were conducted. We estimated between 12 and 30 participants at each one. Peasants cannot be forced to stay during an entire session. Some informants leave the meeting early, others join the crowd. Meetings often started with a small number but ended with a large crowd attending. Active participants are usually limited to a core of some 10 to 12 persons, while the others voice their agreement or disapproval. Provocative questions or statements tend to draw more listeners into the debate. We assume a core of ca. 300 peasants actively participating in the group discussions. In addition we carried out a number of individual interviews. Information obtained in fieldwork for other purposes confirmed our findings.

peasants during the previous 20 years and particularly the recent seasons, we could make use of anthropological methods of "iterative data generation and analysis" (Beebe, 2001: 1, 60–82), and apply techniques of "triangulation" (Atkinson and Hammersley, 1993: 205–232) to test the probability of responses.[1]

Group discussions[2] usually started with a long and informal talk about agriculture, problems in climate, in cultivation, in soil fertility and other issues related to environmental problems. We realised that peasants generally quite exact and detailed knowledge not only about the problems of environmental degradation, but also of the reasons for it and the chain of causes and effects creating a self-reinforcing process of degradation. Thereafter the debate was led over to discussing possible remedies, and peasants were asked where they could get help in planning conservation measures.

Peasants generally in these discussions showed that they understood the problem very well. They saw it in the context of their village and its experience of long term degradation of soil fertility and erosion. Many farmers also acknowledged the gradual but continuous diminishing of plots due to population growth. Others refused to accept a population problem. Some peasants insisted there was enough land to distribute to new young families, if only the authorities would authorise it. Others expected a remedy from a redistribution of land. In the long run, however, the problem of scarcity of land was well understood, and seen as a problem aggravating environmental hazards.

Asked for their needs, for why they requested teaching on the environment, they invariably first quoted their need for precise knowledge on technical solutions and material assistance in implementing them. Asked why they did not approach the Development Agents of the Ministry of Agriculture for help, they admitted they knew these were professionals who had technical knowledge and also had access to the necessary inputs and other forms of aid for environmental programmes. Usually a long debate followed—of which we as outsiders often understood only a small fraction. Examples were quoted showing negative experience with such projects. At some point, some elder would usually summarise the debate for us, explaining that these people were professionals, but that their services generally turned out not to be in the peasants' interest. As one elder in a village near Butajira explained: "We ask them to help us, they come, and they even offer us a package of environmental protection measures, including subsidies. They make a plan, they take over, they command us to do this, do that. They always arrange it so that we have to do the work, but in the end the benefits accrue to them..."[3]

Peasant Experience

In different places, essentially the same experience with extension agents emerged: peasants do not want to consult the extension agents because they have experienced

1. For more methodological information on qualitative research, see Atkinson and Hammersley, 1993; Beebe 2001; Babbie 1992; Devereux and Hoddinoff, 1993; Spradley 1980.
2. Group discussions were conducted in connection with supervision of teachers, near Wolkite and Endeber and Butajira in May 1998, near Shashemane and Nazareth in August 1998, near Nazareth in August 1999 and near Durame in June 2000. Individual interviews were conducted during the same time period in different places.
3. Group discussion in a village near Butajira, May 30, 1998. Obviously, a quotation mark here does not mean a directly recorded quotation. The debate was held in Guragigna language, with a translator summarising but not translating word for word what was said; and with me taking notes to record it in summarised form, as far as possible preserving the original tone, but certainly not the exact wording.

a pattern in which these agents establish a command structure. Peasants are coerced and forced to do the practical work. Peasants resent deeply that the planning is taken over completely by the experts, and that it interferes with their cultivation cycle and agricultural practice. An old peasant in a village near Endeber, who obviously had followed the international news and trends, summarised peasant experience with state authorities in a rather drastic way: "In your country, he said, you may have "good government". But here, government comes always "with the barrel of the gun".[1]

In August 1999, another issue was prominent in peasant complaints: at that time, we were told, many peasants were in prison because they could not pay for the fertiliser they had taken on credit in spring. Peasants greatly resented the involvement of the *kebele* (peasant associations) and the development agents in enforcing the repayment of debts to newly privatised distribution companies.[2] This complaint has become more frequent since 1999. More peasants in more areas appear to have experienced the same trend. In the elections of 2000, demands for repayment were used selectively to pressurise peasants into voting for the ruling party.[3] In 2001, voters complained in many areas that only those who were known as supporting the opposition where forced to repay, and put in prison if they could not—while for their supporters the authorities found reason for extending the time for repayment.[4]

We should not omit to mention that we came across one village[5] where peasants in a rather informal group discussion expressed only satisfaction with the extension service and their advise on ecological issues as well as on fertiliser use. They knew of some people having problems with repayment, but said that those who had been arrested were already released. These peasants seemed to accept that the fertiliser had given them increased harvests and hence incomes. Those who nevertheless failed to repay would have to face coercive measures.

It would be too easy to dismiss such a difference in only one village as a result of peasant suspiciousness or fear of repercussions. Nor could we observe this as a particularly fertile area where, due to good soils or moisture, irrigation or rainfall or a combination of these, crops responded better to fertilisers than in the neighbouring villages. We would rather tend to explain the contrast in responses as a result of this village being given better services from the extension agents. This could be due to the fact that the place was situated close to the main road, and close to a major town, and hence easy to reach for frequent visits by the agents. It could also be the merit of a particularly good team of development agents. Other factors may also have contributed to a response which differed markedly from other places. As we cannot claim a sample of villages large enough to calculate representativeness or statistical margins of error, we can only note one exception—leaving open the causes for their deviant response.

Some peasants also complained that the kebele had forced them to take fertilisers on credit, on the advice of development agents, to be applied even on land that they considered not suitable for cultivation and fertiliser application. As a result, they claimed, the harvest on such land was in some cases not even sufficient to repay the

---

1. Group discussion in a village near Endeber, May 16, 1998. I asked the translator whether he had put the peasant's words into a "modern" language form; but he insisted that the peasant used the terms he might have heard on the radio.
2. Group discussions near Nazareth, 5 and 6 August, 1999.
3. Interviews and group discussions with peasants near Durame, 22–26 June, 2000.
4. Interviews and group discussions with peasants near Nazareth on 25 February, 2001 and near Holetta and Muger on 4 March, 2001. See also the election reports.
5. Near Nazareth on 6 August, 1999.

costs of the fertiliser.[1] Yet they were not only advised, but even forced to apply fertilisers.

Such experience indicates that peasants have no confidence in the agricultural extension service, nor in the rural *kebele* or peasant associations. Nor would they expect a complaint with higher authorities to lead towards improvements. One might ask, why peasants do not find other channels to complain and to enforce their rights—be it at public meetings, through professional associations, through political channels, in the press or even by enforcing their rights in the courts. European peasants would have many avenues open to demand their right to decide for themselves on how to organise environmental protection on their fields. Raising publicity to exert public pressure would be a major way. Linking with other interest groups, in labour unions, in the environmental movement, in solidarity groups, in sports clubs, cultural societies, even in religious social services they could expect to find support for such basic demands. They could even expect that other groups might some day demand the peasants to deal effectively with environmental problems caused by agricultural malpractice and by rural population pressure. An alliance of such interests could well compel both the peasants and the authorities to seriously tackle environmental problems. But it would be done in a way that helps farmers and allows them to introduce environmental protection without disrupting their cultivation cycle, their production and their life adaptations.

Such social mechanisms, which negotiate the interests of different groups with the demands of new—in this case ecological—challenges are critically lacking in Ethiopia. The history of environmental conservation is full of examples showing that there was no lack of concern for the environment—either among peasants or among the authorities. But all programmes were implemented on the basis of orders from above, and administered without taking peasant interests into account. Bringing environmental measures into harmony with peasant concerns was not even attempted, either at the central or at the local level. The ideology of peasant participation through the peasant associations was taken as sufficient. It systematically replaced the negotiating process.[2] Peasants were made to participate in the work—not given a chance to negotiate their concerns. In 1986, a high official in the Ministry of Agriculture in Addis Ababa, asked about peasant participation by an FAO delegation, answered: "We have the experience when it comes to ensuring participation, we know our peasants. You tell us the technical solutions and provide the funds, and leave the rest to us. We know how to make the peasants participate".[3] Such attitudes seem to have returned to the rural scene after 1993. It may thus be worthwhile to have a look at the peasants' experience with environmental issues during the previous years.

Experience with Environmental Protection

The Ethiopian agricultural extension service has considerable experience with ecological protection measures. In the 1970s and 80s the Ministry of Agriculture built

---

1. Oral information in Addis Ababa, from a relative of an involved peasant, August 1999.
2. A thorough study on peasant participation in the Mengistu period was undertaken in 1985–1986, interviewing over 800 peasants randomly selected in two districts—Achefer in Gojjam and Shebadino in Sidamo. It concluded that peasant participation in local level planning had become impossible, and measures to promote local democracy were perceived by peasants as repression and arbitrary interference (Mulugeta et al., 1987/1991: ix, 3, 167–68)
3. My summary from a meeting at the Ministry of Agriculture in 1986.

up an impressive capacity for soil conservation, afforestation and erosion control. The World Food Programme (WFP), particularly their programme 2488, assisted this campaign by providing "food for work" to stimulate peasants' efforts. The Ministry carried out a wide campaign to rehabilitate forests and build protection schemes for the most affected river catchments.

The extension service bore a major responsibility for putting the scheme into practice. Specialists went as planners from place to place to implement the campaign for soil conservation. The agricultural extension agents on the spot had the task of mobilising the peasants, motivating them for voluntary work on the schemes, or for work which was paid in food, and organising their "participation", with the help of the local peasant associations.

Extension agents were trained in prevention of environmental degradation. A Swiss team of experts from the University of Bern, led by Hans Hurni, built up research stations to experiment with suitable technologies. They developed and continuously refined a package of environmental protection measures suitable for Ethiopia and easily applicable for extension agents.[1] The team worked out a handbook, issued by the Community Forests and Soil Conservation Development Department of the Ministry of Agriculture in 1978 (in Amharic, English edition 1986) under the title "Guidelines for Development Agents on Soil Conservation in Ethiopia".

The book was distributed free of charge to the "Development Agents" and the employees of the Natural Resources Conservation and Development Departments in Ethiopia. It offers an easily understandable and applicable guideline for analysing soil qualities and potential for ecological degradation, and for planning the scientifically necessary conservation structures and implementing them. The book was very well designed in terms of technical recommendations and pedagogical preparation: it gave practitioners an easy approach to define which measures should be taken, which terraces, bunds, gullies and ditches should be constructed. But the book does not even touch questions of peasant interests or of adapting environmental measures to their needs. It is assumed that knowledge of technical solutions is needed, not adaptation to local production structures and social needs. It is assumed that peasants are searching for remedies, that they want technical skills and accept solutions planned for them. There is no hint that such plans could interfere with peasant practice or local needs. In almost every chapter the book refers to necessary long term maintenance, which is assigned to the local people. But nowhere does the book ask whether local people are interested in maintenance and willing to do the necessary work, nor whether indeed they have the means to do it.[2] And nowhere are the experts advised in the first place to seek the opinions of the local people on these measures, or to engage in a dialogue on how to make their technical advice suitable to the peasants' needs.

The World Food Programme in Ethiopia supported the campaign of the Ministry of Agriculture consistently throughout the 1980s with its project Ethiopia 2488—Rehabilitation and Development of Rural Lands and Infrastructure. Project 2488 became the largest single food-for-work project in Africa. The campaign of the Ministry, implemented with WFP food-for-work support, developed into a country-wide effort for soil conservation. Its results were seen everywhere, with one river catchment after the other being visibly structured with bunds or bench terraces along the horizontal contours of the landscape. With afforestation projects, area enclosures, river catchment rehabilitation, soil reclamation, gully recoveries, the campaign in-

---

1. Personal information from Hans Hurni, 1993.
2. The book was reprinted in 1995 with no changes in content.

terfered deeply with peasants' adaptation and cultivation practices. Yet the campaign built on an assumption of technical efficiency and social neutrality, as the "guidelines" (Ministry of Agriculture 1986) demonstrate. The WFP evaluation demonstrated the social consequences of such assumptions (WFP/CMI 1994).[1]

The Fuelwood Projects

Also during the 1980s, a series of fuelwood projects was initiated, financed from different donors. The aim was to build remedies for the growing fuelwood shortages in urban centres without depleting forests in the nearer or wider vicinity. In 1989 I participated in an evaluation of two such fuelwood projects, financed by UNSO—the UN office for the Sudano-Sahel programme for environmental rehabilitation. What we saw was projects centrally planned by bureaucrats and forest experts, essentially without due consideration of peasants' interests. Experts had estimated the fuelwood needs of two medium size towns, Nazareth and Debre Birhan, and calculated the size of forest needed to supply the necessary fuelwood. Agricultural and forestry experts identified hillsides in the vicinity of the towns which were only marginally productive, due to deforestation, overgrazing and ecological degeneration. Sufficient areas were demarcated for reforestation. The peasant associations were instructed to organise peasant participation in afforestation.

The Municipality of Addis Ababa had projects of a different size but similar design, coordinated by the Ministry of Agriculture. Other major towns also had their corresponding fuelwood schemes. Towards the end of the decade, the hillsides around many towns began to look green and healthy, forests grew up and gave an impression of greatly improving environments. A closer look would reveal that most of the forests were composed of eucalyptus, ecologically not the best choice, but efficient in terms of productivity.

But the Municipality had to introduce increasingly harsh and costly measures to guard the forests against the local population. Restrictions on firewood collectors to protect the new plantations threatened supplies to local markets. The life of women living on selling firewood at the markets became unsafe as forest guards demanded bribes, blackmailed them or raped them outright with impunity.[2] Towards the end of the Mengistu regime, armed gangs chased the guards away, to engage in regular harvesting, transporting the looted timber on trucks to growing urban markets.[3]

In theory, the project design included a consideration for benefits to the peasants, both from "food for work" or direct payment for afforestation work, and from the sales of timber once the forests became mature and productive. In practice, however, the peasant associations organised peasant participation in the way of the Mengistu regime: peasants were told to hand over the land in the demarcated areas free of charge, "voluntarily". Protests were not heard. Peasants were told they had to contribute their share to socialist development. Complaints about lack of grazing areas were brushed aside: peasants were simply told to graze their cattle somewhere else...[4] Peasants were organised to work on replanting campaigns. The replanted forests

---

1. The report on the evaluation of WFP in Ethiopia avoids criticising past political practice and concentrates on WFP's current performance. However, during the evaluation fieldwork the often disastrous effects of centrally planned and executed environmental programmes became utterly clear—an experience which the report reflects clearly, if only indirectly.
2. Information from interviews in Addis Ababa in 1989 during the evaluation of UNSO fuelwood projects.
3. Information from interviews with peasants in 1989 near Nazaret and Modjo.
4. Interviews with peasants near Debre Berhan and Nazareth in 1989.

were kept in state ownership until the time when peasants were ready to assume the necessary management skills and responsibilities. Some benefits did materialise in the form of food for work or other payments, especially for those few employed in nurseries or administrative jobs. Peasants were told that they would benefit much more once the forests were mature for harvesting. But peasant complaints and protests increased. Peasants resisted the loss of their land, arguing that however marginal it was, they could not afford to lose grazing land—and in some cases even agricultural land—without compensation—as they would face serious harm to their livestock and particularly to the plough oxen.[1] Peasant associations promised compensation, but such never materialised. There just was no land to spare or to redistribute.

Peasants retaliated by stealing wood from the forests, grazing their cattle there against the rules, or even outrightly removing trees to reclaim their land. We heard many individual stories of peasants losing their agricultural viability and their family income through the plantations. Those who had lost agricultural land were insisting that this was still their land, waiting for a chance to claim it back.[2]

The projects had to employ guards to protect the plantations. Trees grew nicely and, in the eyes of the forester, promised a good return and a productivity far above what peasants could have produced through grazing or cultivation. Yet, peasants resisted and looked for a chance to destroy the plantations. One of the projects had to "bribe"[3] peasants by offering them help in building a school, to compensate for individual losses and for the loss of grazing. Still, peasants were not appeased. In the end, the project had to hire guards from other villages, and drive them in project cars over the mountains every day, so they would not have to guard the forest against their own people. In 1989, guards demanded to be armed to be able to repel aggressive peasants (Fantu Cheru and Zethner, 1989).

When the forest approached maturity and harvesting could start in the Nazareth area, armed gangs appeared here and there to harvest timber and drive it to towns for sale, the guards watching it happen powerlessly. So unpopular had the plantation become that strangers were warned not to enter the area after dark.[4] As the power of the Mengistu regime began to falter, it was obvious that the plantations would not survive its fall.

Indeed, in 1993 was obvious from a long distance away that the green cover of the hills surrounding the towns had been dramatically reduced. Naked hills, interspersed with sparse regrowth, were to be seen around Addis Ababa.[5] Yet the new authorities soon re-established the protection measures. The state ownership of the forests was re-confirmed, and the guards re-employed. After a short period of extended and wild destruction, local opposition was once again brought under control. The forests slowly recovered from the damage.[6]

In 1999, officials of the Ministry of Agriculture and employees of WFP in Ethiopia stated that the forests were once again securely under state ownership.[7] The promise to hand them over to the local communities as soon as these are ready to

1. Information from interviews with peasants near Nazareth and Debre Berhan, 1989.
2. In a village near Debre Berhan, peasants took us to their former fields, now enclosed and planted with eucalyptus trees, claiming it was still their land and should be returned.
3. As peasant described it in 1989, near Debre Berhan.
4. Own experience in 1989 during evaluation of UNSO fuelwood projects near Nazareth.
5. Own experience during evaluation of World Food Programme in April 1993.
6. Own observation and information collected during evaluation of World Food Programme in Ethiopia, in April 1993.
7. Information from officials of WFP and in the Ministry of Agriculture in Addis Ababa, August 1999.

administer and control them remained in place.[1] But its realisation has been post-poned time and again. Little is done in practice to enable communities to develop the necessary skills, get people sufficiently trained, or to create a legal base for taking over the responsibility for the forests. For all practical purposes, unless a radical so-cial and political change of attitudes occurs, the time when local communities will be allowed to take over the ownership and with it the benefits, appears to be post-poned indefinitely. To one who knows the history of these fuelwood projects, it does not appear astonishing that peasants are bitter about the very existence of the for-ests, however productive and environmentally sound and beneficial they may be.[2]

The Fate of the Environmental Protection Structures

Even before 1991, many of the structures built by the Ministry of Agriculture were destroyed by local peasants. They complained about the structures and, while they did not dare to resist the appeal to work on their reconstruction, they tried to do the work as superficially as possible, so it should not last. Asked why they resented them, peasants explained that stone bunds give shelter for mice and rats, and that they cannot turn the plough on small corners between bunds and plot borders, con-fining considerable parts of their land to fallow. This is certainly a serious disadvan-tage of the bunds, which were planned along horizontal lines but irrespective of how they crossed through individual plots. But the resentment was deeper than that.

Because the bunds were immensely unpopular, peasants were usually ordered to work on a field at the other end of the village. Returning home in the evening, they would get furious when they saw what others had been doing on their fields.[3] As plans were made for a whole catchment area at a time, planners would not consider themselves obliged to, nor even able to, take individual wishes or needs into consid-eration. This was left, in theory, to the peasant associations who were supposed to convince peasants, and to compensate those who might suffer undue losses. In prac-tice, planners as well as peasant association leaders did not care, nor did they feel able to find remedies. In the name of efficiency, adaptation of environmental protec-tion to household farming patterns and individual needs was sacrificed (WFP/CMI, 1994).

For the planner, the important aspect was to get the job done, to report the catch-ment rehabilitation as completed and move on to the next. For the PA chairman, what mattered was to meet the expectations of the higher authorities, on whom their position and power depended. As soon as the planner had moved on, nobody cared about the further fate of the structures. Maintenance was generally given very little attention. The soil conservation handbook assumed that maintenance was in the in-terest of local peasants, and could safely be left to the peasant associations (MoA, 1986). In practice, neither the Ministry nor WFP or other donors gave it any prior-ity. As late as 1998, an internal evaluation of WFP critically remarked that the project Ethiopia 2488 was giving very little attention to post-construction protection and maintenance (WFP, 1998: 7). In many places, peasants did not even wait until

1. Information from officials of the Ministry of Agriculture in Addis Ababa, August 1999.
2. Ethiopian history offers examples of promises being postponed indefinitely, community projects being turned into state farms. We refer to the farms in Awasa and in Arba Minch, which were started around 1960 as com-munity development projects (with pensioned soldiers in Awasa and settlers in Arba Minch) who were prom-ised ownership as soon as initial investments were in place and the farms became viable. This never happened, the soldiers and settlers ending up as farm labourers on state farms. See Pausewang 1983 p. 50.
3. Peasants freely reported about such practice when, in 1993, they were asked why structures did not last. Ex-perience from WFP evaluation in Ethiopia in 1993.

lack of maintenance removed the structures. As soon as the planner had left, the campaign was forgotten and peasants silently removed the structures on their own fields without much concern.[1]

In 1991, when the Mengistu regime fell, peasants in many regions acted swiftly to remove whatever remained of the hated structures. They chopped down tree plantations, either to get firewood or to get some income from selling it, or just to get rid of all the remnants of a hated regime. In a village near Kobbo, in Wollo,[2] a peasant association leader told me that they had completely chopped down a communal orchard which had a very good yield , was a good asset for nutrition and gave a reasonable cash return. Asked why they did not distribute the trees, or in other ways protect the orchard as an asset, he said that as long as there was an orchard, any new authority would claim it. Removing it gave the peasants a better chance at least to be able to use the land. They did not want any new cooperative, and they feared an available asset would increase the chances that new authorities might insist on forming one.[3]

Environmental Protection in Post-Mengistu Ethiopia

In 1993 I visited rural areas in Ethiopia as a team member in an evaluation of the World Food Programme. In many places, there was hardly anything left of the structures constructed. It may be hard to judge whether as much as 25 per cent of the assets created had been left intact (WFP/CMI, 1993: 36). Mainly plantations with trees which could be coppiced (such as eucalyptus) survived the destruction and looting of forests. In all, the evaluation found that WFP, by leaving implementation to the government without questioning the official version that peasant associations represented genuine participation, had in practice supported a programme that was executed against local interests and the users' needs. From affected peasants we heard lots of complaints about the agents implementing the conservation programme.[4] We learned about the strong resentment felt towards a programme that manipulated peasants into doing conservation works against their own will and interest (WFP/CMI, 1993).

After the fall of the military regime, WFP's project 2488 was reformed and revived in Ethiopia, supporting environmental conservation measures with food-for-work, to provide food for the poorest through a "self-targeting process" in which people who had other opportunities would not resort to this kind of jobs. To enforce food security, an emergency "shelf" of projects can be activated in times of food deficit. Food-for-work programmes can be started immediately, and can offer alternative access to food for the poorest food deficit families. The evaluation remarks that "by now decisions are likely to be made with farmers' participation, thus greatly improving chances that assets will be maintained" (WFP/CMI, 1993: 37).

An interim evaluation of Project Ethiopia 2488 (WFP, 1997) in 1997 makes a strong argument that the programme is now based on a local level participatory approach. It celebrates the "local level participatory planning process" as a major step forward (p. 13) and criticises that current activities are very limited in relation to the

---

1. Peasants in Wollo and Lasta reported on such practices when interviewed in 1993.
2. Subsequent to the administrative reorganizaztion introduced by the EPRDF government, the area is now located in Tigray region.
3. Interview in April 1993, during field trip for evaluation of WFP in Ethiopia.
4. Interviews with peasants in different places in Debre Tabor, Lalibela, Kobbo, Kombolcha, Dessie areas, April 1993.

needs, and therefore need replication all over the country (p. 11). However, in 1998 another evaluation of WFP critically remarks that the programme had given far too little emphasis to maintenance (WFP, 1998).

Recent experience in Ethiopia[1] leads me to doubt whether there has been any move towards participatory planning that could secure peasant consent and owner-ship of the environmental rehabilitation programme. The new authorities again assume and command peasant support and organise participation as labour contributions, but not as participation in planning processes or political decisions. The questions remain: Who is planning—and for whom? Who is delegated by the peasant associations to represent peasants? Whose interests are taken into consideration?

Alternatives

Why, then, did peasants in 1998 ask the teachers of ENWEYAY for training in environmental problems? Obviously not because they lacked knowledge on the expertise offered by the extension system. Rather, they based their request on the experience with the ENWEYAY teachers: 'Here is a group which offers us a debate in which we can participate, in which our opinions matter, in which we are allowed to clarify our needs. They may help us to gradually find solutions which correspond to our interests and our preferences, (see Pausewang, 1996 a) while the state experts and development agents only give us orders and take from us all responsibility....'

It might be difficult to generalise on the basis of a few random discussions with groups of peasants. But they provide the data necessary to employ methods of qualitative research such as triangulation and iterative data analysis, thereby revealing a consistent pattern. This pattern fits into experience gained in other contexts in Ethiopia before and after the fall of Mengistu's government. The new central government promised democracy, decentralisation of power and an administration closer to the local people. But practice shows in many contexts that the authoritarian local structures were revived, in the peasant associations as well as in local administration and in the elections at local level. The experience from the group discussions thus corresponds with tendencies reflected in the reports from election observation in 1992, 1994 and 1995 (Pausewang, 1992, 1994; Tronvoll and Aadland, 1995; Poluha, 1995). It also mirrors the trend reported from the reconstruction of peasant associations after 1992 in Northern Shoa (Aspen, 1995, 1997). Certainly, the description of the land redistribution process in Amhara region, as it was implemented in rural areas in Yefat (Ege, 1998), fits neatly into an emerging picture of a revival of authoritarian structures in peasant associations and peasant relations to local authorities.

Reports from recent elections in rural areas paint a rather gloomy picture of close control which kebele officials and party cadres have been able to re-establish over peasants.[2] The elections in May–June 2000 demonstrated a growing repressive potential in the hands of rural kebele officials. Peasants were threatened they would lose access to fertiliser, credit or other services if they voted for an opposition party.

1. The events during the elections of 2000 and 2001 demonstrate that local administrative structures are again built up to control the peasants, not to give them a voice. Communications are again firmly established as command flows from top downwards, not from down upwards. See the different reports from the Norwegian Institute of Human Rights on the elections in 2000 and 2001.

2. The Norwegian Institute of Human Rights (Oslo) followed the democratisation process during the period of preparation for the elections. Starting from the candidate registration in November—December 1999, it included the re-election in Southern Region on June 25, 2000, as well as local elections in February 2001 and in Southern Region in December 2001. A concluding analysis of the democratisation process, ten years after the fall of the Mengistu government, is in publication and will be available in 2002.

Many of them were beaten, threatened with imprisonment, or arrested under dubious pretexts if they refused to support the ruling parties. By March 2001, in the local elections, this potential of repression had visibly increased, and had reached even Addis Ababa with unprecedented strength. From many areas we heard complaints that supporters of opposition candidates were refused normal citizen rights, and lost access to community services and to protection of their personal security. Food distribution was used again to punish supporters of opposition parties, according to peasant complaints (Aalen and Pausewang, 2001; Pausewang, 2001). The election in Southern Region in December 2001 left no doubt that peasants were once again becoming resigned to the power of local authorities (Aalen and Pausewang, 2002).

A particularly alarming and novel means of repression occurred in the March 2001 election: local party cadres tell peasants who support an opposition party blankly: "The Constitution says that the land is the property of the government. We do not give our land to those who betray us. Let your party give you land—if they have any..."[1] In a society where 85 per cent of the population live from agriculture, land is the most precious resource for food production. Access to land is a question of life or death for an Ethiopian peasant. Where such a kind of threat is brought forward to prevent people from voting for any opposition, participation seems a far cry indeed.

Ethiopian peasants have no practical experience of having a voice outside of their close neighborhood. At the time of the landlords, they were terrorised by their local spies, their chika shum, and their local army ("*Netch labash*"). They enjoyed a brief spell of freedom after the land reform of 1975. For about two years, peasant communities were empowered to make decisions of importance concerning their region, their occupation, and their habitat. For a short interval they were able to develop institutions to facilitate collective decisions. The peasant associations, as they were established by the land reform proclamation of 1975, were genuine representations of local communities. In those parts of the country (mainly in the South) where the land reform was implemented with little delay, they were established early by peasants assisted by *Zemetcha* students. They were—with few exceptions—really autonomous administrative institutions of peasant communities who made their decisions as best they could in an open debate. Peasant associations had very considerable responsibility and authority, they mobilised peasant involvement and expressed peasant interests (Pausewang, 1983: 9–13, 105). At that time, in 1976, peasants could send an administrator packing, telling him to mind his own business, and come back when they called for him: "Now we are in charge here in our village..."[2]

But starting from 1977, their autonomy was curbed and gradually dismantled. Peasant autonomy did not fit into the DERG's concept of a centrally controlled society. The peasant associations were maintained, but their elected leaders were removed and replaced by agents of the state, controlled through political cadres. Their autonomy was replaced by a tight structure of control from above (Pausewang et al., 1990: 38, 213).

After the fall of the DERG in 1991, the peasant association leaders were systematically replaced with new leaders. But the structures remained the same. Peasant associations were renamed rural kebele, and the authorities soon re-established their control through their own cadres.[3]

---

1. Interview with peasants, Northern Shoa, on election day, March 4, 2001.
2. Interview with peasants near Nedjo, Wollega, March 1976; information confirmed by the Administrator in Nedjo, Jonathan Isaac.
3. As observed in Tronvoll and Aadland, 1995: 2, 30.

The Quest for Empowerment

The experience of ENWEYAY teaching, of teachers inviting to a free debate, may well have touched some strings in the memory of older peasants. This experience of a free discussion, which encouraged them to voice their views and interests, without any fear of control or repercussions, may have inspired peasants to ask for a similar approach in the pressing issue of environmental problems.

Seen in this light, the peasants did not ask for technical knowledge on how to control environmental degradation. They know what is wrong, they know in general terms what should be done. What the peasants really ask for, might be paraphrased as a way to involve the technical specialists in a free and equitable debate in which peasants themselves can develop a plan for environmental protection based on their own premises, with technical advise and cooperation from the experts. What they need is not technical plans, but a debate in which the experts contribute their technical knowledge to a planning process guided by the peasants' interests. They hope that such a debate will lead to a plan that they can implement together, and adjust to their needs and preferences.

When they asked ENWEYAY for advice on environmental protection, what they meant was a process to engage the experts in a debate on equal grounds. What they really demanded was a process like the one used in the ENWEYAY teaching, in which their voices are heard; their rights are taken seriously; they can feel that their interests, knowledge, and opinion matter; they are allowed to take responsibility; they are empowered and enabled to have influence; they are allowed to decide their own environmental protection measures; they can demand, reject, or amend, the advice of the technical experts, on the basis of their own priorities and needs; they are the masters, not the objects, of their own environmental rehabilitation programme.

The lesson from this experience, of course, extends beyond a particular local environmental programme. It reflects an experience of a general need for administrative structures which translate democracy into local level practice. It is not sufficient to write democracy into the constitution, when local administrative structures function according to old and well established authoritarian practice. Where authority expresses itself in the ability of a civil servant to impose his will over others, democracy cannot be tolerated in practice. Where it is, in the eyes of the public as well as of himself, a sign of weakness if an administrator yields to demands for change from the public, questions will neither be invited nor tolerated. Where people expect that they have to obey the orders of their administrators or face harsh punishment, debate cannot thrive. And where people experience daily that their opinions do not matter, they search for ways to get around administrative decisions and to sabotage unpopular plans and projects, rather than offering alternatives or contributing ideas.

Parenthetically, we may note that peasants everywhere in the world have both positive and negative experience with extension services, depending on the agents' relations to the state. For example, a study in Norway in 1964 found that Norwegian extension agents changed their activities with changing technological and political opportunities. The service was created in the 1920s to assist small farmers to make a living by exploiting their limited resources as best they could. This worked to the benefit of small subsistence farms until the state changed its policies after World War II and started to rationalise rural production and to modernise the largest farms, in line with new technological possibilities. Now the agents found it more rewarding to help the big farms to increase their production with the help of labour-saving technology and inputs, and lost interest in giving service to the small farms. With bitterness, small farmers felt left alone and exposed to growing pressure to close down their farms and move to town to become industrial workers (Jacobsen, 1964).

The latter alternative—industrial work—is clearly not a possible solution for Ethiopian peasants. They have only one choice: to feed themselves on their land as well as they can, with the help of extension agents, or, if need be, in defiance of their advice.

The experience of ENWEYAY, seen in this light, points to a central issue: environmental (and other development) programmes will never succeed as long as they are implemented in the context of a structure which the peasants do not experience as their own. But they will not consider it their own unless they are able to plan it themselves, in the context of an open debate in a democratic atmosphere. Seen in this light, the problem is twofold. In the first instance, peasants demanded a democratic debate to come to meaningful ways for planning environmental protection. Ecology demands local democracy. In a wider perspective, their demand reflects a need for a general change of local administrative culture. Without local democracy, a public debate in which peasants can reflect and ferment their own interests, neither ecological problems nor other issues are likely to find acceptable and practicable solutions.

The quest thus underscores the need for institutions like ENWEYAY, which teach people that they have a right to participate in the debate. People must be conscious that they have a right to be heard, that planning is in tune with their interests, that it is done for them and on their premises. Administrative officers will not change the style of their relations to peasants unless peasants demand to be heard, and, more importantly, unless the general administrative climate is gradually changed to respect their demands. But such a change will not come by itself; administrators will not readily give up their prerogatives of enforcing their views on peasants. Unless peasants are prepared to insist on their rights and demand influence and responsibility, which they have as a constitutional right but not according to local practice, the latter will prevail.

Peasants have to expect resistance from people wielding authority in the local administration. They will have to be prepared for a fight, which might cost some of them dearly. Thus, teaching them to demand debate and influence, is not an easy responsibility. But it is the only way to ensure a steady growth in influence for local peasants. Authorities have to understand that ecological protection and other administrative and practical measures will only be successful the peasants are allowed to "own" them, to debate them, and then to implement them. An open debate also offers a "carrot", a tangible advantage to the central authorities. Working with peasants is much more efficient and gratifying than trying to enforce decisions from above. And a government which ensures peasant democracy can expect genuine peasant support.

III

Alternative Loci
of Power

Civil Society Organizations in Ethiopia

Dessalegn Rahmato

Introduction

There is currently a growing interest about "civil society" in Africa among people in academia, in international organizations, and donor agencies. The donor community in particular is keen to promote voluntary institutions in the belief that the road to democracy in Africa lies not in revolutions and class struggle but in the active involvement of civil society in the political process. Indeed, such is the current enthusiasm for the voluntary sector that it is often seen as the most important instrument for promoting sustained political reform, responsible governance, and pluralism. According to the World Bank, for example, civil society organizations "hold the greatest promise of success ... in building and rebuilding of state structures and institutions" (1998: 24). Civil society is expected to play in Africa the same role that the bourgeois revolution did in the capitalist West. The World Summit on Social Development held in 1995 placed considerable responsibility on civil society for improving the world environment for the economic and social development of the poor nations of the world (UNRISD, 2000). Among some proponents, civil society institutions are viewed not only as separate from the state but also as opposed to it because what is inherent in each of them is considered to be diametrically different. While civil society, it is believed, tends frequently towards democracy, the state in Africa is always prone to despotism. Thus the "deepening of civil society" in Africa through the pressure of globalization and international support to civic institutions will, it is believed, accelerate the pace of democratization.[1] The excitement with which the donor community has embraced the concept makes it appear as if someone had just discovered a magic formula called "civil society" which would painlessly make African governments more accountable.

But donor interest in strengthening civil society in African countries and elsewhere must be seen in a wider context and not just as another Western panacea for solving the problems of bad governance and underdevelopment. This interest is a recent, post-Cold War phenomenon and reflects a broad agenda of political and economic change that donors are keen to promote in these countries. The link between civil society and democratization that donor agencies insist upon converges, conveniently, with the goals of structural adjustment programs (SAPs) supported by the agencies themselves and imposed on the countries concerned by the IMF and the World Bank. Indeed, it is quite evident that the political agenda underpinning donor support to civil society is closely related to that of structural adjustment. SAP encourages the greater integration of African economies into the world economy, which is dominated by the donor countries, on conditions set by these same countries. It also calls for a minimal role for the state and a strong non-state sector con-

---

1. For the current literature relating to Africa, see references in Kasfir, 1998; see also Bratton, 1989: Hyden and Bratton, 1992. Hume and Edwards, 1997 deal with NGO-state relations. For civil society and donor response, see Van Rooy, 1998.

sisting of civil society and private enterprise. As we try to show further below, and as most policy analysts and economists in the donor countries as well as elsewhere also recognize, civil society in Africa is not capable of maintaining itself without a heavy dose of external assistance. Similarly, given the dominance of Western and Japanese multinational corporations in the world economy, the private sector in Africa will remain a marginal and ineffective force in the continent. In brief, the end product of donor concern with civil society is not so much greater democratization and development as greater dependency of African countries on donor powers and institutions.

Civil Society

There is a wide range of definitions attached to the notion of civil society among contemporary students of the subject but it will take us too far to review the existing literature in such a short discussion as this. Instead I shall view civil society in terms of a variety of autonomous, voluntary institutions which provide services to individuals and which articulate public interests. Civil society institutions occupy the space intermediary between the state on the one hand and the lowest unit of social life, the family, on the other. Such institutions place demands on the state for goods and services, promote the broad interests of their constituencies, and help extend the social space between the state and the individual. Civil society cannot be conceptualized outside of the framework of formal organizations; this means that it includes the organizations of the poor and the dispossessed just as much as those of the middle classes and the professionals. A robust civil society should protect the individual from the overwhelming power of the state. I shall argue that the foundation for democratic and accountable governance lies not so much in discrete civil society institutions but rather in popular, mass-based civic movements. In Ethiopia, civil society institutions include NGOs, advocacy organizations, professional associations, cooperatives, trade unions, religious organizations, and the independent press. I have excluded political organizations and business firms, but business institutions such as chambers of commerce and employers' associations should be considered as part of civil society. At present civil society institutions in Ethiopia can play an important role in promoting public awareness, but this is a much more limited role than securing democracy which is what donor agencies and others expect civil society to accomplish.

Readers may note that our definition of civil society excludes informal (or traditional) organizations that are common in both rural and urban areas,[1] and ethnic-based self-help and development associations, which were active during the imperial regime though under constant scrutiny by the authorities. There is not sufficient evidence to indicate to what extent the latter were conscious of the larger public interest or whether they were solely concerned with undertaking their stated objectives. Such organizations were operating under restricted conditions in the imperial period and were closed down at the time of the Derg, so we have no way of knowing in what direction they would have evolved and whether they would have been concerned with greater citizens' demands or with their own 'primordial' interests had there been a more open environment. This is the main reason that in Ethiopian circumstances the issue must remain, as it were, hanging in the air. Be that as it may,

---

1. Within the NGO sector in Ethiopia, civil society is taken to mean "formal and informal groups and associations that are not of the public and business sectors" (Code of Conduct: 5).

there is considerable debate on whether ethnic organizations should be included as part of civil society, with little prospect for consensus on the issue (Kasfir, 1988: 6–8).

On the other hand, there has not been sufficient comparative debate about informal and formal organizations in Ethiopia, and the differences and similarities between them, and the ability of the former to grow into the latter. Informal organizations (idir, iqoub, etc.) have so far been examined from what may be termed a functional approach. They have been seen as viable institutions providing financial services to social groups that have no access to formal savings and credit institutions (Dejene, 1993), or as useful instruments for local-level development activity (Bekalu, 1997; ESSWA, 1998). There is very little discussion about the institutional capacity of the organizations, their internal governance, and their ability to transcend their narrow objectives and articulate public demands. Civic organizations, on the other hand, are formally organized and usually legally registered, with specific but broad objectives, more or less participatory internal administration, and the autonomy to act beyond the immediate interests of their members or constituencies. Informal organizations do not meet most of these criteria. Civic bodies have a public function beyond their specific objectives, but this is not the case with informal institutions. I should note, in defense of informal institutions, however, that they do play an important role in shielding the individual and the family from the intrusions or depredations of the state. Through the instrumentality of informal institutions the humble individual is able to establish solidarity with his/her neighbors, and create an alternative realm of discourse where the "public transcript" is criticized, ridiculed or rejected (see Dessalegn, 1991). Traditional structures are resilient, much more so in many ways than formal organizations, and they are not easily "captured" by the state, which again is not the case with formal structures.

Civil Society Organizations in Ethiopia

For the purposes of this paper, we may divide civil society institutions in Ethiopia into four broad categories. These are: 1. Non-Governmental Organizations (NGOs). These consist of local or international organizations engaged in relief, development or both. NGOs provide services, channel funds, carry out development projects, and frequently engage in advocacy work. 2. Advocacy organizations. These consist of rights-based institutions and institutions committed to the protection of the environment, wildlife,[1] etc. 3. Interest group institutions. Under this category we find professional societies, trade unions, cooperatives, chambers of commerce, employers associations, and cultural societies. 4. Community organizations. These consist of neighborhood groups, and citizens' and youth organizations. In this section, I shall focus on a select group of organizations and briefly examine the extent to which they have been able to influence state action and public attitudes. Due to space limitations I shall leave out such important and long-established organizations as the Ethiopian Teachers Association and the Ethiopian Chamber of Commerce.

---

1. The Ethiopian Wildlife and Natural History Society is perhaps the oldest environmental protection organization in the country.

Non-Governmental Organizations[1]

Let us first begin with NGOs since these are the most visible institutions in the voluntary sector we are concerned with. There are only a limited number of studies on NGOs in Ethiopia, and most of them focus on the activities of the organizations, especially in the area of relief and rehabilitation, and their unhappy relations with the government.[2]

The tragic famine of the early 1970s in the north of the country, which grew to be beyond the ability of the state to manage, forced the imperial government to open its doors to NGOs. At the time, and through much of the 1970s, there were not more than twenty or twenty-five NGOs operating in the country, mostly in relief and rehabilitation. All but one or two of these were church-based organizations and only a handful were of local origin (see UNECA). A decade later came the devastating famine of the mid-1980s, which again stretched the resources of the state beyond its limits, once more compelling the government, this time the hard-line military Derg, to allow a large influx of Western NGOs into the country. The Derg grudgingly recognized that without large-scale assistance from the donor community, and the intervention of NGOs, it would be faced with a tragedy of mammoth proportions. As it turned out, the famine was a colossal disaster on all counts, and it is now assumed that far more lives would have been lost had it not been for the massive assistance provided by NGOs. This inauspicious beginning and the continued association of international NGOs with disaster and disaster relief have, I believe, tarnished their image and left a residue of resentment in government circles and sections of the informed public. It is as if Ethiopians, or rather the urban elite, never forgave these organizations for forcing their way into the country at a time when both state and society were overwhelmed by tragedy.

But this is only one side of the story. The growing involvement of NGOs in the country, first in relief and rehabilitation, subsequently in the development field, has its reverse side in the increasing inability of the state to meet the basic needs of the people and to provide essential services. The capacity of successive governments to deliver the benefits of development programs, in particular to the long-suffering rural population, has fallen far short of their public commitments. In the last three to four decades, the crisis of public finance, made worse by war and civil conflict, and a shrinking tax base, has reduced the ability of the state to invest in development or to sustain public programs. This deficiency must be seen against a background of a declining economy, loss of natural resources on a large scale, and the depreciation of the country's exports in the world market. The net result has been deepening poverty, growing unemployment and more frequent food crises. The greater the decline in state capacity, the greater the stature of NGOs among the needy public. Thus in the eyes of the government, NGOs, far from being a welcome partner, become a daily reminder of its own inability to play the dominant role in service delivery and the development effort. In short, these two circumstances, i.e. the unpropitious entry of NGOs into the country on the one hand, and the deflation of the stature of the state on the other, continue to sour NGO-state relations.

In the latter part of the 1980s, there were no more than sixty-five to seventy NGOs in the country. Thus the rapid growth in numbers has taken place after the change of government, in the last six to seven years. There are at present over 350

---

1. By NGOs I mean organizations that have signed operational agreements with DPPC.
2. See Agri-Service 2000; Bekalu, 1997; Campbell, 1996; Clark, 2000; Tegegne, 2000; UNECA, n.d.; Van Diesen and Walker, 1999; and Zegeye, 2000.

registered local and international NGOs engaged in a variety of activities in the country. Voluntary organizations that are not legally registered—and there are quite a few of them—are not included in this tally, nor are those set up and operating in the regions. New organizations are being established every year. CRDA, the main umbrella organization for NGOs, now has over 160 full and associate members, of which over 40 per cent are local NGOs.[1] The number of local NGOs has also increased dramatically since the fall of the Derg. In the 1980s, there were only a handful of local NGOs and almost all of them were church-based organizations. The table below summarizes information based on unpublished DPPC data sources.

Growth of Local and International NGOs 1994–2000

NGOs	1994	1996	1998	2000
LNGOs	24	96	160	246
INGOs	46	96	119	122
Total	70	192	270	368

As the table shows, the strength of local NGOs has increased from 34 per cent in 1994 to 67 per cent in 2000. However, most local organizations today are small in size, and involved primarily in mother-and-child care programs, and health and social welfare services. In general, the NGO presence in Ethiopia is much less visible and less assertive and the scope of their work more restricted than in many African countries, despite the greater population size of the country and the greater extent of poverty and food insecurity.

Figures cited by CRDA show that in the period from 1984 to 1996 NGOs provided relief assistance on the average to 6.5 million beneficiaries each year, or about 14 per cent of the rural population. In 1990 alone, 13 million beneficiaries are said to have received assistance from NGOs. The volume of food aid distributed by them ranges from 1.5 million quintals in 1984 to 5.1 million in 1992. The development projects undertaken by NGOs in the 1990s, estimated to have cost 2.5 billion Birr, are believed to have benefited 26 million people, both rural and urban, and created 14,000 employment opportunities (CRDA, 1998: 7–9). It is not quite clear what the benefits consist of and what their impact has been on beneficiary livelihoods. There are no accurate figures indicating how much resource the organizations have brought into the country, but a recent study, citing UNDP sources, estimates that in 1996 five per cent of the country's external assistance (or US $35 million) was provided by NGOs. UNDP figures show an increase in external assistance provided by NGOs over the period 1991–1996, "but it is unclear whether this reflects improved data capture" (Van Diesen and Walker, 1999: 7). The same document notes that DPPC's estimate of the annual budget of NGOs is about 400 million Birr (US $55 million). The evidence from DPPC sources also shows that over 49 per cent of NGO resources was invested in rural development and agricultural projects, 8.7 on health, 7.5 per cent in urban development, and 6.2 per cent on environment; less than four per cent each was spent on water and sanitation, and education. Most of the NGO resources has been invested in four regions: 23.4 per cent of investment has gone to the Amhara Region, followed by the Southern Region (20.6 per cent), Oromia (20.3

---

1. The information contained here comes from CRDA 1998, CRDA membership directories, and CRDA News, the monthly bulletin of the organization.

per cent) and Addis Ababa (17.6 per cent). Marginal regions such as Beni-Shangul and Gambella have attracted very little NGO attention (DPPC figures cited in CR-DA, 1998: 13; see also Zegeye, 2000). The high investment in rural development and agriculture reflects the greater concern of NGOs for food security, which was the main justification for their involvement in the country in the first place.

Despite the positive figures noted above, I believe the overall impact of NGOs, measured against the resources they have mobilized, is quite disappointing. Development projects run by many NGOs have done little to improve the livelihood of the communities concerned. NGOs have been very good at emergency operations and the delivery of food aid to vulnerable populations, however their interventions in the field of development have not been equally successful. Opinions gathered for Christian Aid by Van Diesen and Walker (1999: 31–33) shows that NGOs' achievements have been limited, and that they would have been more effective if they had invested more resources in the education and health sectors. I should add here that NGOs have operated, since the 1970s, in an unfriendly policy environment and this has definitely contributed to the limitations of their performance.

But what about the intangible qualities of NGOs: have these been transferred to government structures and the voluntary sector in general? NGOs are reputed to be more accessible to the poor and the marginalized, and to reach people in more inaccessible areas. Their other qualities include efficiency and flexibility, the use of innovative methods to solve local problems, and skills in promoting participatory practices. It is quite true that *in comparison with the government* many NGOs are efficient and flexible. They are more likely to employ innovative methods albeit on a small scale, though the claim that NGOs are keen innovators needs to be taken with a pinch of salt. While some have successfully employed new ideas to deal with old problems, most rural programs run by NGOs are almost uniform in conception and approach, so much so that one gets the impression that they have copied each other's blueprints. On the other hand, NGOs have made greater efforts to promote participatory approaches. The government now says it is committed to the participatory approach but it is debatable whether this is the influence of the NGOs. In contrast, state structures, including those charged with managing development programs, have become more bureaucratic in the last two or more decades, and few state officials are willing to consider innovative approaches to program design and management. On the other hand, while they may be more accessible to the poor than government institutions, few NGOs are well rooted in the communities they serve. Indeed, quite often, they are looked upon by the poor as benevolent outsiders who may withdraw their assistance at any time.[1] Finally, NGOs do operate in the more inaccessible parts of the country, but so does the government; there is hardly any NGO site that does not have a government presence. Bratton has argued that voluntary institutions in Africa have broadened their interventions in the period since the 1970s to fill the gap left by the state. He talks about the "retreat of the African state" creating opportunities for the growth and influence of civil society (Bratton 1989). The political experience in Ethiopia is quite the opposite. Far from "retreating", the Ethiopian state has been undergoing a massive expansion since the 1960s. Both during the Derg and the present government, the ability of the state to intervene at the local and household level, and in every part of the country, has been greatly enhanced.

---

1. According to Clayton et al. (p. 7), "recent NGO impact studies and evaluations provide little evidence to suggest that (NGOs) actually are more effective than governments in reaching the poorest with development assistance".

There are those who argue that civil society should consist of organizations whose objective is to influence public policy, and should exclude institutions which are solely engaged in service delivery (Blair, 1997). Most NGOs in Ethiopia would not qualify as civil society organizations on the strength of this definition. Few of them consider policy advocacy as one of their main responsibilities. Where NGOs have ventured into advocacy, it has often been over safe issues such as, for example, promoting the rights of the child, and campaigning against cultural practices harmful to women. The organizations are not keen to challenge the state on any issue or even to draw attention to the need for alternative approaches or for reforms in public policy. They are a cautious lot, and while they may be privately critical of policy decisions, they are content to work within the policy framework and through state structures. The government is particularly hostile to NGOs taking up policy advocacy, and this has been one of the reasons why most of them have shunned it. It is perhaps fair to add here that the responsibility for taking the lead in policy advocacy rests on local NGOs; international NGOs can only play a supportive role.

There is nevertheless a growing feeling among NGOs that they should not be restricted to relief operations and running development projects, but that they should make an effort to influence policy and speak for the rights of the disadvantaged. On the other hand, there is very little advocacy experience in the country and few NGOs would know what to do even if the policy environment was not discouraging. Many local organizations, for example, are ill equipped to undertake advocacy activities at present: they lack organizational capacity and are poor in program planning and management. While the *Code of Conduct* that was recently drawn up by NGOs carefully avoids mentioning advocacy as part of the mission of the NGO sector, the fact that the code is now accepted as the main instrument of NGO self-regulation by both voluntary organizations and the government is seen as a significant step in the right direction. To date, there have been few occasions when the government has consulted the NGO community in the formulation of policies relevant to the community. Important policy measures such as those on Water and Food Security, for example, were drawn up without close consultation with NGOs, which have invested considerable resources in both sectors. Only in the health sector has the government shown any willingness to consult and collaborate with NGOs. It is true that NGOs are represented in some government initiated consultative committees responsible for program review and other tasks, but these are not policy making fora nor does representation provide the opportunity to make an input in program design.

Advocacy Organizations

At the end of 1999, there were about a dozen rights-based advocacy institutions in the country, but many of them were small in size, with little or no experience, and organizationally vulnerable. It is worth noting that such institutions would have been unthinkable at the time of the imperial or Derg regimes neither of which tolerated voluntary organizations except those that we have described as informal and traditional. The main concern of advocacy organizations centers on what may be described broadly as "rights" issues: enhancing civic awareness through civic education, promoting respect for the rule of law, and protecting the rights of women. Such significant social and economic issues as the environment, poverty, and education have not yet attracted institutional advocates. It is interesting that in a country where environmental degradation occurs on a large-scale and poses a major threat to economic development, and where abject poverty is widespread and growing in intensity, there are few voluntary institutions actively engaged in environmental advocacy or in promoting the cause of the poor.

The two advocacy organizations which have attracted considerable public support are the Ethiopian Human Rights Council (EHRCO), and the Ethiopian Women Lawyers Association (EWLA). Both are membership organizations and both would be described as agents of civil society by any definition. EHRCO, which describes itself (wrongly in my opinion) as a "humanitarian organization", is the first human rights organization in the country. It was established in 1991, shortly after the fall of the Derg and the establishment of the present government. EHRCO stresses that it is a non-partisan organization committed to promoting the rule of law and the democratic process.[1] One of its main activities is monitoring human rights violations in the country and disseminating its findings to the public by means of periodic reports detailing acts of unlawful imprisonment, torture, extra-judicial killings, and violations of property rights. These reports have had wide readership but they have angered the government which has disputed the reports' accusations claiming that they are based on false evidence and politically motivated.

EHRCO's local membership, which is made up of academics, professionals and businessmen, is estimated to be over 500, and it has support groups active in a number of West European countries as well as in North America. It has established links with such major international human rights bodies as Amnesty International and Human Rights Watch. In terms of size of membership EHRCO may appear small but it has succeeded in putting the democratic credentials of the government under close scrutiny. Moreover, it has made the rule of law and the democratic process a public issue requiring the active concern of all citizens. This is no mean achievement given the country's culture of governance and the tradition of successive governments of leaving the public out of the political equation.

The government tried to silence EHRCO from the early days of the organization but without much success. Initially it refused to approve the Council's application for registration alleging that EHRCO is a political organization and should be registered as such. A media campaign to brand the organization as an anti-government political movement and to discredit it in the eyes of the public in the mid-1990s backfired and may in fact have enhanced the stature of the organization. Later, the government decided to establish its human rights commission and ombudsman office to compete with EHRCO but the initiative has yet to bear fruit. In 1996, the state-owned Commercial Bank blocked EHRCO's account and the organization had to rely on public donations to cover its basic expenses and maintain its activities. The Council sued the Bank but the court was reluctant to handle the case. International donors, no doubt pressured by the government, were unwilling to provide financial support or speak up on its behalf. The Swiss Ambassador to Ethiopia, whose government had earlier provided funds to EHRCO, was quick to dissociate himself publicly from the organization when the latter published one of its earliest documents criticizing the government's political record and accusing it of failing to live up to its stated democratic objectives. The Ambassador in effect endorsed the government's view that EHRCO was not an impartial organization and was engaged in partisan politics. Many of the major diplomatic missions, including the U.S., were expressly unhappy with EHRCO. It is quite telling that Western donor agencies which placed so much emphasis on civil society as the best hope for fostering democratization in

---

1. The discussion is based on EHRCO documents which are listed in the References.

Africa felt it prudent to kowtow to the government when it decided to take punitive measures against the one and only human rights organization in the country.

In mid-1999, EHRCO's application for registration was finally approved and its bank account was unblocked soon after. The move came as part of the government's effort to woo the voluntary sector following the war with Eritrea. Since its legal registration, the organization has become more active outside Addis Ababa and has been able to establish a number of branch offices in other parts of the country. While it is too early to judge at this point there is no evidence that EHRCO's efforts have had any impact on the process of law enforcement and the conduct of government authorities. EHRCO does not provide legal assistance to the public: it does not represent aggrieved persons in court nor offer legal advice or support to those who may seek it. It is on the strength of its reports and documentation that it hopes to achieve its main objectives. Due in part to government hostility and harassment, EHRCO's activity has been confined to Addis Ababa and its range of functions fairly limited.

EWLA was established in the mid-1990s by a group of women lawyers to defend women's rights through the legal system, to raise public awareness about the plight of women, and to agitate for reforms promoting gender equality.[1] Its main activities consist of legal aid to women, public education and advocacy for legal reforms, and research and documentation. The organization has three main branch offices outside Addis Ababa (in Assossa, Bahr Dar, and Nazret), and operates through eleven committees at the regional level, and twelve voluntary committees at the zonal and woreda levels distributed throughout the country. Committee members are given a short para-legal training and encouraged to take an active role in protecting women's rights in their localities.

The legal aid program, which is probably one of the most central of EWLA's activities, provides a wide variety of legal advice and counseling to women, including court representation by EWLA lawyers. The service is offered free of charge to all that come seeking help. While the overwhelming majority of EWLA clients are women, a few men have also sought legal aid, not for themselves but on behalf of their female relatives. About 85 per cent of the cases brought to EWLA involve marital conflict, and the rest consist of rape, abduction, robbery and theft, and assault and battery. Over 4,000 women have received legal aid since EWLA began the program in 1996; most of the women were from poor and disadvantaged social backgrounds. Many of the women who came seeking EWLA support heard about the organization either through EWLA's public education program transmitted over the broadcast media, through word-of-mouth, or through the organization's advertising campaign. EWLA has had some notable successes in court and this has enhanced its stature among women.

The main aim of the public education program, another important component of EWLA's activities, is to help bring about change in public attitudes to women. The program consists of several activities carried out in the capital and the regions, including workshops and seminars involving law enforcement officials, judges, women and concerned individuals; educational material broadcast on radio which is particularly aimed at encouraging women's rights activists; and leaflets and posters. The program has been instrumental in gaining EWLA wide publicity and raising EWLA's profile especially among women who have been victims of marital injustice and gender discrimination.

---

1. The discussion that follows is based on EWLA documents; see References at the end of the book.

EWLA has also invested in legislative reform. While the goal is to bring about the amendment of laws discriminating against women, the main focus so far has been on the reform of the Family Law which was enacted in 1960 during the imperial regime but which remained in the statute books until the second half of 2000. EWLA submitted a draft amendment of the Law to the federal and regional legislative bodies in 1996, but it was not until July 2000 that a new Family Law was finally enacted. While the organization did not succeed in getting all its recommendations accepted by Parliament, the new law that was passed by the legislature provides significant improvements on the earlier one (EWLA, 2000). It is to the credit of EWLA that the reform of the Family Law became a public issue and that the government felt compelled to revisit the legislation. EWLA was also actively engaged in promoting women candidates in the parliamentary elections that took place in May 2000.

It is too early to judge the impact of EWLA's activities on women and the policy process. As far as its legal aid program is concerned, many women are now aware that they can turn to EWLA if they feel they have been victims of gender-based injustice. In this respect, it is filling an important gap and providing an invaluable service. A recent EWLA publication states that in "those regions where EWLA operates with full time staff ... EWLA is almost a household name. The offices have been enjoying tremendous public support and respect" (1999: 9). On the other hand, it would be too much to expect a comparable success in its effort to change public attitudes to women; such change may come about after decades of struggle by women and their allies and through the instrumentality of a vigorous and mass based feminist movement. With respect to legislative reform, EWLA has a long and difficult task ahead of it.

Professional Associations

In comparative terms, there are fewer professionals and professional societies in Ethiopia than in many African countries, and this is obviously a reflection of the greater underdevelopment of the country and the much lower level of urbanization. The repressive environment of the past half-century, which is the period of the modernization effort in the country, has been detrimental to the growth of associational life. The imperial regime was very mistrustful of formal voluntary institutions, including professional bodies that could hardly be suspected of harboring a hidden agenda, though a small number of associations were allowed to function. The Derg, in contrast, was altogether hostile, seeing in civil organizations the hand of imperialism or counter-revolution, and as a consequence almost all professional associations were closed down or went into hibernation in the 1970s and 80s; the Ethiopian Medical Association is perhaps one of the few exceptions. We have very few studies about professional societies in this country and it is therefore hard to determine accurately their numerical strength; we also do not have adequate knowledge about their activities (see Habteselassie, 1998). According to a survey of science and technology professional associations carried out by the Ethiopian Science and Technology Commission in 1998, there were thirty-two associations in the science and technology sector, and seven in the health sector; the survey also includes a small number of societies in other areas. If we add to this figure societies in the liberal professions and other fields, the total number of organizations in the country may reach over seventy-five. However, many of the organizations have small membership, and their activities do not go beyond annual meetings and the occasional publication. Furthermore, there are only a limited number of associations whose objectives go beyond the narrow interests of their members and which are keen to raise issues of wider public concern.

Established in 1992 by a group of distinguished Ethiopian economists, the Ethiopian Economic Association (EEA) is arguably the most active and visible professional association in the county. Like all other professional societies, the advancement of the professional interest of its members is an important objective of EEA, although the organization also seeks to improve the quality of education in institutions of higher learning, and to influence the process of economic policy making. Its monthly round table debates bring together policy makers, academics, businessmen and interested professionals to discuss topical economic issues and government policies related to them. The forum attracts on a regular basis a relatively large audience, both economists and non-economists, and is becoming an important fixture of the Addis Ababa intellectual environment. The organization publishes a bimonthly bulletin in which a limited number of articles appear in Amharic, and an English language biannual journal. Most of the articles in these publications and the annual conference proceedings are critical of the government's economic policy. There is a strong concern among contributors and active members of the organization that the economy is not showing any significant improvement, that an increasing number of the population is facing severe poverty and hardship, and that the country is being marginalized in the global market.[1]

EEA's activities are confined to Addis Ababa, and economists and others in the rest of the country have no opportunity of participating in its programs. The organization does not promote a particular school of economic thought; reflecting the diversity of its members, the views expressed in its publications are eclectic and lacking in novelty and creative adaptation. In common with economic bodies the world over, there is a strong tendency to rely on quantitative methods, and limited theoretical debate on broad development issues. As the president of the Association pointed out in his address to the organization's seventh general assembly in 1999, there is no way of knowing for certain whether EEA's efforts have made any impression on economic policy making. It is evident that, at present, these efforts appear to have made very little impact on decision-makers. He notes, however, that the willingness of senior government officials to take part in the organization's debating forum should be taken as a positive step in the right direction (Economic Focus, August 1999). But the issue is much more complex than is suggested in the president's address. To begin with, EEA has not really made a coherent intervention in the policy arena. To influence policy, it is not enough to hold discussions among a select group of professionals, which is what EEA has been doing so far, on the contrary, it requires a diverse set of activities including extended debate of policy options in the mass media, winning the support of important stakeholders such as local and international investors, and lobbying decision makers. Secondly, EEA does not speak for all professional or academic economists in the country, hence it does not have as much weight in policy making as it thinks it should. Thirdly, economic policy is not made in a vacuum, on the contrary, it is the outcome of struggles among strong vested interests which frequently are not impressed by eloquent discussions and 'scientific' research findings.

---

1. See *Economic Focus* 1997–1999, *Ethiopian Journal of Economics* 1992–1996, and the annual conference proceedings 1992–1998.

Trade Unions and Cooperatives

The trade union movement in Ethiopia has had a history which was, in retrospect, the result of false perceptions and an exaggerated sense of worth. Its formative period goes back to the early 1960s, when leaders from a number of individual labor organizations decided to form the Confederation of Ethiopian Labour Union (CELU). The earliest trade union, the Railway Workers Union, was established in the 1940s, but it was not until the late 1950s that other workers' organizations were formed to represent workers' interests. These unions were weak and pliable organizations led by opportunistic and corrupt officials who frequently were not workers themselves (Sileshi Sisaye, 1979). By the end of the 1960s, CELU had a membership of some seventy thousand workers (Seyoum 1969) but only a small percentage of these were active members. From the 1960s to the present, the numerical strength of the working class relative to other classes has not grown significantly and modern sector workers constituted, then as well as now, a very small percentage of the country's population. In the early 1970s, for example, there were 100,000 working men and women employed in the modern economy and the public sector, and by the 1990s the number had risen to not more than 250,000; the population of the country according to the 1994 census was fifty-four million. And yet, all governments since the 1960s have given the trade union movement a significance and power far beyond its actual potential, and over-reacted whenever its members threatened to carry out, or undertook, work stoppages or made efforts to free themselves from government tutelage.

The imperial regime kept a watchful eye on CELU's activities and the leadership knew that the threat of violent suppression was always hanging over its head for any action it took that was not approved by the government. The Derg was more forceful; after having violently smashed CELU's attempt at a general strike in 1976, it purged the trade unions of their leaders and replaced them with ones that were zealous supporters of the government and its ideology. The present government has been much less violent than the Derg but equally unwilling to tolerate an independent trade union movement. Its favored tactic since the early 1990s has been to force a split in trade unions considered hostile to its policies and then give its support in favor of leaders friendly to it. On occasions, independent minded leaders have been harassed, thrown in jail on trumped up charges, or forced to flee the country. In brief, the trade union movement, which should have emerged as an independent force defending the rights of working people, has been kept as a docile instrument of state policy by successive governments since the 1960s.

Rural cooperatives have also had a short and turbulent history. The cooperative experience during the imperial regime was very limited, and the credit for a national program of cooperative formation, involving millions of peasants must go to the Derg which actively promoted what were then called service and producers cooperatives as part of its agricultural socialization program. Unlike their earlier counterparts, cooperatives under the Derg were not independent institutions but rather tightly controlled by the Party and the Ministry of Agriculture. Moreover, membership in cooperatives was not voluntary but rather imposed, and members as well as non-members resented both institutions, particularly producers' cooperatives (Dessalegn, 1993). The latter were quickly disbanded following the mixed economy reforms of 1991 and except for a few heavily subsidized, model enterprises, which remained functioning for some time, almost all producers' cooperatives disappeared without a trace, their members returning to private farming within a short period of time. When the Derg fell in 1991, there was a wave of looting, arson, and destruction of property in the countryside, and service cooperatives were one of the chief targets of this violent agitation (Dessalegn, 1994). Thus the cooperative experiment of the Derg period was unpopular and unproductive, and ended in bitterness and violence.

The present government was initially hostile to cooperatives, which it saw as an instrument of the Derg; it imprisoned a large number of leaders of cooperatives throughout the countryside soon after it came to power in 1991. It was not until several years later that there was a change of government attitude. The cooperative proclamation issued in 1995, which has since been replaced by another one issued in 1998, provides the new policy framework under which cooperatives are to be set up on an individual and voluntary basis. Under the Derg, membership in service cooperatives, though not in producers' cooperatives, was neither individual nor voluntary. It was the Peasant Association (PA) rather than the individual that was a member of service cooperatives, and the individual peasant, who of course was a member of the PA, had no choice in the matter. The new cooperative policy is in some ways a radical departure from the past. At present, membership is voluntary and individual, and any member has the right to withdraw if he/she wishes to do so. There is also a profit sharing arrangement in which individual members receive dividends at the end of the year depending on their contribution and involvement in the activities of the institution.

Cooperative societies now provide a wide variety of services to their members. Responsibility for managing input supply is gradually shifting to the societies, and in the long run this may well become one of their most important tasks. Another area of involvement is grain marketing. The societies purchase grain from their own members at the time of harvest when prices are low and sell to members at a later date when prices are higher. This enables peasants, especially those in food deficit areas, to have access to grain when they need it most, and the profit thus gained supports the societies. Moreover, society members stand to benefit if they purchase from their own organization since their dividend is based on how much they have participated in cooperative services. Cooperatives also provide consumer goods, which they sell to their members at slightly lower prices than the local trader. Grain mills and veterinary drugs are also some of the other services they also provide. Some cooperatives are involved in seed multiplication and distribution schemes on contract with their members; others have had some of their members trained as para-veterinarians to manage the cooperatives' small veterinary clinics. These are good examples of societies taking over some of the tasks of the public sector. The marketing activities may also be taken as further evidence of cooperatives taking over roles to fill the gap between local needs and the weak private sector.

However, cooperative societies, including those that are better organized and more endowed, face a wide variety of serious difficulties. To begin with, the agents of the Cooperative Promotion Office (CPO) that are now active in cooperative formation are not peasants themselves but civil servants and agents of the government. Cooperative promotion requires dedication, zeal and local commitment, all of which are strongest if the promoters and the beneficiaries are one and the same people. Secondly, the societies were born large: most cooperatives in the regions have a membership of over 1,000 people, making management a difficult undertaking. Small cooperatives are easier to manage than large ones; they also provide members with the opportunity to acquire management skills. The short-term weaknesses include lack of managerial skill among cooperative leaders, insufficient working capital, and inadequate storage capacity. But the most fundamental problem of rural cooperatives at present is that they are not independent bodies, rather, in common with Derg practice, they are tied to the government. The CPO in each region, which is responsible for organizing and monitoring the societies, has replaced the Ministry of Agriculture, which during the Derg period was charged with the same responsibility. Moreover, while they do not formally intervene in the organization and management of the cooperatives, the regional parties have considerable influence over the leadership, many of whom are quite likely to be party members themselves. In addition, many, if not all, CPO staff are party members and will no doubt promote the interests of the party as they carry out their official duties. In brief, cooperative societies do not have an independent voice, are not able to serve their members adequately, and cannot speak on behalf of the wider interests of their constituencies.

Nevertheless, despite these discouraging developments, the societies should not be dismissed as docile instruments of the state, and many of their members appreciate the services they are providing, limited though they be. In the long run, with sufficient experience and a more committed and conscious leadership, rural cooperatives will begin to put demands on the state for goods and services, and play a more assertive role in articulating the broad interests of the peasantry. In the circumstances of this country, which has had no history of independent peasant movements, cooperative societies provide the only avenue open to the peasantry to create an independent force to defend its rights.

Constraints Facing Civil Society Institutions

The growth of civil society institutions has been greatly hampered by a variety of what may be called "external" and "internal" constraints, the former referring to the policy environment, and the latter to resource access and managerial capacity. The absence of a favorable policy environment, which remains the most difficult constraint to overcome at present, has been responsible for restricting the terms and terrain of activity of the voluntary sector in Ethiopia.

Until recently, the government was hostile to independent institutions such as NGOs and rights-based advocacy institutions. International NGOs in particular, some of which had provided support to the government when it was still an insurgent movement, and which had hoped for a policy environment more favorable than that of the Derg, were very disappointed with the unfriendly outlook of the new government (see Campbell, 1996). Initially, the government was of the opinion that NGOs, especially international NGOs, were not really needed in the country and that they could be replaced with local, party-controlled organizations, which would be safe and friendly. Moreover, the government was suspicious that independent institutions were part of the opposition and were actively working to undermine its authority. There has been a marked improvement in NGO-state relations in the last couple of years, and part of it may be attributed to the government's desire to win the support of the voluntary sector following the Ethio-Eritrean war. Nevertheless, the government still does not wish to accept NGOs and other civic institutions as real partners in a common endeavor.

The state sets the rules governing the activities of civil society organizations, but what is most disturbing to the voluntary sector as a whole, and the cause of continuing friction between the two is that the rules are vague, ambiguous, and subject to arbitrary interpretations by the regulating agencies (CRDA, 1997). The requirement that civil organizations have to renew their registration every year gives the state immense power over the voluntary sector and has effectively stifled critical and independent initiative. Moreover, the wide array of government agencies, from the federal to the regional level, that are involved in the registration, regulation and monitoring of civic organizations, and the lack of transparency on their part continues to exacerbate relations between the government and the institutions. These bureaucratic hurdles, some of which have been put in place on purpose, have hampered the growth of civil society. On the other hand, the state is actively promoting its own parallel or rival organizations often under the control of the regional parties; some of these include NGOs, women's organizations, and trade unions. This reinforces the suspicion held in the voluntary sector that the state does not have confidence in independent institutions and may be planning to replace them at some time in the future. Finally, the government is reluctant to consult stakeholders in the preparation of policies and legislation, and a good case in point is the new NGO law now being drafted in the Ministry of Justice; officials have so far been unwilling to involve the NGO sector in the preparatory effort.

A major "internal" constraint has do with the lack of secure access to resources, which includes both funds and physical assets on the one hand, and competent human capital on the other. The private sector in Ethiopia is underdeveloped and fragmented, and lacks the capacity to play a leading role in the economic sphere, much less in social and political change. It is confined in the main to small and medium-scale activities because it lacks the capital and the market to invest in large-scale operations. Government control of the economy, in the form of a wide array of public and party-controlled enterprises, continues to hamper the growth of private investment. The dead hand of the state bureaucracy weighs heavily on the business community as a whole, but state officials are particularly hostile to local capital and often discriminate in favor of multinationals. In the developed countries, civil society relies for much of its support on foundations and philanthropic organizations established by successful businessmen or socially conscious business firms. In Ethiopia and other African countries, on the other hand, civil society organizations cannot turn to local philanthropists and instead are dependent on international donor agencies for financial and other assistance; the private sector in these countries plays only a marginal role in sustaining civil society. Quite apart from the unwelcome dependence on external agencies, this may compromise the independence and effectiveness of the organizations concerned. Moreover, international donors are often willing to support organizations that actively support economic and political objectives acceptable to them (i.e. the donors), and which they themselves are actively promoting in the countries concerned. For example, in many countries of Sub-Saharan Africa, civil society organizations committed to the promotion of "economic liberalism" (i.e. the capitalist economy) are the most sought after by the major international donor agencies, including those from the Nordic countries (see J. Hearn 1999); those that are engaged in activities whose objectives may not fully conform to the ideology of "economic liberalism" are frequently ignored. In Uganda, donors have focused their attention on service giving NGOs, which, according to one study, have very little impact on the democratisation process (Bazaara, 2000).

A second kind of resource that is also in short supply is organizational and intellectual capital. As noted earlier, many of the civic organizations in the country are fragile bodies lacking in sustainable managerial capacity. The brain drain that has been going on since the latter half of the 1970s has seriously depleted the country's trained human power, and nowhere is this more keenly felt than in the voluntary sector, in particular advocacy institutions and professional societies. Civil society institutions cannot hope to grow and influence public policy without a secure organizational foundation, which requires capable management, and an innovative intellectual leadership.

Other limitations that may be briefly noted include the following. Firstly, most civil society institutions are concentrated in Addis Ababa and their activities are confined to the capital; the exceptions are NGOs and cooperative societies. While the capital does have a disproportionate influence on the country's economic and political life, focusing one's attention here serves only the interest of the urban elite. Secondly, voluntary institutions operate under a cloud of uncertainty, never sure whether they will retain their legal status from one year to another. Thirdly, civic institutions have not yet internalized democratic culture, especially the culture of tolerance and constructive debate. Fourthly, there is no dialogue between civil society organizations and the state; the latter often does not believe the organizations have legitimate claims and deserve to be heard. Fifthly, there is no adequate medium to inform the public of the activities of the voluntary sector. The independent press is inexperienced, lacks professional staff, and operates on a shoe-string budget. It is largely concerned with current politics and sensational issues, and is ill equipped to serve as a vehicle for public education. Without a professionally competent, vigorous and public-spirited press, civil society institutions will have limited influence.

Conclusion

We do not have an adequate yardstick to determine the influence of voluntary organizations on public policy and the democratic process. Nevertheless, we can make broad conclusions without having to worry about quantifiable measurements. At one level, we see little evidence that in Ethiopia decision-makers as a body are willing to listen to the voluntary sector or are ready to recognize that it has legitimate claims. Indeed, among some government circles, civic institutions are still considered as part of the political opposition and regarded with hostility. At another level, it is evident that some of the advocacy groups have aroused public interest and are attracting public support, though the "public" we are referring to is in the main the Addis Ababa public. As noted earlier, for instance, EWLA's legal aid service is actively sought by a good number of women who feel they have no other recourse for redress of grievances. Thus despite their limited experience, civil society institutions have made a modest impact on public attitudes.

Under present circumstances, civil society institutions can do no more than promote public awareness and stimulate public discussion about democratic rights and responsible governance. To expect them to achieve more than this is to misjudge their capacity, and to place on them unwarranted hopes and exaggerated expectations. Discrete civic organizations, however potent they may be, do not on their own bring about policy reforms, rather it is civic movements that have the potential to achieve such results. To be able to have a meaningful impact on the democratization process, or to promote good governance, Ethiopian civic organizations would have to transform themselves into civic movements. The term "civic movement" may sound inelegant but it refers to the active engagement of the broad public, including the laboring classes, in support of popular causes. The narrow boundaries of individual organizations will have to be transcended so that instead of, for example, a human rights organization, a women lawyers' association, a cooperative, etc., we can begin to talk about a human rights, women's or cooperative movement. Such movements can only be built on widespread public awareness, and active popular involvement. This does not mean individual organizations will have to disappear, rather it means that each one of them will have to function as part of a broader social initiative for a wider set of public benefits. A civic movement may be likened to the coming together of many streams to form a mighty river.

There is another side to the coin that should not be lost sight of. If civil society is to be the active and positive element in social change, the orderly "dis-empowerment" of the state will be necessary, and this will not be possible without the modernization of the economy and the society. By "dis-empowerment" (a term I use reluctantly for lack of a better alternative) I do not mean the total loss of power of the state, for then the state would cease to exist, but rather its disengagement from many sectors of social and economic life so that it ceases to be, as it is at present, the only active force in society. Civil society will remain gelatinous, to echo Gramsci, as long as the state continues to maintain overwhelming power. The vacuum left by the retreat of the state would have to be filled by civic institutions and the private sector.

What then does the "deepening of civil society" mean in these circumstances? If civic institutions are to broaden their ability to influence the democratic process and public policy, they will, in the short to medium term, have to aim to achieve two inter-related goals: the first is to enhance their operational and leadership capacity, and the second to promote greater cooperation among them. The lack of managerial capacity and of experienced and flexible leadership is the single most serious limitation of the voluntary sector in general. On the other hand there is at present a fragmentation of voluntary institutions, which is obviously the legacy of the repressive environment of the last fifty years. Civil society in Ethiopia, such as it is, does not speak with the same voice nor does it share the same goals. It is therefore important to enable the individual organizations to engage in more dialogue among themselves and to support each other at every opportunity. The objective is to enhance greater confidence and a greater sense of security within the voluntary sector.

In the short to medium term, civil society organizations should strive to extend the available political space for independent civic activity, and one way to do that is to continue the struggle to ensure respect for the rule of law, and the right to free association and advocacy. EHRCO, for example, is right in placing strong emphasis on respect for the rule of law, for this is the basis for the growth of civil society and for democratic governance. On the other hand, it is clear that relative to most African countries, civil society institutions in Ethiopia are less developed, less active and much fewer in number. There is thus an urgent need for a multiplicity of voluntary organizations committed to a wide diversity of public causes.

A robust civil society does not emerge as a matter of course but is the result of sustained civic investment by individuals, groups and communities. By civic investment I mean the effort, time and resources invested by each social actor to enlarge the opportunities for the self-activation of citizens and citizens' groups. As is evident from the present state of civil society institutions, Ethiopians have not made sufficient civic investment, though there are now grounds for cautious optimism.

The Role of NGOs in Promoting Democratic Values

The Ethiopian Experience

Kassahun Berhanu

Introduction

This paper explores the record of NGOs in Africa in general and Ethiopia in particular. Their official aims have for some time now included supporting and strengthening democratic values and attendant practices. In the article I attempt to capture and reflect the view from below—i.e. the perceptions of beneficiary groups of NGO activities. I start by presenting a brief account of the NGO phenomenon as such. I then present a brief account of the relatively recent emergence of NGOs in Africa and in Ethiopia in particular. Following this I appraise government–NGO relations; a special section reviews the record of NGOs in Ethiopia in relation to advocacy and the promotion of democracy. I round off by discussing some impediments to progress in this work.

The NGO phenomenon

The need to address a wide range of problems adversely affecting vulnerable groups prompted the emergence and growth of NGOs as we experience them today. The immediate aftermath of World War Two was a landmark in this regard. Massive dislocations and destruction transcended the reparative capacities of states, requiring resources and structures commanded by agencies outside the state domain. The fifties and the sixties thus witnessed the emergence and rapid proliferation of NGOs whose stated goal was to extend support and assistance to people in need. Churches and missionary societies based in the developed countries were pioneers in this regard. In addition to their evangelical aspirations, they embarked on the task of catering for the poor and the needy, the disabled and the displaced, all of whom lacked one or another type of support and care.[1]

Bratton (1989: 571) suggested classifying NGOs according to a number of attributes such as size (big, medium, small); origin (indigenous, foreign); behaviour pattern (regime-conforming, regime-critical); central activity (relief/welfare, development); and orientation (secular, ecumenical). NGOs were seen as non-political, non-profit-making and autonomous entities with potentials for positively transforming social life. Padron (1987: 70) defined NGOs as all organisations located outside the state domain and the structure of government. But his definition failed to take account of the now established concept of "Third Sector". This defines NGOs as distinct not only from the state, but also from businesses and corporations whose major orientation and activities are predicated on the "profit" motive. NGOs

---

1. For a chronological summary of the evolution of modern voluntary humanitarian action, see De Waal (1997: 66–68).

hoped originally to attain their objectives through working in partnership with pertinent stakeholders, i.e. governments (Bratton, 1989: 582). They were also portrayed as specialised agencies with a considerable degree of professionalism, flexibility and innovativeness (Getachew, 1990: 9).

NGOs in Africa

NGOs emerged in Africa on the eve of the nationalist struggles for independence. The period that followed the independence of the ex-colonies created a vacuum in the provision of public services precipitated by the withdrawal of personnel and funding from metropolitan sources. The capacity of the nascent post-colonial African states to provide services therefore steadily diminished. In many of the newly independent countries, expatriate Church organisations and missionary societies tried to bridge the gap by running schools, hospitals, vocational training centres, etc. To this end, they made use of their connections with philanthropic organisations and foundations in the developed countries of the North.

At a later stage, NGOs run and manned by Africans began to emerge as voluntary agencies of various denominations. As Kajese (1990: 11–13) noted, the emergence of the majority of these was not a result of a natural evolution from traditional forms of association peculiar to the indigenous societies in question. Present-day African NGOs are modern phenomena deriving their motivation from foreign sources. Their rapid proliferation in several countries, stimulated by a considerable flow of foreign funding, attests to this. According to Fowler (1991: 54–55), Kenya experienced a 260 per cent growth in the number of non-Church foreign NGOs and a 115 per cent increase in the numerical size of local NGOs, between 1978 and 1987. Similarly, indigenous NGOs in Botswana grew by 60 per cent between 1985 and 1989.

NGOs in Ethiopia

Traditional voluntary humanitarian practice in Ethiopia is as old as the society itself (Pankhurst, 1958). In traditional Ethiopian society, the burden of catering for the needy and disadvantaged was the responsibility of the extended family, religious institutions like the Church, and indigenous social organisations, whose actions were predicated on cultural and philanthropic values. This is a traditional non-governmental method of voluntary action (Kassahun, 1994a: 3; CRDA, 1998: 4). The practice of charity and mutual self-help motivated by religious teachings and/or under the aegis of social organisations took place during times of stress, and social events like death, marriage, and birth. Many of these organisations managed to endure and survive the effects of "modernisation". They continue to co-exist alongside their modern-day counterparts, the NGOs.

The presence of NGOs in Ethiopia is a relatively recent phenomenon. Prior to the 1970s, only a few NGOs were involved in Ethiopia.[1] Several of them were ecumenical in orientation, foreign-based, and mainly engaged in social welfare and community development programmes of limited scope. They mainly addressed problems affecting vulnerable groups such as the disabled, orphans, the aged, and

---

1. Among others, the Ethiopian Red Cross Society (1935), the Menonite Mission (1946), the EECMY (1960), the Cheshire Foundation (1962), the Ethiopian Family Guidance Association (1969), Agri Service (1969), and Hope Enterprise (1971).

the poor. They provided relief aid, education, health, and vocational training. The overwhelming majority were concentrated in Addis Ababa; their presence in the rest of the country was negligible. These first-generation NGOs in Ethiopia functioned in close co-operation with government departments. Government officials presided on the organisations' decision-making bodies as presidents and board chairpersons and members.[1]

The Famines of 1973–74 and 1984–85 and the Resulting Boom in NGOs

The proliferation of NGOs in terms of size and scope of operations was a consequence of the two great famines of the mid-1970s and mid-1980s. These famines were prompted by different factors, both natural and man-made. Their severity varied throughout the country. Nevertheless they caused involuntary mass migration, huge losses of life and property, and a host of other disruptions.

Famine is not new to Ethiopia. Historical records tell of famines on a massive scale as far back as the ninth century (Sen, 1981: 86; Pankhurst, 1992: 5).[2] However, the 1973–74 and 1984–85 famines were unique in that they attracted a massive influx of NGOs with the intention of alleviating the widespread suffering.

The 1973–74 famine was brought to the attention of the international public through extensive humanitarian appeals supported by broad media coverage which detailed the extent of the catastrophe. An organisational network was formed, to co-ordinate activities and synchronise programmes and intervention policies. The Christian Relief and Development Association (CRDA) was created as a membership organisation of ecumenical NGOs in 1973. In the process, some indigenous NGOs came into being. Between the mid-1970s and 1990, the total number of NGOs operating in the country grew from below 30 to over 100 (CRDA, 1998: 5). About 220 international and local NGOs operated in Ethiopia in 1997. A year later, in 1998, the number of NGOs had risen to 270 (CRDA, 1998: 5). Although this number may seem considerable, the same source reveals that there were 54,000 NGOs in South Africa and 700 in Zimbabwe at about the same time (CRDA, 1998: 5). The comparatively low level in Ethiopia illustrates the domestic constraints of various kinds with regard to forming NGOs. Among those that operate in Ethiopia, international and particularly Northern NGOs constituted 54 per cent of the overall total, thus outnumbering their indigenous counterparts.

NGO interventions in the mid-70s coincided with the termination of imperial rule in Ethiopia. Notwithstanding the initial support by the socio-political and economic reforms of the new *Dergue* regime, a period of disillusionment followed the high-handed nature of governance exercised by the *nouveau regime*. Subsequently, Ethiopian society witnessed the progressive and steady shrinking of socio-political and economic freedoms. At the same time, politically instigated insurgencies escalated in several parts of the country. The State responded to the growing popular discontent by ruthless and arbitrary violations of basic human rights and democratic freedoms in a manner unprecedented in the history of Ethiopia in the twentieth century. Another famine in 1984–85, triggered by the vagaries of nature and armed conflict, accounted for a new cycle of NGO influx. Their efforts and participation in

---

1. Thanks are due to Ato Yohannes Welde Gerima for this information.
2. On the causes, scope and attendant effects of famine, see also Pankhurst, 1966; Mesfin, 1984; Dessalegn, 1985; and Fasil, 1990.

emergency life-saving operations were commendable. They also initiated and supported many rural development schemes in the subsequent years, which created some off-farm employment opportunities.

Appraising Government-NGO Relations in Africa

Having briefly outlined the genesis and proliferation of NGOs in Africa and Ethiopia in particular, I want now to discuss the relations characterising the interaction between governments and NGOs in Africa.

The first generation of NGOs attempted to alleviate human suffering. They offered extensive support and care to groups affected by both man-made and natural disasters. As a result, donor governments and international institutions assumed that NGOs had the vision and capacity to address such situations. Brodhead is of the opinion that such a perception warranted their recognition as dynamic players (1987: 1). In time they came to be viewed as agents of popular empowerment that could encourage and support ordinary people to define their needs and actively participate in decisions affecting their lives (Freire, 1970; Gran, 1983). However, experience showed that such expectations were largely without substance. Perceived NGO shortcomings gradually attracted criticism from various quarters (Pronk cited in Hellinger, 1987: 137; Duffield and Prendergast, 1994; De Waal, 1997). The next generation of NGOs, which emerged in the seventies and eighties, sensitive to changes in popular and donor sentiment, shifted their mandate and focus according to what was considered important at the time. Their areas of concern varied from relief/rehabilitation to development and democracy (advocacy, empowerment, human rights).

The success of NGOs depends very much on the response of the political authorities. Without government support, they can hardly accomplish tangible results. Tegegne (1994: 28) noted that NGOs enjoy substantial freedom when working in democratic socio-political settings. They participate in development debates, the setting of development priorities, and act as a mouthpiece articulating the aspirations of vulnerable and marginalized target groups. According to Bratton (1989: 572), the NGOs gained a reputation for effectiveness and efficiency not as a result of their own merit and accomplishments, but from people's disillusionment with the effectiveness of state intervention in addressing pressing concerns and the failure of governments to deliver the "public good".

When governments failed to meet the most basic and legitimate needs of society, the people saw in the NGOs an alternative vehicle of transformation. But this perception of NGOs as agents of transformation and conduits of resources earned them the envy and suspicion of power-holders. They saw the NGOs as competitors in the fight for space and constituencies, and were quick to respond by regulating and monitoring NGO activities through a host of control mechanisms.[1] NGOs that earnestly sought to bring about changes commensurate with their stated mission, found that they had to struggle against discontented governments. In this unproductive climate, several NGOs opted for subservience, sacrificing at least in part their underlying and declared principles and objectives. Several NGOs capitulated and were de facto co-opted, and became reduced to appendages of the bureaucratic structures of

---

1. In order to control the autonomous existence of NGOs, a number of African states introduced legislation aimed at ensuring the administrative co-optation and regulation, political appropriation, deregistration, etc. of NGOs. See Fowler (1991: 64–69) for cases in Kenya, South Africa, the Sudan, Uganda, among others.

the state. Unfortunately, in many developing countries there are NGOs willing to submit to the wills and whims of authoritarian regimes. At times, NGO compliance contradicts and undermines their expressed "goals". Fowler (1990: 40) states that there are few African NGOs who managed to influence political developments, save those already sanctioned by the state apparatus.

Another factor promoting subservience was the disconnectedness of NGOs from indigenous African society. Despite their claims to good relations to the local people, their de facto "rootlessness" left them in limbo. They had no other alternative than to succumb to the whims and wills of governments and donors. The donors held the purse strings and could force NGOs to conform to the desires of officialdom, which undermined NGO autonomy.

Many NGOs resorted to opportunism or subservience, which they euphemistically labelled "pragmatism". Such opportunism can be seen in a wide array of factors, such as the urge to preserve personal and institutional interests. This results in a lack of commitment to uphold publicly professed ideals and principles. They are ready to make political calculations deemed necessary to ensure survival. NGOs take recourse to such measures in spite of their "apolitical" and "neutral" pretensions. However, as Getachew (1990: 20) pithily observes, the significance of the NGO phenomenon is as much political as it is economic. Mainstream establishments, among which political regimes stand in the forefront, have to sanction NGO operations. The need to obtain legal recognition and operational space forces NGOs to maintain good relations with the centres of power. Depending on the concrete situations in which they embark on their activities, NGOs often end up confirming the regime, regardless of the regime type, in the hope of preserving their respective goals and priorities.

De Waal (1997: 6) has lamented the apolitical pretensions of NGOs arguing that they are futile. Without a will to act politically, it is impossible to positively transform societies. De Waal finds support in Getachew who recommends that NGOs must move into the political arena in order to facilitate the participation and representation of grassroots groups in decision-making and political processes (1990: 20–21).

The tendency to retreat from anything political has influenced the attitudes of several Northern NGOs (NNGOs) and their counterparts in the developing world, though with variations in terms of inducement and mode of co-optation.[1] Governments and donors in the North used their control over funding and other resources to browbeat "non-conformist" agencies and personnel into submission. Those in the South employ instruments of governance (legislation, regulation/deregulation, repression). As a consequence of this, Beets et al. (1988: 49) called for safeguards against arbitrary state encroachments on the autonomy of NGOs. They recommended that NGOs need a motivated staff, which could provide support in popular struggles for access to resources and land.

The dependence of African NGOs on foreign funding led to a corresponding reliance in other respects, too. This included conceptualising and defining problems to be addressed, setting priorities, and designing strategies deemed instrumental for attaining goals. Often traditional organisations have been dismantled in this process, (both by omission and commission). In consequence, much indigenous knowledge was lost. Uncritical and blind emulation of alien ways of thinking and doing things

---

1. Kajese (1990: 83) speaks of "a growing anxiety over whether international NGOs managing huge grants from their home governments enjoy autonomy and independence vis-à-vis the policy of their donors".

replaced their roles as custodians of traditions. The presumed "rootedness" of African NGOs in their societies was proved to be little more than empty talk.

The intention here is not to suggest that NGOs should adopt a confrontationist stance in their relations with governments. Belligerence and assertiveness might be counter-productive. But if NGOs become subservient, and go for self-aggrandisement even at the expense of their declared principles and underlying ideals, they lose out on both sides and capitulate. Hence there is a need for striking the right balance between the two extremes—of accommodation and confrontation.

In spite of these problems, justice is due to NGOs. They have saved lives in emergency situations through providing relief assistance. In the more long-term perspective, they facilitated access to health services, and increased food security through "Food For Work" employment opportunities. Moreover, their inputs by way of contributing to rehabilitation and developmental purposes must also be commended.

The Balance Sheet: NGOs and Democracy in Ethiopia

Democracy obviously means different things to different people and societies, and interpretations and practical applications differ. A general consensus seems nonetheless to prevail as to its main tenets. In the Ethiopian context and as applied here, democracy is understood as the enrichment of societal life by political freedoms and civil liberties anchored in the rule of law. It also signifies a process of open dialogue and debate that affects the setting of priorities, the forming of common values, and decision-making (Sen, 1999: 7) on the basis of transparent consultation and consensus. Democracy is also closely related to the concept of empowerment of vulnerable groups and local communities in NGO areas of operation.

Empowerment refers to the enabling of individuals and groups to make their own decisions about their own future (Calvert and Calvert, 1996: 175). This implies that people should participate, on the basis of agreed upon mechanisms and procedures, in decision-making processes that impinge on their lives.

So how have NGOs acted in relation to democracy-promotion in Ethiopia? In what follows, I attempt to address the following questions:

a) What is the role of NGOs operating in Ethiopia in sensitising local people and beneficiary groups to their legal and legitimate democratic rights?

b) What measures have been taken and which approaches have been employed to assist people to realise these rights?

c) What roles have NGOs played in Ethiopia to induce the authorities to acknowledge the legitimacy of people's needs and demands, and what have they done to enhance official accountability and transparency

A survey conducted in 1994 (cited in CRDA, 1998) indicated that 72 per cent of all NGOs operating in Ethiopia were engaged in welfare programmes in the form of service delivery on a subsidised basis. There was no long-term strategy for "self-sufficiency" and sustainability in place. Of those remaining, 22 per cent aimed at improving the quality of life and productive capacity of target groups, and providing assistance of a purely relief nature in emergency situations (6 per cent). The number of NGOs that registered their programmes as focusing on issues related to human rights, advocacy, and democracy was less than 10 in 1995 (CRDA, 1995). There is no convincing evidence that these few have made even modest attempts to follow this up.

Almost all NGOs operating in Ethiopia, and the indigenous ones in particular, draw the bulk of their funding from external sources such as multilateral institutions and donor governments. The Ethiopian government has also contributed through providing administrative support in the form of facilitating access to goods and services, providing land for building physical infrastructure, and extending duty-free privileges for importing items officially approved as relevant to on-going programme components. Voluntary support by individual citizens, private firms and public organisations (PVOs) based within the country is minimal. This accounts for the apparent dependence of the Ethiopian voluntary sector on external sources of support.[1] Thus the whole exercise has become a resource-led process. While it cannot be denied that these organisations have saved lives, created community assets, and enhanced awareness, the diffusion and entrenchment of democratic values is insignificant at best.

The balance sheet thus shows an utterly disappointing record. If advocacy is to be understood as trying to change policies that negatively impinge on the well being of target groups, NGOs in Ethiopia have not made positive contributions. The Ethiopian NGO sector has shown no progress worth mentioning to promote policy/legislation governing its existence and operations. Nor are there visible traces of achievements in terms of beneficiary empowerment originating from NGO involvement. According to a survey I conducted on 19 NGOs in 1994 (Kassahun, 1994b), beneficiary participation in all organisations was limited to implementing decisions made by agency officials. Beneficiaries were practically never involved in identifying needs, planning, monitoring and evaluation of activities. They attested that they were not represented in any of the decision-making bodies and forums even for consultation. Asked whether they ever made demands to this end, they said that it never occurred to them; they viewed their relations with the agencies as one between providers and recipients. But far from nursing grudges for being left out, the overwhelming majority were grateful for the aid provided by the agencies and the occasional job in one of the projects. In spite of the fact that the situation in the 19 NGOs cannot be taken as representative of the overall state of affairs that prevailed across the board, there is no evidence that conditions across the board are fundamentally different. Many NGOs have not made the slightest attempt to support the beneficiaries' aspirations for self-empowerment.

In as much as the NGOs themselves are entangled in a vicious circle of dependency on donors and governments, target groups persistently find themselves at the receiving end of agencies posing as patrons. This explains why NGOs shy away from embarking on activities pertaining to empowerment and advocacy, which they consider political no-go areas.

A case in point is their failure to act when a window of opportunity arose during the change of regime in 1991. At this time, the "Transitional Period Charter" and "Constitution of the Federal Democratic Republic of Ethiopia" provided a legal avenue to promote democratic values and practice. But no attempt was made by NGOs, apart from a few notable exceptions such as the Ethiopian Human Rights Council (EHRCO) and the Ethiopian Women Lawyers Association (EWLA), to put the pledges and solemn declarations of the post-Dergue regime to the test.

In the post-Mengistu era, the Ethiopian Human Rights Council (EHRCO) was formed in October 1991 with the declared objective of monitoring the situation of human rights in the country. True to its stated principles, it "systematically and at

---

1. Regarding resource allocations in cash and kind for the different NGO programmes covering the period between 1973–1997, see CRDA (1998: 24).

great risks to its officers, managed to monitor and report on human rights violations by the government" (Mutua cited in EHRCO, 1995: viii-ix). Since its founding, EHRCO has compiled several hundred pages of "regular", "special" and "urgent" reports on violations. This was mainly done on the basis of evidence collected through its independent investigations. Simultaneously, EHRCO demanded that the government bring the culprits to book and redress the wrongs inflicted. In making such attempts, the organisation braved the threats and pressures of party zealots and government bureaucrats who worked hard to discourage it in various ways.

The Ethiopian Women Lawyers Association (EWLA) was formed in the mid-1990s. In line with its stated objectives, it strives to sensitise the general public on the plights of women resulting from such abuses as administrative, legal and social discrimination, abduction, rape and domestic violence. EWLA is also preoccupied with lobbying the government to introduce legal reforms and to do away with unfair and discriminatory legal provisions that negatively affect the rights of women. Counselling, and representing disaffected women in court litigations constitute the legal aid component of its activities.

Identifying the Impediments

Several factors account for the inability of NGOs to act as catalysts of change through imparting democratic values. I will only discuss the following: policy environment; social and organisational factors; entrenchment of institutional and personal interests; and NGO dependence on governments and donors. What implications do they have on the promotion of democratic values?

Policy Environment

The legal basis for the establishment and operation of NGOs and public associations is enshrined in Articles 404–482 of the Ethiopian Civil Code promulgated in 1960 (IEG, 1960). Legal Notice 321 of 1966 provided further elaboration to some of the pertinent provisions in the civil code. The formation of NGOs and their operations were treated on the basis of these legal instruments. However, none of the articles in either instrument mentioned NGOs as they are understood today. A cursory look at some aspects of these legal provisions will identify the implications for the promotion of democratic values.

According to Legal Notice 321/1966, registration regulations for associations are incorporated into the "Internal Security Act" issued by the Minister of the Interior. This denotes that security was accorded primacy over and above other considerations. In the face of these laws, a quest for transformation would be improbable. These prohibitive provisions are also responsible for the bureaucratic delays and hurdles experienced by NGOs applying for official recognition, which is a prerequisite for starting operations.

The provisions of both the Civil Code and the Legal Notice governing the establishment and activities of public associations still remain in force. Save for some insignificant modifications, there is to date no full-fledged legislation in place to deal with NGO matters. While it cannot be ruled out that something is in the making, there is no information on any concerted legal struggle waged by NGOs in Ethiopia to secure binding legislation that could curb the arbitrary, unwarranted and destructive practices of officials. The lust for controlling and regulating NGO activities dominates the thinking and practice of the government. Concurrently, the docile disposition of the voluntary sector in Ethiopia encourages the authorities to persist in their efforts.

Social and Organisational Factors

Most NGOs in Ethiopia emerged in response to the 1973–74 and 1984–85 famines. They were therefore not homegrown, indigenous developments. Their programmes were not designed to address fundamental societal concerns on a long-term basis, or in line with local realities. Most of them simply extended their ad hoc interventions of the famine years without further ado. Their leaders and staff are mainly taken from the cosmopolitan elite, whom target groups and communities tend to view as outsiders and external benefactors. They lack the necessary constituency of support, which renders their position increasingly vulnerable to pressures from power centres. In Ethiopia, several NGOs have been de-registered through discretionary decisions of state officials.

The statutes and by-laws of almost all NGOs provide for the existence of appropriate bodies and organs (General Assembly, Board, Executive Committee), and demand that leading positions are to be elective and that beneficiary representation is ensured. In reality, however, the founder-directors of many NGOs are vested with overwhelming powers, which enable them to make decisions single-handedly. The internal modus operandi of several NGOs is therefore undemocratic in the sense of not allowing participation and expression of divergent views (Kassahun, 1994b).

Entrenchment of Institutional and Personal Interests

NGOs operate within the context of rules and regulations and codes of behaviour laid down by mainstream establishments (donors and governments). They have shown marked tendencies to preserve narrow institutional and personal interests. Under conditions where the primary concern is to ensure survival at whatever cost, they avoid as far as possible encounters that could antagonise the wielders of power. In as much as institutions have the desire to continue operating legally, their functionaries and personnel also want to maintain their employment and other benefits accruing to them. The same applies to the founder-leaders of NGOs. This appears to be the dominant trend in most NGOs in Ethiopia. As Tegegne (1994: 28) has argued, NGOs in Ethiopia pursued their strategy for survival by forging closer relations with the central government bureaucracy than with local groups and institutions. Hence the NGO preference to stay close to the locus of power whatever the ramifications. As Fowler (1991) noted, only a few NGOs in Africa have democratic structures allowing for the control of their actions by those whom they serve. Besides this, many NGOs have developed the habit of making themselves readily available to be manipulated and commandeered by the power elite.

Dependence on Governments and Donors

The overwhelming majority of both expatriate and local NGOs in Ethiopia depend on governments and donors for the bulk of the financial and material resources deemed essential for carrying out activities. According to Hellinger (1987: 137), their involvement in joint projects funded by governments posed a threat to their independence and long-term survival. This is substantiated by Weston (1994: 14) who recognised that NGOs entangled in such a situation failed to distance themselves from economic and social policies with negative bearings on the poor. The dependence of NGOs operating in Ethiopia on donors and governments can make them indifferent to unpopular measures even when these run counter to their stated objectives.

Concluding Remarks

To a large extent, African NGOs are replicas of the post-colonial states in that both are products of "modernisation". Unfortunately, "modernisation" has failed to tally with conditions prevalent in African societies. Such pretensions to "modernity", which both African political regimes and non-state players lay claim to, undermined in effect structures of traditional wisdom and indigenous knowledge. On the other hand, "modernity" enabled conventional, albeit unrealistic, approaches of defining and addressing problems to gain ground and currency. But it is these approaches that constitute the whole essence of the "up-rootedness" of the indigenous state and non-state players. This does not mean that Africans should exercise some kind of autarky by way of distancing themselves from everything that is foreign. The growing interdependence of peoples and cultures of the world necessitates co-operation and positive exchange. But the slavish imitation of approaches and strategies tends to render efforts towards transformation futile.

The contribution of NGOs in Ethiopia towards the emergence and consolidation of democratic values has been insignificant. This failure to enhance democratic values, even in favourable environments, is quite strange. It seems that a policy of "laissez faire" is considered the safest way of ensuring survival without antagonising the wielders of power. As Hovde (1992: 8) noted, the traumatic experiences of the Dergue era caused NGOs in Ethiopia to be overly cautious, "enormously fearful, lacking in confidence and unsure of their mission". Hence, there is a need to redefine their roles in a manner that necessitates shift of focus. They still need to develop approaches and strategies to facilitate conditions for democratic transformation.

Decentralization in Ethiopia

Two Case Studies on Devolution of Power and Responsibilities to Local Government Authorities

Meheret Ayenew

Introduction

Since 1991, Ethiopia has been experimenting with a policy of regionalization, which is aimed at devolving governmental power from the center to the regions. The policy has created nine ethnic-based regional state governments and two autonomous administrative areas that comprise the Ethiopian federal structure. All the regions are given a considerable degree of internal self-rule, including the authority to raise local revenue and administer their own budgets and development plans. Each region has a number of zonal, *wereda* and *kebele* tiers of administration to which it must transfer responsibilities and resources to promote decentralized governance at all levels of government. The main objectives of Ethiopia's regionalization policy are to enable the different ethnic groups to develop their culture and language, manage socio-economic development in their respective areas, exercise self-rule and bring about an equitable share of national resources among the regions. Lately, it has become increasingly evident that the shortage of trained personnel and inadequate institutional and administrative capacity that many regions are experiencing have hampered efforts to institutionalize decentralized governance and promote balanced development in the country.

From a theoretical perspective, decentralization has become an essential political agenda to provide opportunities for people at the local level to be involved in determining their economic and political choices. Over the years, politicians and development policy makers have argued that decentralization is necessary to empower local communities to be responsible for their development. Further, decentralization is directly and indirectly associated with many aspects of good governance, including consensual decision-making, equity, representation, accountability and responsiveness of public institutions to community concerns. These positive aspects of democratic governance have added to the theoretical and practical appeal of decentralization as an attractive political program to bring government closer to the people. In addition, 'the failure of the centralized state' has rekindled a great deal of interest in the inter-relationship between decentralization and democracy. Accordingly, many governments have embraced the policy of decentralization as a means of advancing participatory development and governance (Olowu, 1993; Wunsch and Olowu, 1993; Litvack et al., 1998). The current regionalization policy in Ethiopia appears to have been guided by a similar vision, but the results so far have been mixed.

Some preliminary studies on Ethiopia's decentralization experiment suggest that the *wereda* level of government does not exercise sufficient decision-making power and self-rule to act as an autonomous local government entity. Formally, the *wereda* level of administration is a legally recognized independent local government authority and has been given powers and functions guaranteed by the different regional constitutions. In practice, however, it does not exercise sufficient local autonomy on budgetary, economic and social affairs and is tightly controlled by zonal administrations in each region. Inadequate administrative and personnel capacity to carry out socio-economic functions and a poor revenue base are the main reasons for the continued dependence of the *wereda* on the central and regional governments. In addition, lack of independent taxation authority and restrictions on raising local revenue or imposing tariffs without the approval of the regional government have curtailed effective self-government at the *wereda* level (Fenta, 1998; Meheret, 1998; Tucker, 1998).

This article argues that Ethiopia's current decentralization process has not brought about adequate devolution of decision-making power and responsibility to the *wereda* tier of government. At present, zonal administrations supervise the work of all *wereda* governments. Politicians and administrators at the zonal level are appointed by regional governments and are thus accountable to them rather than to the people. What needs to be emphasized is the fact that community development and governance at the *wereda* level are dictated by the non-elected zonal administrations. This has rendered the present system of regional and local government structure top-down, and that in turn has undermined the accountability and responsiveness of public officials to the community.

A democratic local government that is accountable to the people and that enhances public participation in governance is a *sine qua non* for effective decentralization. The extent of decision-making authority and fiscal and budgetary autonomy at the local level are major criteria that are increasingly being used to measure the success of official decentralization policies in bringing about democratic self-governance. In this paper, the same parameters will be used to assess the extent to which Ethiopia's regionalization policy has promoted democratic local governance and participatory development at the *wereda* level.

Methodology and Organization of the Study

This is an exploratory study to look into the decentralization of resources and responsibilities to the *wereda* level of government in Ethiopia. The study will assess the extent to which this level of local self-administration exercises democratic self-governance, including accountability and responsiveness of local government officials to the people, representativeness of elected councils, popular participation in governance and independent decision-making power on matters pertaining to social and economic development and the local budget. It will also attempt to identify major problems and challenges to democratic and decentralized governance at the *wereda* level since the country's transition from a military-cum-civilian dictatorship to an ethno-linguistic-based federal state structure.

The *wereda* level of administration is taken as the focal point for this study because of its strategic place in the present state structure. First, with an average population of around 100,000, the *wereda* is a viable unit of government for meaningful democratic governance and socio-economic development at the local level. In the past, it has been retained as a unit of administration largely for the maintenance of law and order. Second, the fact that there are about 550 *wereda* administrations makes it the most ubiquitous tier of local government and a logical choice for a study aimed at examining whether regionalization has led to effective decentralization in this country.

This article is based on case studies of Dessie Zuria in Amhara regional state and Tiyo/Assela *Wereda* in Oromia regional state. The former is found in southern Wello administrative zone while the latter is found in Arssi administrative zone. These two areas, which are found in two of Ethiopia's biggest regional states, were selected because the observations drawn can be relevant for other parts of the country. However, given Ethiopia's enormous size and diversity, one must be careful not to make assertions claiming to have universal applicability for the whole country.

While collecting primary and secondary data for the research, the writer held discussions with different stakeholders, including *kebele* officials, municipal officers, *wereda* administrators, elected councilors and heads of NGOs in both Tiyo (Assela) and Dessie Zuria *wereda*. All of them cooperated in providing information on the state of local governance in their respective areas, and shared their views on what needs to be done to consolidate democratic local governance. One of the most important issues that repeatedly came up in the discussion was the problem of predominantly rural *wereda* councils supervising urban municipalities. Town residents resented the fact that municipalities did not have their own councils that would be responsive to the needs and concerns of urban constituencies.

Apart from field observation, official reports and publications were used to prepare the socio-economic and demographic profile of both Assela and Dessie Zuria. The federal and regional constitutions and other laws were reviewed for the purpose of examining the formal powers and duties of the *wereda* levels of government vis-à-vis the federal, regional and zonal administrations. In addition, the same sources were also used to sketch the formal institutional framework and inter-governmental relations between the *wereda* and the other tiers of government in the Ethiopian federal structure.

Theoretical Discussion: Approaches to Decentralization

There are two important approaches to decentralization, *viz. administrative decentralization and political decentralization*. It is necessary to discuss some important aspects of these two approaches in order to assess the impact of the official decentralization policy on democratic governance and self-rule in Ethiopia. Such a discussion can provide a proper framework for examining the extent of democracy and decentralization at the *wereda* level. In addition, it will help in assessing the effective transfer of decision-making authority and responsibility from the central government to this level of administration.

The essence of *administrative* (bureaucratic) decentralization is intra-government transfer of authority and responsibility among units of administration within the same organizational hierarchy. It is a *deconcentrated* form of administrative organization that involves delegation of responsibilities and functions by central headquarters to field offices. This is a bureaucratic-administrative arrangement whereby the authority to make decisions is retained by central headquarters. Since they are highly regulated by central administrations, local governments and branch offices are limited to executing policies and plans formulated by central authorities. Their discretion in matters of decision-making is very much restricted. Lacking independent legal existence, local authorities exercise delegated authority that can be revoked by the center when circumstances precipitate such an action. In sum, *administrative decentralization* cannot promote democratic self-rule and participatory development because it does not confer decision-making authority upon local communities and institutions of governance. Hence, this model has limited use for studying the contribution of official decentralization policies to democratic self-government and local decision-making by lower tiers of government (Smith, 1980; Rondinell, et al., 1989; Davey et al., 1996).

Political decentralization, on the other hand, refers to the territorial division of state power. It is a popular governance arrangement aimed at achieving complete *devolution* of decision-making power and transferring political responsibility to subnational governments. This model of decentralization is most often practiced in highly decentralized political systems, for example, federal states. In such a political structure, sub-national governments have an independent legal existence guaranteed by constitutional arrangements. Often, there are legal provisions to prevent any undue interference by central governments in matters determined to be of local jurisdiction. In federal systems, the independence and autonomy of the constituent units are so important that authority and responsibility are constitutionally shared between the central government and other subsidiary units of government, which can be states, regions, provinces and chartered municipalities. Such a division of state functions and responsibilities is the hallmark of genuine decentralization.

Apart from legal guarantees for autonomy, politically decentralized governmental units have independent revenue and taxing authority, and can prepare and approve their budgets and socio-economic development plans without having to seek central authorization. Further, they can also have elected councils/legislative assemblies and executive administrations primarily accountable to the electorate. Independent revenue powers and the presence of elected councils answerable to the citizenry constitute important yardsticks for devolved local government. These two aspects of political decentralization have the single most important advantage of advancing democratic self-rule and popular participation because decision-making authority is effectively transferred from the central government to local government structures (Smith, 1985; Slater, 1989).

In the debate on democratization, the contemporary discourse on state structures examines the relationship between decentralization and democracy. There is a linkage between the two, as decentralization enhances public participation in administration and politics. Such participation constitutes part of the democratic process because it empowers communities to influence public policies. More important, the direct linkage between democracy and decentralization is often emphasized because decentralized structures offer the people greater avenues for participation and opportunities to subject public officials to popular control and accountability. In modern politics, the closer a political system gets to such direct participation and the more people it offers an opportunity to influence policy making, the more decentralized and democratic it is (Crook and Manor, 1991; Barkan et al., 1998).

From the preceding theoretical discussion, it can be inferred that it is *political* rather than *administrative* decentralization that can transfer decision-making authority and responsibility to sub-national structures of government. The decentralization program of any government must be guided by the principles of political decentralization and the measure of success must be its contribution to democratic self-government at the local level. By the same token, the current regionalization policy of the Ethiopian government must be evaluated from the perspective of conferring decision-making authority and responsibility upon the *wereda* administration. A brief historical discussion of past attempts at decentralizing the Ethiopian state is necessary as a prelude to assessing the prospects for the *wereda* becoming a viable unit of democratic local governance.

Historical Background of Decentralization in Ethiopia

The policy of decentralizing government and development is a relatively new phenomenon in the Ethiopian political landscape. Throughout most of its recent history, modern Ethiopia has been a highly centralized unitary state because the politics of nation-building has been anchored in creating a strong, centralist state that jealously guarded its sacrosanct central power. In particular, the two post-World War II Ethiopian regimes, including the Haile Selassie government and its successor the Derg, paid only lip service to any serious program of decentralization and the country has largely remained a centralized polity. The current difficulties in instituting a working federal structure and a democratic political and economic order can be partially explained by the legacy of insufficient experience in decentralized governance and administration.

The first move towards institutional decentralization in Ethiopia dates back to the imperial era when the Haile Selassie I government submitted to the then parliament the *Awraja* Local Self-Administration Order No. 43 of 1966. The draft bill proposed to grant administrative autonomy to 50 *awraja* governments drawn from the majority of the country's fourteen provinces. Despite strong resistance from parliament, the program was implemented in 17 selected *awrajawotch*[1] on an experimental basis. Each *awraja*'s economic potential to become a self-sufficient administrative area was a critical consideration in the selection process. The policy could be considered a typical administrative measure aimed at easing bureaucratic congestion at the center rather than a serious decentralization experiment to bring about effective self-government. Among other things, a chief administrator for each *awraja* was appointed by the central government. In addition, the authority of the *awraja* government to raise revenue and utilize it for development was limited. The policy did not have much impact on decentralization in Ethiopia mainly because the imperial parliament failed to pass the local government finance bill. Given these major shortcomings, it was unlikely that the policy would have promoted genuine local self-government (Cohen, 1974).

The Derg had no better record than its predecessor in decentralizing the Ethiopian state. For a long time, it too steadfastly held to a highly centralized and unitarist state. With the introduction of radical socialist policies in the mid-1970s, including the nationalization of rural and urban land, the regime established Peasant and Urban Dwellers Associations that were empowered to carry out social, economic and judicial functions in defined jurisdictions. These mass organizations enjoyed significant autonomy and served as popular institutions of governance and participation, at least in the early days of military rule. Later, they were stripped of their autonomy and independence because the regime converted them into state bureaucratic accessories geared towards implementing central directives.

The intensification of ethnic/civil wars in the country and the increasing resistance to military rule compelled the government to consider some kind of decentralization in the early 1980s. It established the Institute of Nationalities to draft a new constitution that would help in reorganizing the post-monarchist Ethiopian state. Following the establishment of the Peoples' Democratic Republic of Ethiopia (PDRE) in 1984, Tigray, Afar and the Ogaden became autonomous administrate regions. Eritrea was given a special autonomous status. This did not make much difference in the long-running civil war in Ethiopia's rebellious province, which became

---

1. *Awrajawotch* is the plural form of *awraja*.

a separate state in 1991. All the regions slated for autonomous and decentralized administration were the country's most unstable and troubled regions affected by ethnic insurgency, drought and famine (PDRE, 1987; Clapham, 1988).

The Derg instituted an authoritarian state that did not lend itself to participatory governance and development. The regime maintained a monolithic government and party structure which kept a tight rein on the economy and society. The Workers' Party of Ethiopia (WPE), organized according to the Leninist principle of 'democratic centralism', put in place a highly regimented system of agricultural and economic management and pursued a policy of forced collectivization and coercive resettlement of the drought-hit rural peasantry. All these policies were reminiscent of authoritarian rule and antithetical to democratic governance. Towards the end of its reign, as we have seen, the Derg granted autonomy to carefully selected provinces afflicted by ethnic and nationalist strife. This was a clear demonstration of the fact that decentralization was not a policy to which the regime was fully committed but was adopted as a matter of expediency to deal with the problems of ethnic insurgency and political instability (Andargatchew, 1993; Keller, 1988).

Following the fall of the Derg, the Transitional Government of Ethiopia (TGE) was established in 1991 under the leadership of the Ethiopian Peoples' Revolutionary Democratic Front (EPRDF). The country was divided into twelve self-governing ethno-linguistic regional states and two special autonomous administrative areas. The number was later reduced to nine regional states following the controversial merger of the numerous ethnic and nationality groups encompassing many regions in the south into one regional government. Ethiopia was declared a federal republic following the adoption of yet another new constitution in 1995. At present, Tigray, Afar, Amhara, Oromia, Somale, Southern Nations, Nationalities and Peoples (SN-NP), Benishangul-Gumuz, Gambella and Harrari national regional states; and Addis Ababa and Dire Dawa city administrations comprise the Federal Democratic Republic of Ethiopia (FDRE). Apart from ethnic and linguistic diversity, Ethiopia's regional states are vastly different in terms of population and territory. For example, the regional state of Oromia, with an estimated population of nearly 22 million and an area of 353,000 sq. km., contrasts with that of Harrari regional state with a population of 150,000 and an area of about 311 sq. km. Table 1 presents data on population and area of the nine regional states and the two autonomous administrative divisions (TGE, 1992; MEDAC, 1998).

Table 1. Population, Area, Number of Zones and *Weredawotch* of National Regional States of Ethiopia

S/N	National Regional State/ Administrative Area	Population 1998/1999	Area in '000 kms²	Number of Zones	Number of *Weredawotch*
	Tigray	3,358,358	60.2	4	35
	Afar	1,131,437	77.0	5	28
	Amhara	14,769,360	188.8	10	130
	Oromiya	20,012,952	360.0	12	176
	Somale	1,978,600	215.9	9	47
	Benishangul/Gumuz	492,689	46.8	3	13
	SNNPRS	11,064,818	112.0	9	76 (estimate)
	Gambella	194,755	26.1	4	8
	Harrari	143,587	.31	3	19
	Addis Ababa	2,341,964	.54	6	28
	Dire Dawa	277,245	1.6	4	23
	Total	55,765,765	1089.1	66	556

Source: MEDAC, Department of Regional Planning and Development, 1998.

Each regional state government has been given a considerable degree of self-rule, including an elected regional council and an executive administration. In addition, each region can also be considered as having semi-sovereign status because it has a constitution, a flag and a regional language to be used in schools, courts and public administration. It is also empowered to prepare and approve its own budget and economic plans and programs (FDRE, 1995).

Both the federal and regional state governments have legislative, executive and judicial functions. As in any other federal system, state sovereignty has been constitutionally apportioned between the central government and the nine regional states that constitute the Ethiopian federation. In addition, central and regional government powers and responsibilities have also been defined in the constitution. Accordingly, national defense, foreign policy, currency, inter-regional trade and citizenship are major functions left for the central government. Regional governments are made responsible for executing economic and social development policies, strategies and plans of the region, and establishing and administering a regional police force and maintaining public order. The constitution further stipulates that "all powers not given expressly to the Federal Government alone or concurrently to the Federal Government and the states are reserved to the states" (FDRE, 1995).

The current Ethiopian state structure has five tiers of government, viz. the federal, regional, zonal, *wereda* and *kebele* levels. The 1995 federal constitution, which is Ethiopia's fourth, recognizes only the federal government and regional state governments and does not mention the last three. An earlier legislation, Proclamation No. 7/92, makes reference to all and assigns powers and duties to each of them. All echelons of government below the regional level are the responsibilities of regional state governments, and their organization, powers and functions are defined in regional constitutions. Article 39, sub-article 3 of the federal constitution can be broadly interpreted to provide for a considerable degree of self-rule when it states that 'Every nation, nationality and people in Ethiopia has the right to a full measure of self-government which includes establishing institutions of government in the territory that it inhabits...'. Both the federal and regional constitutions provide for periodic democratic elections and popularly elected councils at all levels, active citizen participation in government and the establishment of local government administrations that will be transparent and accountable to the electorate. The diagram below demonstrates the Ethiopian state structure as provided for in both the federal and regional constitutions (TGE, 1992; FDRE, 1995).

Main Features of Decentralization in Ethiopia

Ethiopia's current system of state structure can be characterized as ethnic federalism because ethnicity and language are used as major criteria in creating sub-national governments. One of the criticisms leveled at the present ethnic-based regionalization policy is that there has not been effective devolution of power and responsibility from regional governments to lower levels of administration. The point is made that regional governments are still dominant and exercise significant control in the affairs of sub-national levels of government, including zonal, *wereda* and kebele administrations. On the other hand, proponents of the policy argue that it has laid a strong foundation for a federal system of participatory governance whereby public officials will be held accountable and responsive to the needs of the citizenry. Whatever the merits of the controversies surrounding ethnic federalism in Ethiopia, it is obvious that the evolving system manifests certain problems. It is important to consider these structural and administrative deficiencies because they will help in assessing the prospects for an effectively decentralized governance system in this country.

Figure 1. Organizational Structure of the Five Levels of Government of the Federal Democratic Republic of Ethiopia

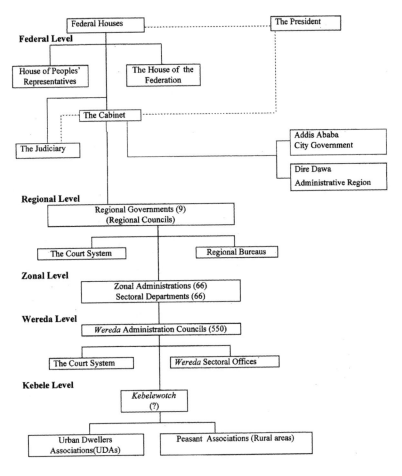

An Experiment in Authoritarian Ethnic Federalism

From an institutional perspective, the current federal structure in Ethiopia can be characterized as authoritarian ethnic federalism. The term "authoritarian" is used here to depict the tight control exercised by central authorities over the lower orders of governance. An important feature of this evolving system has thus been central government control of regional state governments through the instrumentality of single ethnic-based parties that are affiliated with the ruling EPRDF. Each region is ruled by an ethnic-based party that has established structures at the level of zones, *weredawotch* and *kebelewotch*. The overwhelming majority of elected and appointed local government officers and administrators are members of the ruling party. As earlier pointed out, since the regional ethnic-based party is a member of the ruling EPRDF coalition, the system maintains a monolithic structure that ensures the heavy influence of the center on the periphery.

The present authoritarian political arrangement can engender consequences with far-reaching implications on the governance structure that is evolving today. First, it will reinforce upward accountability both among party functionaries and administrators throughout the system. Second, it will make it difficult for multi-ethnic political parties outside of the EPRDF coalition to have a level field in politics and play a constructive role in the future of this country. Third, it will accentuate vertical integration between the center and the regions rather than horizontal or inter-regional cooperation among regions. All these features militate against the institutionalization of decentralized governance and an administrative machinery that will be accountable to the electorate. In sum, ethnic federalism in Ethiopia will take hold only if the political system is sufficiently democratized and allows a wider latitude for participation.

Heavy Regional Dependence on the Central Government

Another manifestation of the top-down character of ethnic federalism in Ethiopia is the heavy dependence of the regions on the federal government for budgetary allocations. There are two possible explanations for this state of affairs. First, central government monopoly over the most lucrative revenue sources has rendered regional and local governments financially weak and thus dependent on the center. Second, the economic underdevelopment of the country, the paucity of national revenue sources and the limited capacity to mobilize adequate resources for development have accentuated the fiscal dependence of the regions on the central government. Over the past few years, regional governments have been able to finance only an average of 17 per cent of their expenditures from their own revenues while a hefty 83 per cent was given to them by the federal government in the form of transfers. The data in Table 2 show the gap in revenue share of the federal and regional state governments between 1994/95–1999/2000 (Meheret, 1998; Brosio and Gupta, 1997).

Table 2. Revenue Share of the Federal and Regional State Governments in Ethiopia 1994/95–1999/2000 (in millions of Eth. Birr)

Year	Share of the Federal Government	Share of Regional State Governments	Total	% Share of the Federal Government
1994/95	5026.3	886.6	5912.6	85
1995/96	5836.5	1129.4	6965.9	84
1996/97	6525.0	1352.4	7877.4	83
1997/98	6817.6	1595.2	8412.8	81
1998/99	7846.0	1516.1	9362.1	84
1999/00	8616.7*	1813.9*	10430.6	83
Average	6778.2	1382.2	8160.2	83

*Estimate
Source: Budget Department, MEDAC, December, 1999.

Top-Down Approach to Federalism

A great deal of top-down leadership and management can be observed in Ethiopia's on-going experiment in federalism. In addition to their dependence on the federal government for budgetary transfers, regional governments are also subject to substantial control by the center. Formally, all regional states have been given wide-ranging powers and responsibilities and are expected to manage most political and economic matters on their own without the interference of the federal government. In practice, however, the country's lack of experience in managing a federal system and the wide disparities among the regions in terms of administrative and managerial capacity has prompted constant central government interference in regional matters. The key unit that plays the role of a clearing house for regional matters is the Regional Affairs Bureau within the Office of the Prime Minister. Apart from political control, the bureau provides administrative and technical support to the emerging regions, and undertakes the implementation of socio-economic projects on their behalf. As an executive arm of the central government, it also bears much of the responsibility for regional government and spearheads important policy decisions affecting the regionalization process in this country.

The extent of supervision and monitoring of regions by the central government varies from one region to another. Regional governments that have sufficient administrative and institutional capacity, including adequate trained manpower, a relatively developed infrastructure and sufficient local resource base, enjoy a relatively higher degree of autonomy and independence than those with serious shortages of trained manpower and finance. For example, Amhara, Oromia and Tigray are not subject to the same degree of interference and supervision by the center as the manpower-deficient regions such as Gambella, Afar, Benishagul-Gumuz and Somale.

Considerable Differences among the Regions

An important characteristic of the emerging federal system in Ethiopia is the existence of significant differences among the regions that constitute the federation. The country's regions are vastly different in terms of population, area, and level of economic and infrastructure development. The allocation of budgetary and national revenues on the basis of geographical and demographic factors obviously favors bigger regions. The challenge for many federal systems is to correct regional disparities and bring about even and balanced development among the different regions. Unless governments are able to provide equal development opportunities, the persistence of regional economic differences can generate resentment that can threaten the viability of the federal arrangement.

To sum up the discussion of the nature of the evolving federal state structure in Ethiopia, it can be said that the top-down approach to federalism cannot facilitate devolution of power and authority to lower levels of administration. It was also observed that the regions are heavily dependent on the central government for budgetary support. This has necessitated close monitoring of regional issues by the central government, especially in regions with inadequate administrative and institutional capacity. It is against these general observations that the extent of decentralization of power and responsibility to *wereda* levels of administration must be examined.

Decentralization and Democracy in Ethiopia: Two *Wereda* Case Studies

As mentioned earlier, the purpose of this study is to assess the extent of decentralization in Dessie Zuria and Tiyo/Assela *Wereda*. Background information and the socio-economic profiles of each of the local government units were prepared following two brief field visits by the author. The existing governance and administrative structures are also reviewed for the purpose of assessing the institutional and organizational capacity of the two *weredawotch* for effective self-government. A review of the legal status, functions and responsibilities of the *wereda* level of government is presented below as a prelude to discussing the extent of devolution of power and responsibilities in these two *weredawotch*.

Powers and Responsibilities of the *Wereda* Level of Government

The *wereda* is a multi-purpose local government unit in the current state structure in Ethiopia. Although not mentioned in the federal constitution, it is recognized by all regional constitutions and has been given elaborate powers and responsibilities. As an autonomous self-governing unit, it has an elected council, executive committee and administrative structure. Formally, this level of government can prepare and approve its own budget, prepare and implement economic and social development projects, set up and manage public services and exercise democratic decision making at the local level. In addition, it has an independent court structure and has been given the authority to mobilize the people for participatory governance and development. This list represents significant indicators of devolution of power, including local autonomy, decision-making and responsibilities. What is not clear is the extent to which these are exercised in practice. The following discussion is intended to provide answers to these and related questions.

Socio-Economic Profile of Dessie Zuria *Wereda*

Dessie Zuria *Wereda* is found in South Wello administrative zone. It is the zone's most populous *wereda* with nearly 230,000 inhabitants. It comprises 45 peasant associations. There is an elected council that acts as a legislative body. Its membership size of 120 is admittedly too big for the *wereda*'s estimated population of 230,000. This body meets three or four times a year. Out of the total council membership, 13 constitute the executive committee whose function is to oversee the day-to-day administration of the *wereda*. Only two of these are women. In terms of educational qualification, out of the 13 standing committee members, three have completed high school, five are farmers and have completed grades 7–8, 5 are former civil servants and teachers, whose educational qualification is above grade 12. Eleven of them are members of the EPRDF while two are independent or have no party affiliation.

The executive committee and the general council serve for a simultaneous term of five years. About 110 of the 120-member council or 92 per cent are members of the ruling EPRDF. Only eight of the council's total members are women. This represents a mere 7 per cent compared to their share of more than 50 per cent of the total population in the area. All members of the *wereda* executive committee are paid a monthly salary of 120 Birr, which is the same amount paid to a kebele chairman.

Dessie is the capital of South Wello administrative zone. It has a population of about 120,000. In 1999, the Dessie municipal administration had a total of 189 permanent and 250 contract employees. The 13-member *wereda* executive committee is also responsible for supervising the management of the town. The chief town officer is a member of the *wereda* council and is answerable to it.

Dessie Zuria *Wereda* has extensive formal powers and responsibilities. It is responsible for running all socio-economic development in the area including agriculture, health, education and infrastructure development. In practice, however, it is subject to the control and supervision of the zonal administration and the regional government in matters ranging from budget preparation and approval to undertaking socio-economic development projects, for example, building schools and clinics. In interviews with the chairman of the *wereda* council, it was learnt that the *wereda* could prepare its own budget but this had to be submitted to the zonal administration for approval. It cannot implement the budget without securing formal approval from the zone and the regional government because it receives its budget appropriation from this higher authority in the form of transfers. This can be cited as evidence of the restrictions placed on the *wereda*'s fiscal autonomy and independence.

The *wereda*'s powers and responsibilities are also limited in many other ways. For example, it does not have the authority to introduce taxes and impose new tariffs without the approval of the zonal administration. Its spending authority is limited to amounts not exceeding 30,000 Birr and all expenditures above this figure must be authorized by the zone. In addition, all economic and social plans have to be submitted to the zonal administration and instructions for their implementation have to come from the same office.

An important feature of zonal control over the *wereda* is the practice of gimgema or evaluation. Although periodically conducted by the zonal administration, its purpose is not clearly established. In the early years of EPRDF rule, it used to be frequently exercised; but, its significance has diminished in recent years for reasons that are not clear. According to some *wereda* officials, gimgema is a democratic exercise intended to evaluate the performance of the elected council and ensure its accountability and responsiveness to the electorate. It is an essential practice intended to investigate allegations of corruption and abuse of authority by elected officials.

The benign view is that the potential use of gimgema keeps local councilors on their toes and instills in them a strong sense of public service and accountability among the leadership. In practice, however, it has proved to be an effective weapon to weed out members whose allegiance to the party line might be in question. This is especially true in light of the fact that the initiative to conduct gimgema usually comes from within the executive committee. There is very little popular interest and public involvement in it at the local level because most often it is stage managed by and among the local government leadership, ostensibly to settle scores. Hence, it will be too simplistic to generalize that the practice has the democratic feature of holding public officials accountable for their tasks; the more so in a country where the people have very limited avenues to air their grievances and complaints against public officials. In other words, in a political culture where 'whistle blowing' is virtually unknown, the practice of 'gimgema' can only represent a strong fist of central authority over local autonomy because it is largely a top-down process and there is very little popular community initiative in the exercise.

An important issue that needs to be addressed is the legal status and function of municipalities in the evolving local government structure. Most municipalities and urban centers in Ethiopia are not recognized as distinct authorities of local administration. As such, they are subject to dual authority. On the one hand, lacking separate legal status, they are supervised by predominantly rural *wereda* councils. On the other hand, they are subject to the technical and administrative supervision of zonal Bureaus of Works and Urban Development (BWUD).

Dessie municipality, which is part of the Dessie Zurea *Wereda* administration, is supervised by the *wereda* executive committee. The town does not have an independent legal existence. As mentioned earlier, the chief town officer is a member of the *wereda* executive council. He is a salaried officer and is made responsible for the day-to-day running of the municipality assisted by an executive committee and sectoral offices operating in the town. He has the dual role of being a member of the EPRDF and a public administrator.

The relation that Dessie municipality has with the *wereda* administration is fraught with problems and is a major factor constraining the autonomy and independence of the former. Most matters pertaining to the municipality's governance and administration, including its annual budget and work plan, have to be approved by the *wereda* council. Apart from occasional grants from the regional government—mainly for infrastructure, including street maintenance and repair, garbage collection, etc.—the municipality is self-financing and does not receive any subsidy either from the *wereda* or the zonal administration. The lion's share of its revenue comes from business taxes and licenses. Given this reality, it is not clear on what basis the *wereda* council acts as a supervisory authority over municipal affairs. As long as it is under the authority of the *wereda* administration, the municipality's problems are likely to receive secondary attention from a council whose membership has an overwhelmingly rural background.

The *kebele* is the lowest tier of administration in Ethiopia's state structure. It is an important unit of local administration. However its role and function in the current system of government are not clear. In many instances, *kebelewotch* (sing.: *kebele*) have served as basic units of grassroots democracy and enhanced community participation in governance. At present, there are no clear authority and functional relationships between the *kebelewotch* on the one hand and the *wereda* administration and the municipality on the other. In addition, there is a problem of jurisdiction as to whether *kebelewotch* are under the *wereda* or the municipal administration. In relative terms, the status of rural *kebelewotch* is clear because they are under the supervision of the *wereda* administration. However, urban ones are subject to dual supervision by the *wereda* council and the municipality.

Kebelewotch have virtually become neglected areas of government in Dessie Zuria *Wereda*. It was observed that there was no functioning *kebele* administrative structure in place to serve the community and no budget was allocated for activities to be undertaken at that level. Many of the *kebelewotch* in Dessie were under-staffed and under-financed, and thus unable to deliver services to the community. Because most of them were not functional, town residents increasingly flocked to the central municipality for all kinds of services. This has overstretched the municipality's limited financial and personnel capacity. More important, it has also caused a great deal of bureaucratic congestion and inconvenience to the community.

Tiyo/Assela *Wereda* Administration

Tiyo is one of the twenty *weredawotch* in Arssi Administrative Zone, Oromia regional state, with an estimated population of 142,000. The *wereda* council has 165 elected members, an average of one representative for about 860 people. This is a rather large assembly. It has an executive committee of 13 members, of whom only one is a woman. Of these, six have completed grade 12, and the rest can only read and write. Only three are party members of the Oromo People's Democratic Organization (OPDO), a local affiliate of the ruling EPRDF coalition.

Assela is the main town in Tiyo *Wereda* with an estimated population of nearly 50,000. The town has 14 *kebelewotch* organized into 2 *kaftagna*. Each *kebele* sends two representatives to constitute a 28-member town council. There is an executive committee of seven members out of which three—the chief town officer, the deputy town officer and the secretary—carry out the day-to-day affairs of the town on a full-time basis. Only these three permanent officers are paid. The rest serve voluntarily and most are civil servants and teachers in local schools and serve on a part-time basis. The municipality has 75 permanent and 58 contract employees. Out of the total permanent labor force, 3 are illiterate, 25 have completed grades 1–6, 41 have completed grades 9–12 and only 6 are above grade 12.

Legally, Tiyo/Assela *Wereda* has the full powers and responsibilities that any autonomous local government could have. In reality, however, it is under the general supervision of the zonal administration and has several restrictions placed on its authority and autonomy. For example, most issues ranging from budget preparation and approval to carrying out socio-economic development in the area have to be endorsed by zonal sector offices. As in Dessie zuria, *gimgema* is often practiced and remains a potent weapon to insure the subordination of the *wereda* to the zonal and regional administrations. As earlier pointed out, the practice is often resorted to in order to serve the political purpose of purging individuals whose loyalty to the party might be in question. Far from being a democratic means to enhance answerability and responsiveness of public officials to matters of public concern, this practice has reinforced upward accountability. As a result, the needs and concerns of the electorate receive only secondary attention.

The town of Assela is subject to a great degree of control by the *wereda* because as a municipality it does not have a separate legal existence. The budget of the municipality and all development and infrastructure plans of the town have to be approved by the same body before they are implemented. Despite the fact that it is a separate administration both geographically and functionally, the municipal council cannot introduce new tariffs or taxes without obtaining approval from the *wereda* administration. In addition, although elected by the town dwellers, the municipal council and its administration are supervised by the *wereda* council and must report to it. As in the case of Dessie municipality, most *wereda* councilors have a rural background and have little appreciation for urban problems. This has meant that urban problems are often neglected and municipalities do not receive sufficient resources to solve the social and economic problems of the residents.

Rural and urban *kebelewotch* in Tiyo/Assela *Wereda* administration are in a state of limbo and provide practically no services to the community. They do not have clear functions and roles and their relationship to the *wereda* and the municipality has not been clearly defined. *Kebelewotch* have become dysfunctional because they are under-financed and under-staffed. They receive no financial and material assistance either from the *wereda* or the municipality. Most of them function as part of the administrative structure of the *wereda* administration and have lost their distinct character as basic units of grass roots governance.

Factors Constraining Democratic *Wereda* Government

From the preceding discussion, it can be observed that the *wereda* tier of government does not have complete autonomy and decision-making authority. It lacks sufficient institutional and resource capacity to exercise effective self-government. Apart from historical and political reasons for the persistence of centralization tendencies in Ethiopia's state system, there are more fundamental constraining factors that have impeded progress towards the institutionalization of democratic *wereda* local government. Some of these constraining factors are discussed below.

Dearth of Trained Local Government Personnel

The greatest challenge in institutionalizing a functioning decentralized system of *wereda* government in Ethiopia is the serious dearth of skills and expertise in the areas of basic management, project management, budgeting and finance, human resources management and service delivery. At present, most *wereda* administrations are staffed with people who have only secondary or elementary school background and no practical experience in local government administration. The overwhelming majority of *wereda* councilors can only read and write. Equally important is the fact that most *wereda* government personnel are far from familiar with the concept of public service or government responsiveness to the needs and concerns of the citizenry. Such awfully inadequate personnel capacity and lack of awareness about the potential role of decentralized governance does not augur well for institutionalizing meaningful self-government and bringing about sustainable socio-economic development at the local level.

Weak Revenue Base

One of the real tests of an effective self-government is adequate financial strength. *Wereda* administrations in Ethiopia are financially strapped mainly because they cannot generate sufficient revenue from local sources. This has primarily meant that their hands are tied when it comes to undertaking meaningful community development at the local level. Most of them lack either secure sources of revenue or their tax base is so narrow that only a miniscule portion of their budgetary requirements is met from their own revenue. As suggested elsewhere in this article, the primary explanation for this state of affairs is the fact that almost all well-paying revenue sources are monopolized by either the central or regional governments leaving very little for the *weredawotch*. In addition, restrictions placed on the *wereda's* ability to raise additional revenue and to introduce new taxes contribute to its extreme fiscal and financial weakness.

Heavy *Wereda* Financial Dependence on Regional Governments

The fiscal and financial independence of local governments is a critical factor affecting their autonomy and effectiveness in addressing the problems of their constituency. *Weredawotch* in Ethiopia are heavily dependent on both central and regional governments for financial and budgetary subsidies. This study has brought to light the reality that in both Dessie Zuria and Assela/Tiyo, the *wereda* governments could cover only a maximum of thirty-five per cent of the budgetary expenditures from revenues they collect from the area. The situation at the national level is pretty much the same. According to some preliminary studies nearly 65–70 per cent of the annual budget of most *weredawotch* in Ethiopia comes from the regional government in the form of transfers or outright grants. Such financial dependence has serious implications for the autonomy and independence of *wereda* governments in Ethiopia.

Poor Awareness of the Proper Role and Function of a Responsive Local Government

Most *wereda* administrators and councilors see their roles as representatives of the central government and the party. As such, carrying out government and party orders takes precedence over community concerns and needs. This is perfectly understandable given the fact that the majority of *wereda*-level personnel got their jobs in the first place primarily because they are either members or sympathizers of the ruling party. However, this does not help at all the evolution of an independent local government system that is responsive to the people at the local level. In conjunction with the serious problem of heavy financial dependence of the *wereda* on the regional government, government/party dominance of local government can only reinforce upward accountability. Given this situation, it will be a long road before a democratic *wereda* self-government that is responsive to the needs and concerns of the community emerges in Ethiopia.

Non-Representativeness of *Wereda* Government Councils and Executive Leadership

Representativeness is an attribute of a democratic local government. The term is used to refer to the participation and presence of different groups and interests in the leadership and management of local governments. *Wereda* governments in Ethiopia are sorely lacking in this respect. This limited study has revealed that the governance and leadership structures of both Dessie Zuria and Assela/Tiyo *Wereda* were highly unrepresentative. The councils and their executive leadership did not adequately represent women, community and religious organizations, private businesses and NGOs. All of these elements of civil society can make tremendous contributions to effective self-government and to instilling democratic traditions at local level. Apart from rendering governance more democratic and representative, involvement of different organizations and interests promotes popular participation and enhances the role of the *wereda* as facilitator rather than as the sole actor in the governing process.

Conclusion

The professed goal of regionalization in Ethiopia is to progressively transfer the delivery and management of public services from the central government bureaucracy to democratic sub-national governments. However, one needs to differentiate between rhetoric and reality in the ongoing process of regionalization in this country. The constitution and the various policies provide for the formal transfer of powers and responsibilities from the central government to regional, zonal and *wereda* levels of administration. In reality, however, there has been very little devolution of authority and functions from regional governments to *wereda* levels of administration because zonal administrations, although not constitutionally recognized, have been super-imposed and act as brakes on the autonomy and independence of *wereda* governments. It is no exaggeration to say that zonal administrations in Ethiopia's local government system have become an albatross that stifles *wereda* level democracy and self-rule. As such, *weredawotch* do not have sufficient decision-making authority to serve as autonomous institutions of decentralized governance, nor do they manage public and community services on their own without strict guidance and supervision by zonal administrations.

The emerging pattern of decentralized government and administration is hierarchical and top-down because the chain of command flows from regions to zones, *weredawotch* and *kebelewotch* in an unbroken line. This has affected the independent decision-making power of the *wereda* level of government. Formally, the *were-*

da government has been given full powers to exercise complete decision-making authority. In practice, however, commands and instructions flow from top to bottom in an unbroken bureaucratic line from the regional government to the zones, *weredawotch* and *kebelewotch*. The bureaucratic chain of command has limited the local discretionary power and decision-making authority of the *wereda* tiers of government.

The shortage of adequately trained local government personnel is a major constraint on the capacity of the *wereda* to evolve as a viable unit of self-rule and democratic governance in Ethiopia. The vast majority of *wereda* government councilors and municipal officers have a low level of education and training. The shortage of qualified local government and municipal personnel is one of the serious impediments to instituting an effectively working decentralized administration and governance system. It is absolutely necessary to attract merit-based and professional personnel in order to provide efficient public service and to improve the quality of local governance at the *wereda* level.

A typical feature of *wereda* government is that it is top-down. Although formally elected, most *wereda* councilors and administrators have been able to secure their positions because of their membership of the ruling EPRDF. This has generated a great deal of upward accountability. This will not help the emergence of a democratic self-government system that is responsive to local demands and needs.

One of the goals in focusing on the *wereda* level of government has been to promote equity and fair representation of all social groups in local administrative and governance structures. In this regard, very little has been achieved in Ethiopia. The representation of different segments of society and organizations of civil society in policy-making and administrative processes of *wereda* governments is extremely low. In addition, there is very little community involvement and participation in *wereda* administration and municipal management. There is lack of awareness both among elected and appointed local government personnel that NGOs, private business organizations and many other elements of civil society can partake in development and the provision of services to the community.

Wereda governments in Ethiopia have a poor revenue base. This has to change in favor of a more decentralized fiscal system by enhancing the taxing power of these administrations. In addition, they must be given authority to charge user fees for services and to mobilize local resources for development. These measures can enhance *wereda* revenue capacity so that they can undertake meaningful development on their own. The resources generated from the locality must be used strictly within the area in an accountable and transparent manner. People will be motivated to participate in socio-economic development when they see their taxes and contributions translated into tangible benefits.

Finally, a true measure of decentralization of resources and power to the *wereda* must be its contribution to advancing democracy. In this regard, *wereda*wotch in Ethiopia have fared poorly and leave much to be desired. The participation and representation of the general population in the power structures and processes of governance at this level are crucial elements in the democratization process. Decentralized *wereda* government can promote democratization when the people are empowered to decide on economic and political issues affecting their well-being. Putting in place institutional and legal mechanisms for ensuring the accountability and responsiveness of public officials to the needs and problems of the citizenry is a concrete manifestation of democratic governance at the *wereda* level.

IV

Alternative Voices

Mengistulore
Oral Literatures Depicting the Man, His Regime, Officials and Proclamations

Fekade Azeze

Introduction

This study deals with issues of governance as expressed in oral literature in Ethiopia during the last 150 years or so. It investigates the oral literature that portrays the Derg and its leader Colonel Mengistu Hailemariam. Jokes and couplets that depict the man, his colleagues, the party, the Ethiopian Revolution, the Derg, democracy and the various proclamations are collected and investigated. An effort has also been made to trace the multifarious voices from the early years of the regime up to its demise in 1991, and to reveal the unheeded responses to some of its major policies.

The study focuses mainly on the reactions of the toiling masses residing in rural and urban settings. For they are the ones who suffer most from the atrocities committed by various irresponsible officials and cadres running the state bureaucracy. It is also true that most of these people do not read and write at all. They mainly receive information and articulate their views orally.

Unlike the small educated section of the community, which occasionally expresses its views in the electronic and print media, the talented among the uneducated public express their views via oral poetry, jokes, idiomatic expressions, anecdotes, and nicknames. Their views are transmitted quite easily from one corner of the country to the other. Nowadays, with relative improvement in transportation, the widespread use of the telephone, the radio and TV, such expressions travel from a bar in Addis to another in a regional capital, then to a local drinking place (the *täjj* or *tälla bét*) and then to a remote community or village drinking place and vice versa. One can even say that, fairly often, they move faster than the products of the press.

In the olden days, emperors, kings, governors, and local officials reportedly used to ask *"erräñña men alä?"* (meaning, "What do shepherds say?"). If there are things that have gone wrong in the community, if there are prophecies of what is to come, critical and prophetic views are said to be expressed in the songs of young shepherds. Oral tradition has it that Menelik benefited a lot from the views, criticisms, and warnings of these shepherds. Thus, it could be said that there was a tradition of governance in Ethiopia which always gave room and paid attention to these voices.

However, there does not seem to be much enthusiasm for and devotion to oral traditions in general and *oral literature* in particular in Ethiopian social science publications. As far as I know Ethiopian historians writing and publishing in Amharic are more inclined to use *oral literary sources* than most expatriate and national academics writing and publishing in English. In the writings of the latter, we seldom hear ordinary men and women voicing their views on the political, economic and social events that constitute their history. It is hoped that this paper will contribute towards narrowing this gap.

Sources

The study is based on: (1) data I have been collecting in Addis Ababa since the late sixties and from Northern Shäwa during the years 1992 and 1996; (2)data I obtained from Wällo by hiring as enumerators fourth year university students native to that area; (3) collections of different oral literary materials in relevant BA and MA theses available at the Institute of Language Studies, the Institute of Ethiopian Studies and Kennedy Libraries of Addis Ababa University; and (4) material obtained from term paper assignments I have been giving to my graduate and undergraduate students attending my classes in oral literature. Since these students come from the different regions of Ethiopia they have enriched my collections in the last ten years or more.

My personal collections of couplets (although some of these are triplets and quartets, I shall refer to them as couplets hereafter for the sake of convenience), jokes and other oral literary material related to peasant life and issues of governance have not yet been systematically organized. Though I cannot give an exact figure now I believe they exceed one and a half thousand.

Analysis of Oral Literature Collections

The jokes and poems found in the above works deal with numerous topics. Mengistu the man and leader, his colleagues, the Derg, the Workers' Party of Ethiopia (WPE) and the Commission which established it, Peasant Association committee members and leaders, government officials and cadres of the last and present regimes are the topics for these jokes and poems. Proclamations on land, resettlement, cooperatives, national military service have also inspired many oral poets. Poems, jokes, anecdotes, sayings, and graffiti depicting the red terror, the literacy programme, the *zämächa* (campaign) of students to the rural areas, the war between EPLF-TPLF and the Derg and other social, political and economic issues are found in these works too.

Since one cannot deal with all of these topics in depth and in detail in this short paper, I have chosen to discuss some of the folklore that directly deals with Mengistu first. The proclamations, the officials, the party and its cadres, the Derg, the qäbälé and other institutions shall be discussed. The central argument of the presentation is to indicate, yet again, to government officials, literary and social science researchers and policy makers the importance of listening to unheeded voices such as these.

Generally speaking, governments do not seem to have much respect for the opinion of peasants even on matters that deeply affect their material and psychological lives. They are not known to consult the people concerned on matters pertaining to the implementation of the various proclamations they manufacture on their behalf. They did not, for example, frankly discuss the best ways of distributing land on the basis of the Land Proclamation of 1975 before rushing to arbitrarily implement them during the unsettled social and political situation of the early years of the revolution. The same holds true for the running of the *qäbälé* peasant associations, as well as the women and youth associations. Their views on villagisation, resettlement, national military service and producers' cooperatives were not solicited, either.

Frankly speaking, the idea of holding unrestricted and free discussion with peasants does not occur to most officials. They do not even envisage the worst scenario and try to benefit from the views of peasants. For example, let us say they knew for sure that they were going to implement the villagisation programme whether peasants liked it or not. Why did not they frankly tell them this, and then ask their opinion on how to implement this very policy which peasants found despicable? They would have naturally and surely come up with suggestions which would in the end have been less damaging to them and more honourable to the officials themselves.[1]

Peasants do not, of course, hold open and free discussions of their own in a community which they know is infested with spies of various tags (ነጭ ለባሽ፥ ፈርማቶሪ፥ ፀጥታ፥ ደህንነት፥ ...) and cadres of all kinds of fake ideologies (fake of course, as far as the peasants are concerned) who visit them to order them around and to assemble them and shower them with a barrage of orders from the central seat of power. So peasants quietly "obey" while expressing their views on various issues in oral literature.

I think the issue has an important bearing on all our social, economic and political problems. The arrogant attitude of the officials on the one hand and the extraordinary tolerance of peasants on the other come out as a dominant feature of the discourse in the poems found in the collections cited above. My interview with some elderly peasants and a close examination of the multitude of couplets, sayings and narratives have led me to think that these are fundamental issues that need to be addressed as soon as possible. The hide-and-seek game or the *Samna—warq* (wax and gold) palaver between government officials and peasants must be, to say the least, drastically reduced. Why I am saying this will be clear from my discussion of the jokes and poems below. Even if my discussion focuses on the days of the Derg and Mengistu, I am certain that there are relevant lessons to be drawn by those in power now.

I will start with the particular and proceed to the general issues I mentioned in passing above. Discussing "Mengistulore"—the folklore told around the personality of Mengistu—is closely entwined with the history of the Derg. The jokes and oral poems told about him are many. I will be very selective in my presentation here and keep the rest for a larger work on folklore and governance in Ethiopia.

One of the earliest jokes I heard about the 1974 Revolution in Ethiopia and which I have remembered since that time was the one told about democratic rights.

Joke 1. *At the outbreak of the Revolution the leading figures of the Derg were three in number. Since their wives come from modest families they think of buying new clothes appropriate for the new status they now hold in society. They enter one of the biggest shops in Addis and ask the owner to bring down from the shelves various clothes that pleased their eyes. The man has to go up and down the ladder repeatedly bringing down some and returning others. In the process, he farts. The three women hold their noses and say "What a shame! What a disgrace!". The man, standing high up on the ladder and looking down at the ladies, retorts angrily, "Your husbands sit at the palace and zip my mouth. And here you are in my owSn shop trying to zip my ass!".*

This was perhaps the first pointer at what was to happen, at least for over 15 years of the Derg period. When the revolution erupted there were many voices which indicated the direction they thought and wished it should take. Perhaps the loudest of these was the voice of the Ethiopian Student Movement whose left wing propensities were quite well known. The Derg on the other hand was composed of soldiers, mainly of low ranking officers, with different educational, social and political background. Another

---

1. Although I translate most of the jokes and couplets cited in this article, I occasionally give the Amharic version for the benefit of Ethiopian readers so that they can get a direct feel of the intended message.

joke that was told at about the same time as the one above described the chairman and two vice-chairmen of the Derg as a confused group. It might also represent the state of affairs during the early phase of the revolutionary process.

Joke 2. *Teferi, Atnafu and Mengistu are driving about in the city with a chauffeur. When they come to a roundabout the driver asks which way he should go. Mengistu replies: "Go to the left!" Atnafu says: "Go to the right!" Teferi adds: "Indicate to the left and go to the right!"*

The joke demonstrates the ideological difference between the two vice chairmen of the Derg and the conciliatory view of the chairman, Teferi. Likewise, there was an earlier joke which depicted all of them as loyal servants of Emperor Haile Sellassie. It goes as follows

Joke 3. *Teferi, Atnafu and Mengistu are taking a walk in the palace after dinner. Teferi slips and immediately says* "የጠቃ አሽከር" *(a customary invocation meaning "servant of Teqel!"; Teqel was Haile Sellassie's horse's name). Teferi gets embarrassed by his own utterance. Since he is not sure whether Atnafu and Mengistu heard him, he asks Atnafu: "Did you hear what I just said?" Atnafu replies "I swear by the name of Teferi, I have not heard". "Teferi" here refers to Haile Sellassie as this was his name before his coronation). When Mengistu is asked in turn, he replies "I swear by the name of Haile Selassie, I have not heard what you said".*

These then are the images of the three persons elected by the 120-man Derg to lead the country at the time of revolution. The joke suggests that the revolution has ironically fallen into the hands of loyal servants of the regime.

There was also a joke that scoffed at the alleged commitment of these leaders to alleviating the economic problems of the Ethiopian people.

Joke 4. *The three are travelling in a helicopter. Teferi looks down at the farms below and says: "If I drop ten berr from here I will make ten farmers happy."*

Atnafu follows the lead and says: "If I drop fifty berr it will make fifty farmers happy."

Mengistu says with an air of confidence and commitment: "If I drop a hundred berr a hundred peasants will be happy."

The pilot turns around, looks at them, and adds: "If I drop the three of you the entire population will be happy."

Their inane solutions to the problem of poverty are sneered at by the pilot who figures here as the voice of opposition to the regime.

When Mengistu's name started to figure in political conversations, rumours began depicting the man as the most revolutionary officer among the members of the Derg. When he started appearing on television and at public meetings jokes portraying his physical features and his educational background became common.

Joke 5. *Three members of the Derg go to depose Haile Sellassie. They politely tell the emperor that it would be good for him and the country if he relinquished his power. The Emperor agrees with their proposition and says "If you can bring* ብስል ሰው *(literally, "a well cooked person" but meaning "a mature person") We are willing to give up Our throne." The next day the delegation returns to the palace and presents Mengistu to the Emperor. The monarch, looking penetratingly at Mengistu, says "But this one is more than cooked, he is badly burnt."*

This is a common commentary, often of bad taste, made especially by highlanders while talking about persons of darker complexion. On the surface describing him as a person with a "badly burnt face" seems to be simply talking about the blackness of his skin. Underneath it all, however, the statement alludes to the low birth and inferior status of Mengistu. In short, the emperor is literally calling Mengistu a slave and hence incapable of occupying a throne which "naturally" belongs to members of the "Tribe of Judah", that is men of royal blood. We know that the distasteful word ባሪያ (slave) was often used as a nickname for Mengistu among his own officials and in the community at large.

There is another story which associates his physical features with his character and political deeds and depicts him as an extra-terrestrial being of supernatural properties.

Joke 6. *A woman takes her sick child to various hospitals but gets no remedies. Neighbours advise her to consult a famous local medicine man, who prescribes a big photograph of the devil and advises her to put this under the mattress of the sick child. The woman searches for the picture of the devil all over the market but fails. It dawns on her that she might as well use Mengistu's photograph for the purpose. Unfortunately the child dies. She goes back to the medicine man and tells him what happened and why. Alarmed he holds his head with his two hands and admonishingly says "Why did not you tell me before using his photograph? ... You know what you did?... You killed the baby with an overdose!!! That photograph was too much even for an adult!!!"*

His educational background is also ridiculed in different jokes. I will cite two of them here.

Joke 7. *In the early days of the revolution the Provisional Military Administrative Council (PMAC, otherwise known as the Derg) was recruiting educated persons to work with it. One day Mengistu was interviewing two returnees from Europe and the following discussion ensued:*
Returnee No.1: "Comrade Chairman, I just completed my M.Sc...."
Returnee No.2: "I also finished my M.A., sir!..."
To which Major Mengistu retorted: "Oh Comrades! We are all in good shape! I too have an M-one!!"

"M-1" is the name of a semi-automatic rifle popular in the army at the time.

Here is another one which delineates a worse Mengistu than the one just depicted above.

Joke 8. *Castro was narrating his experience with taxi drivers in Addis. He had difficulty communicating with them in English. When he talked to the first one in English the only response that came from the driver was "Eh?..." So he could not bring him to the palace. The second one said "Yes" but did not understand what Castro wanted.*

The third one said "OK" and took Castro to the palace. Castro asked Mengistu to explain this mystery. Mengistu was more than happy to explain this. The first one, he said, who replied with only an "Eh? "has completed grade eight. The second one was a tenth grader. The last one who said "Ok!" and drove him to the palace had completed his secondary school education. Surprised with what he heard, Castro exclaimed: "Oh, is that so?" Mengistu replied "Eh?"

Some time after Mengistu had consolidated his power, many jokes began to appear, focusing on Mengistu the man, Chairman of PMAC and the Commission for Organizing the Party of the Working People of Ethiopia (COPWE), Commander-in-Chief of the Armed Forces. Some of these depicted the power he had amassed, the confidence he had developed and the disillusion-ment he experienced with himself, his government, his party and the various policies they pursued.

Joke 9. *Mengistu Haile Mariam, dressed like an ordinary person, enters a small tea shop in a village on the outskirts of Addis Ababa. He asks for tea and the owner returns with a cup of tea and a battery. Mengistu, looking at the battery, says: "I ordered only tea." The owner replies: "Hey JO! When I went to the qäbälé service cooperative shop I too had asked for only sugar. However, they said that I could not buy sugar only. I had to buy some batteries with it."*

Joke 10. *A hungry person living by a river goes fishing for his lunch. He catches a reasonably big fish and goes home happy. When he arrives he discovers he has no oil. He goes to the qäbälé shop, the only one around, to buy some. Unfortunately for him they have none. As he returns home disappointed, he decides to put the fish back in the river. He throws it into the water and starts walking back to his house. Immediately, he hears a loud shout of merriment: "Viva Mengistu!!! Long Live the Revolution!!!" (It is the fish expressing its gratitude to Mengistu and the revolution for creating shortages of oil and thus sparing its life.)*

These two jokes ridicule the shortages and the regulations governing the distribution of consumer goods in the qäbälé shops in the city and the rural areas.

As in Joke 9, Mengistu in another joke travels among the common folk to get to know what they think about him, his government and party.

Joke 11. *A film about the victories of the Revolution was being shown at the cinemas in town. Mengistu went to Cinema Ethiopia incognito to see how the audience reacted when he appeared on the screen. When his image came into view the spectators clapped their hands with incredible vigour and loudness. The man sitting next to Mengistu was also applauding with apparently wild excitement. Mengistu nudged the person and asked him: "Do they really like him that much?" The man avoided the nudge with anger and replied: "Look buddy, are you going to clap or are you going to sit there asking silly questions and getting both of us in trouble?" and continued applauding with even more agitation.*

Joke 12. *Two months after the establishment of COPWE, Colonel Mengistu dresses like a Moslem and sets out on a journey to different parts of the country to assess public response to this event that he considers historic. He takes a taxi from Revolution Square and drives to Bole International Airport. As they approach the airport Mengistu realises that he has forgotten one of his suitcases at the point he took the taxi. He politely asks the driver to take him back. He finds the luggage at exactly the same spot he left it. Stunned by this fact, he says to the driver: "This is incredible!!! I never thought I would find my suitcase. Ethiopia has really changed. Thanks to the Revolution, there are no more thieves on our streets!!!" The driver replies: " You are one hundred per cent right! Since many of the thieves joined Mengistu's commission for the Party, thank God, the streets are relatively much safer now than they were some months ago."*

Joke 13. *On Revolution Day, Revolution Square is very crowded. Guests and members of the diplomatic corps are also heading towards the square. Security staff are waiting alertly for Mengistu's arrival. One of the security personnel observes a donkey lying in the middle of the road by the Estifanos church. This is the road Mengistu will drive along to take his position on the tribune. Security staff try to drive away the donkey but it will not budge an inch. They kick it severely in the hope of making it run away because of the pain. Then they try to pull it away from the street. However, they cannot remove it. They start worrying because they hear motorcycle sirens heralding Mengistu's arrival. A young man who is watching the drama approaches the security staff and volunteers to help them. He bends down and whispers a few words in the donkey's ear. The donkey suddenly jumps up and runs towards the church. Everyone is astonished by the act. The security chief calls the young man and asks him how he did it. The lad approaches the chief and whispers: "I told the donkey that if she does not clear off she will be made a member of the Workers' Party of Ethiopia. That's all I said to her."*

In Joke 11, we see that people cheer their leaders not because they love and respect them but because they fear them and the oppressive power machine they wield. In 12 and 13 the much-trumpeted party is not only disparaged by humans, but it is even scoffed at by an animal generally considered to be stupid. Mengistu's secret journeys in some of these jokes make him taste the bitter fruit of his own policies. They are intended to show that the inflated assumptions and opinions he had about himself, his government and party are, to say the least, groundless. It is interesting to note that whenever Mengistu is portrayed as an ordinary individual participating in ordinary conversations, in these circumstances, he becomes both the object of the joke and witness to his own atrocities without the knowledge of the other character in the conversation. And the hero in the jocular anecdote comes out unscathed by the real Mengistu who is the villain of the joke.

I believe such jokes are first told in the cities. It is also very likely that they are first told by the educated sector of the community that may have created them or adapted them from other sources. There is reason to suspect that a good number of them may have been modified to fit the Ethiopian situation from jokes in the contemporaneous socialist countries. I have presented them here to give the reader a taste of the panorama of political life depicted in one of the genres of oral literature. Most of them are self-evident especially to Ethiopians who lived through those testing times in the country's history, and to social science scholars who have researched and/or read about them. As I tell these jokes now, I personally feel that time has softened their cutting edge. Of course, they cannot have the same force today as they did when they were told when the actual target of the jokes threatening everyone's survival was still in power. However, we cannot deny that these jokes have captured the spirit of the times.

Let us now turn to the major policies of Mengistu and his government that deeply affected the rural community, and the reactions of peasants to these policies.

One of the major goals of the land reform proclamation which came out in 1975 under the title "Public Ownership of Rural Lands Proclamation" was to completely transform the prevailing landlord-tenant relationship by abolishing what it called feudal oppression and establishing a new set of relations based on public ownership of land. It also aimed at boosting agricultural production, contributing towards the creation of work for the rural population, narrowing the gap in income and wealth primarily by distributing rural land. Generally speaking, creating opportunities for rural development was an important component of the Proclamation. Immediate and jubilant reactions of peasants to the Proclamation are recorded in many oral poems that openly expressed their admiration and support to the Derg and its leaders. Among the early ones I shall cite some from Rassa (in Northern Shäwa)

Couplet 01
የመሬት ከበርቴ እርግጣችሁን አውጡ
ታፍኛ የኖረ መጣ ቅብጥብጡ
(Oh! landlords do cry in despair
The valiant peasant, stifled for ages,
Has now risen.)

Couplet 02
ጀግናው አባ ደርጉ ሰፊ ነው ደረቱ
መቶ አምሳ ነው ጡቱ
ጠሬፍ እስከ ጠሬፍ የሚያጠባቱ
(The gallant Derg's large chest has many teats
With which he feeds people from periphery to periphery.)

Couplet 03
ተለቀቀ ብለን ደርጉንም አናማ
የካብታሙን መሬት ሰጥቶን በጉልማ
(We would not scold the Derg
Because it lost its authority;
For it had given the poor the right to farm
The arable land of the wealthy.)

I was told by my informants that the first two couplets were sang following the Proclamation to communicate their pleasure with and approval of the Derg. It was also to declare the awakening and emergence of the poor peasant from years of oppression. The Derg and its Land Proclamation were instrumental for the new lease of life the rural poor began to enjoy. The third couplet I recorded in 1992, about a year after EPRDF took power, further indicates the depth of feeling, appreciation and gratitude that persists up to now.

Peasants of Qobbo Wäräda in Wällo were predominantly tenants during Haile Sellassie's reign. Because of the rights the land proclamation of 1975 gave them they glorified the Derg. They also supported the Proclamation because it made land the property of the people.

Couplet 04

እንግዲህ ባላባት እግዚር ይሁንህ
እንግዲህ ወረሴ እግዚር ይሁንህ
እንግዲህ ተክሌዋ እግዚር ይሁንህ
መሬት አልተገኘም መንደላቀቂያህ (ሞላ፥66)

(Oh landlord, may God help you!
Oh Wärräsèh, may God help you!
Oh dear Teklé, may God help you!
For the land is no more
That used to pay for your lavish expenses.)

According to the informants, the *Wärräsèh* (another name for members or descendants of the Yajju dynasty) owned most of the land in the *wäräda* and especially in the sub-*wäräda* known as Gura Wärqè, and Täklè was one of the persons who bought and owned large private farms in the area (Molla,1993:17). The above couplet is happily announcing the end of the extravagant life for these wealthy persons and their like.

During the reign of Haile Sellassie, land was held communally in many districts in Northern Ethiopia. Each member of a family in these districts had the right to farm on a plot of land that belonged to the head of the family wherever this plot might be. He had the right to trace his lineage any time and obtain his share. However, he could not sell this land or transfer it in any form to someone outside the family. If he died, only his sons had the right to use it. Although land was communally owned it did not mean that everybody in these districts had an equal share of land. Some had bigger plots than others. Those who belonged to or associated themselves with the nobility owned larger plots of land.

The land proclamation of 1975 had significant impact on this tradition and on agrarian relations in the rest of the country. It was proclaimed that "...all rural lands shall be the collective property of the Ethiopian people" (Proclamation No. 31 of 1975: 94). All persons above the age of 18 were promised a plot of land sufficient for their livelihood. On the other hand well to do farmers had to give away some of their land to those who had very small plots and those who had none at all. Moreover it was declared that all farming families should have equal plots of land, as far as possible, and the productivity of land and local conditions should be taken into consideration during land distribution. The Proclamation also had provisions for the establishment of peasant associations at *wäräda*, *awraja* and provincial levels.

One of the principal tasks of peasant associations at the *qäbälé* level was distributing land to its members as evenly as possible. Of course the population of a *qäbälé*, the availability of sufficient land to fulfill the needs of this population, the quality of land available and its location were bound to influence significantly the very act of distribution. That is why we find poems criticising the manner of distribution.

Couplet 05)

እጃችን አውጥተን የመረጥነው ዳኛ
ጉድጓዲቱን ለእሱ ገጣጢትን ለእኛ (ሞላ፥55)

(The judge we elected raising our hands
Took godgwadit for himself and left gätatit for us.)

Couplet 06

ለገመድ ነታቹ ጠጅ ያጠጣ ሰው
ደልዳላውን መሬት ይኽው አረሰው (ሞላ፥?)

(He who bought täjj for the holder of the measuring rope
Ploughed the deldala plot.)

Couplet 07
የኮሚቴ ውሻ እንቅልፍም አይተኛ
ሲለፈልፍ ያድራል እንደ በሽተኛ(ሙሉጌታ፥93)
(The dog of the Committee has no sleep
Throughout the night it barks like a sick man.)

Couplet 08
መሬት ለኮሚቴ መንግስት አምና ሰጥቶ
ተቸበቸብ አሉ ገበያ ወጥቶ::
(Having trusted committee members
Government gave them jurisdiction over land
Look, they are selling it openly at the market.)

In the above couplets committee members elected to lead the community and distribute land are seen favouring themselves. Though they were elected to work in the interest of the electorate they are found taking advantage of their positions by taking the best plots for themselves. Hence the complaints in couplets such as the ones quoted above.

The land referred to as "ገጣጢት(getatit)" in couplet 05 is a very difficult plot to plough because it is rocky. On the other hand "ጉድጓዲት(godguwadit)" and "ዳልዳላ"(däldala) in couplet 05 and 06 respectively are soft, fertile land which are easy to plough and give a good yield unlike the former "ገጣጢት"(getatit) which demands hard labour but gives poor results.

Though selling land is prohibited by the proclamation, couplet 08 states that land was sold like hot cakes. This is to show the level of financial deals committee members struck. Moreover, as indicated in couplet 07, were paid secretly, preferably during the night.

Couplet 09
ደህና ደህና መሬት ባሀርዛፍ ለበሰ
የሚያርሰው አጥቶ ድሃ እያለቀሰ (ሞላ፥ ገፅ 56)
(Fertile land is covered with eucalyptus
While the poor cry in need of land for farming.)

Sometimes it sounds as if it is sheer jealousy or evil nature that prevents the peasant leaders from distributing the good plots of land to others. According to the above couplet fertile land is left unploughed while farmers are struggling with the rocky parts of the land in the community. Maybe it was kept aside for those who could afford to pay fat bribes. However, since these were generally few in number and in all probability had all taken their share already, the best land was often left unproductive because a *qäbälé* chief was waiting for a generous bribe.

These and other experiences force the peasants to retract their earlier glorifying poems and to replace them with those criticising the whole system. This time they refrain from mentioning names of known personalities of the times since it is dangerous to do so. So they speak in general terms and keep the more direct ones until the collapse of the regime itself.

Couplet 10
ምን ያለ ጊዜ ነው የጊዜ ጨብራራ
አይን ያለው ቁጭ ብሎ እውር እያመራ
ከምኔልክ ወዲያ አሳየንም አጤ
መንደሩን ዝዞ የማንም ወጠጤ (ሞላ፥ገፅ 8)
(What a time! An epoch of blinding light!

Where the blind lead, while the knowledgeable sit idle;
We have not seen a real leader since Menilek
The villages are governed by juvenile fools. (Molla, 1993: 08)

The poet goes back to the reign of Emperor Menelik and admires the days of his rule. He states that the days of good governance and justice had gone with him. Even Emperor Haile Sellassie was not spared from criticism, albeit indirectly, in the couplet above.

One of the ways of showing one's resentment under circumstances such as these was by resorting to voluntary migration, in the case of Wällo usually to Awsa. Not finding sufficient reason for staying in his native village because the land allotted to him was rocky and could produce nothing worthwhile, the peasant laments:

Couplet 11

ምን ያለ ጊዜ ነው የጊዜ ጨብራራ
አይን ያለው ቄጭ ብሉ እውር እየመራ
ከምኔልክ ወዲያ አላየንም አጤ
መንደሩን ገዟቸው የማንንም ወጠጤ   (ሞላ፥ገፅ 8)

(Having nothing to bribe the chairman with
I am heading for Asayta leaving my relatives behind;
Let me proceed to Asayta, towards the cotton farms
Since the fertile land of my village
Has been grabbed by the Committee.)

There are also poems that censure the forcible contributions made to the All-Ethiopia Peasant Association (AEPA), Revolutionary Ethiopia Women's Association (REWA), Revolutionary Ethiopia Youth Association (REYA) and other irregular impositions.

Couplet 12

አሥራትን ከፍዬ ማይገማ ቀርቶኛል
ማይገማ ከፍዬ አይመማ ቀርቶኛል
አይመማ ከፍዬ አይሴማ ቀርቶኛል
አይሴማ ከፍዬ ጎንጎን ቀርቶኛል
ለሁሉም ከፍዬ አንድ ብር ቀርታኝ
ጨው አምሮኝ ልበሳ አይኔ ሲቃበበብ
ያቺንም ወሰዱት ለተማሪ ቀለብ(ሙሉጌታ፥ 103)

(Having paid my tithe I still have to pay for AEPA
Having paid for AEPA I still have to pay for REYA
Having paid for REYA I still have to pay for REWA
Having paid for REWA I still have to pay for the "Side-by-Side"
Having paid for all, I am left with only one berr
Craving for a bite, with the flavouring of salt
They snatched my only berr
As contribution for literacy.)

After paying his taxes and various contributions to peasant, women and youth associations the peasant has very little left for living on. The contribution described in the poem as "Side-by-Side" (the Amharic term is literally translated here) refers to the more irregular contributions for drought and famine, and those for national unity and sovereignty (Mulugeta, 1992: 31). It can be concluded from this and many other similar poems that the peasant livelihood is always threatened by forced contributions and donations.

Another major proclamation focusing on the improvement of rural life is the one concerned with establishing cooperatives throughout the country. It seems that the idea of setting up cooperative farms was officially initiated on December 13, 1974 when the PMAC declared Ethiopia socialist. It was also directly mentioned and an article provided for it in the "Peasant Associations Organization and Consolidation Proclamation" of 1975. This document defines the Agricultural Producers' Co-operative Society as "...a society that is established voluntarily by peasant associations" (p. 109, emphasis mine). When the actual proclamation for instituting it appeared in March 1978 under the title "A Proclamation for the Establishment of Cooperative Societies" its structure and objectives had been elaborated.

The organization was established to satisfy the needs of its members, and to make them self-reliant by building socialism, enhancing and sustaining economic development, expanding industries, increasing production, conducting political agitation, and eradicating customs regarded as reactionary. Bringing the means of production under the control of cooperatives and gradually making them collective property was also one of the major aims; this was thought to facilitate the journey from "feudalism" to socialism.

The 1978/79 Guide (የ1971 ዓ.ም መመሪያ) for Peasant Associations declared that peasants should pool their resources, i.e. instruments of labour and land, together and work as members of producers' cooperatives. Although the aims and goals indicated in Proclamation No 31/1975 and the Guide sounded positive, their application left much that was objectionable to peasants. Those who did not want to join the cooperatives expressed their grievances as follows:

Couplet 13
አሁን ገና መጣ የደርገቹ ጉድ
መሬት አንድ አርጋችሁ እረሱ በግድ
ተሠፈረ ግላው በረጅም ገመድ
ማን ጠይቆት ደሀን ቢጠላ ቢወድ
(Now comes the unmentionable villainy of the Derg,
Forcing us to plough the land in common.
The field is measured with a long rope;
Who bothers about consulting the poor man,
On whether he prefers this or not?)

Couplet 14
እንኳን ዉት ተጠምዶ ቢጠመድ በግታ
ግላኝ አይደለም ወይ የሚያያላ ኮታ::
ግላኛው ገራ የተንገበገበ
ኮታውን አሟልቶ ገበያው ጠገበ
(Who is it that fulfils the quota?
Is it not the gelläsäb
Even if the ploughing started toward evening
Let alone in the morning?
The bustling and industrious gelläsäb
Not only meets his quota,
But also keeps the market fully stocked.)

Couplet 15
አምራች አምራች አሉ ስሙ ነው አምራች
ይበተን የለም ወይ ነገ ሲሰለች::

("Producers! Producers!" they cried,
"Producers!" they called;
But aren't they going to disperse
When tomorrow they get bored.)

Nowhere in the proclamation of March 1978 is it declared that joining any of the co-operatives is compulsory. In fact Article Section 1 states that "Farmers in a peasant association *may form* agricultural producers' cooperatives" (p. 42, Emphasis mine). Moreover, as pointed out earlier, it is clearly spelt out in the Proclamation of 1975 that cooperatives are to be organised *voluntarily*. However, there are many critical poems, like the ones cited in numbers 13, 14 and 15, told and sung about these cooperatives. The first complains that the Derg formed cooperatives without consulting the peasants. It states that they were imposed on the community. In the second couplet, aware of the full support promised and provided to cooperatives by the government, the poet confidently declares that peasants who have joined cooperatives are less productive than gelläsäb (private peasant farmers) despite the avenues to services and credit open to them and despite the favourable allocation of fertile land to them.

Perhaps poems depicting the cooperatives at Yetnora are exceptions to this general sentiment. According to Fentaneh and Lakew, Getie's informants, the Yetnora agricultural producers' cooperative in Gojjam (Däbärmarqos, Däjän wäräda) "...was established on April 2, 1979 with 20 members, on a land area of 50 hectares, with 34 oxen...Their initial capital was 11,600 Birr" (Getie,1994:70). Getie writes that, as early as January 1981, the head of state offered his assistance in the area for building planned villages supplied with clean water and a machine for producing oil. Most of this had materialised by 1985. Getahun also indicates that encouraging results were seen in the cooperative by 1984/1985 (p. 65). Getie further states, mentioning three other studies on Yetnora, that "... the peasants of Yetnora received various forms of aid including tractors, fertilizers, selected seeds, farm, oxen, milk cows, building materials, and cash credit from the MOA, AMC, UNICEF, ILCA[1] and other organizations and institutions"(p. 75–76). In short, it was the most favoured cooperative in the country enjoying the political and economic support of the government and some international organisations. Moreover, the personal attention and continuous moral support of President Mengistu Hailemariam helped Yetnora to develop an image of a model for cooperatives in the country. No wonder that it drew the attention of various delegates from socialist countries.

However, things were not as rosy as they were proclaimed to be. Many member peasants were disappointed with the cooperative because of the corruption that was gradually spreading in the organisation. It is interesting, therefore, to examine a few poems that reflect the formation, development and demise of the Yetnora Cooperative. I shall cite especially from Getahun (1992) and Getie (1994) because their collections largely focus on that cooperative. In these poems we hear many voices portraying the complicated events and attitudes of peasants in Yetnora and its environs while the government media were unashamedly and blindly glorifying Yetnora and cooperatives in the country at large.

---

1.   Ministry of Agriculture, Agricultural Marketing Corporation, United Nations International Children's and Educational Fund, International Livestock Center for Africa.

Couplet 16
በወጀል ያላችሁ በእነቢ ያላችሁ በደጀን ያላችሁ
አምራች ተመሥርቷል እንኳን ደስ ያላችሁ(ጌታሁን÷99፤ ጌቴ÷265)
*(Those of you at Wäjäl, Ennäbi and Däjän
Congratulations! Cooperatives are formed)*

Couplet 17
የግብርና አደራጅ ሌቦችን ሰብስቦ
መሬት ለካላቸው ዙሪያውን አካቦ(ጌታሁን÷80)
*(The gebrenna organiser gathered thieves
Moved round the farms and measured land for them)*

In couplet 16 a congratulatory message is sent to peasants residing in Wäjäl, Ennäbi and Däjän who were in the process of establishing cooperatives whereas in 17 the poem desribes peasants organised in cooperatives as thieves. The organisers, here called gebrenna, are employees of the Ministry of Agriculture working with peasants in rural Ethiopia. Each side expressed its views on the very idea of establishing cooperatives more strongly and more freely than was presented in the media. The exchange of opinions in the form of insults, angry derisive remarks, and indecent comments seem to have continued, until the cooperatives dispersed, whenever important controversial issues related to cooperatives cropped up. In the next two couplets we observe members of the newly established cooperatives at Yetnora extending their gratitude for the support they were given, and stressing their determination to strengthen their organisation.

Couplet 18
ግብርናም ለገሠን ምርጥ ዘር እህል
መንግሥቱም ላከልን ማረሻ ወገል
እንግዲህ ምን ቀረን በሉ እንታገል
እድሜ ለአምራች እያልን እንበል እልል።።
(ጌታሁን÷ 99፤ ተቀራራቢ እጌቴ÷ 262)
*(Gebrenna gave us choice seeds
Mengistu sent us farming tools
What remains now except to struggle?
Let us ululate wishing long life to cooperatives.)*

Couplet 19
በልጅግ ጠመንጃ ደርጉ ሸልሞህ
በህብረት ሁነህ ምን ትፈራለህ
ሆ በል አምራች ታሸንፋለህ(ጌታሁን÷102፤ ተቀራራቢ እጌቴ÷ 286)
*(The Derg has awarded you the gun called Beljig
Now that you are united what are you afraid of?
Say Hooray! members of the Cooperative, you will win.)*

According to couplet 19 members were not only supplied with fertilisers, quality seeds, large plots of fertile farms and farming tools as incentives; they were also issued arms to defend themselves and their new organization. Such care and attention definitely endowed the cooperatives with an attractive image and gave impetus to the efforts to recruit members. The achievements documented in many couplets confirm this proposition.

Couplet 20
አስመራ አዲስ አበባ(?) ምን ያረጋል ማርቆስ
ይበልጣል የትኖራ አለው ግርማ ሞገስ(ጌታሁን፥107፤   ጌቴ፥267)

(What worth do Asmara, Addis Ababa, and Däbrä Marqos have!?
Yetnora, the majestic one, excels.)

Couplet 21
ደጇንን ከተማ ከተማ ብለሺው
ማርቆስን ከተማ ከተማ ብለሺው
የእንዳይላሉን ሰፈር የትኖራን ባየሽው" (ጌታሁን፥103፤ ጌቴ፥268)

(You call Däjän a city?
You call Marqos a city?
I wish you saw Yetnora, Endaylalu's settlement!!!)

Couplet 22
ማን አስቦት ነበር እንዲህ ያለ ጉድ
በገበሬው ነጆ ኮረንቲ ማንደድ
እንዲህ ግለኛ ምንድን ታልም ታስብ
ስልክና ኮረንቲ እንደፀሀይ ሲያብብ (ጌታሁን፥103ና 104፤ ጌቴ፥ 263)

(Who had ever thought of this miracle?
Electric light in a peasant hut!!!
Now gelläñña what would you contrive?
When telephone and electricity radiate like the sun.)

Yetnora is interestingly compared with Däjän, Däbrä Marqos, formerly capital of Goj-jam province, and even with Asmara and Addis Ababa. Obviously, the poet is trying to indicate the extent of change that took place at the once dark rural village of Yetno-ra. Installing piped water, telephone lines and electricity there might have never been thought of at all had it not been for the political and exemplary value of the Yetnora Cooperative. No wonder that the poet who witnessed these transformations responded with jubilation. No wonder, either, that he was elated by the performance of the peas-ant farmer. The appreciation communicated in the following two couplets suggests the potential development of the peasant.

Couplet 23
በዘመናዊ እርሻ ያውም በትራክተር
ገበሬው አጨደ ወቃ በኮምባይነር(ጌታሁን፥104፤ጌቴ፥263)

(With modern farming, using a tractor,
The farmer harvested and thrashed with a combiner.)

Couplet 24
አምራቹ ገበሬ ያውለኝ ካንተ ጋር
መኪና እንደበሬ ከምትነዳው ጋር(ጌታሁን፥105)

(Farmer of Yetnora,
You, who drive a tractor like an ox,
Let my sojourn be with you.)

The whole idea of driving, particularly middle sized cars and big trucks, was previous-ly seen as nothing short of a miracle by peasants. The fact that farmers themselves were able to drive tractors and combiners must have been astonishing at first sight.

To conclude this part of the paper I shall simply quote three couplets composed to depict the dissolution of the cooperative.

Couplet 25

እንግዲህ ግለሰብ እንኳን ደስ ያለሀ
የአምራቾች ማህበር ተበተነልህ(ጌታሁን÷111፤ጌቴ÷285)

(Congratulations! gelläsäb[1]
Producers' cooperatives are dissolved.)

Couplet 26

የኔው እንዳይላሉ እግዚአብሔር ያጥናሀ
አምራች ፈረሰና ጉቦ ቀረብህ(ጌታሁን፤111፤ጌቴ÷266 በግም ተቀራራቢ)

(My dear Endaylalu, may God console you!
Cooperatives are dissolved, bribes are no more.)

Couplet 27

እኛ ምን ቸገረን ያ መጣ ያ መጣ
አምራቹ ፈረስ የማታ የማታ(ጌቴ÷270)

(That one came and then that one
But why should we bother?
Our concern is that ultimately
Cooperatives are disbanded.)

Couplet 28

እሁድም ታረስ ቅዳሜም ታረስ
ትዝብቱ ነው እንጄ አምራቹ ፈረስ(ጌታሁን፤114፤ጌቴ÷270)

(It was ploughed on Sunday,
It was ploughed on Saturday, too,
All that did not save cooperatives from breaking up.)

We have tried to show briefly that the two contending groups sing for or against the government and its officials depending on what they believe they have done for or against producers' cooperatives. Getahun has collected 163 poems speaking against producers' cooperatives and 97 extolling them. When the cooperatives were dismantled poems celebrating their dismemberment were sung. Sixty-six of these are documented in Getahun's thesis. These, I think, belong to the 163 poems mentioned above, since they express boundless delight at the ultimate destruction of the cooperatives in the area. Since Getie's 388 poems are not classified by the topics they treat I am unable to easily comment on their content as I have done on Getahun's. I shall, however, come back to this issue sometime in the future.

I must conclude this paper by introducing some of the poems that deal with villagization, one of the measures the Derg took, perhaps to make up for the failure of its policy of forming cooperatives, in the name of transforming rural life and economy. My principal informants in Rasa (Northern Shäwa), Zeqé and Agonafer, stated that they were told that the basic aim of the villagization campaign was to bring people together to sites where they could comfortably share various resources and common services. They both believed that the idea was a noble one. However, the problem, as usual, arose when the local officials tried to apply this arbitrarily. They forcibly moved people from where they had lived peacefully for years without asking for their consent.

Moreover no preparations were made to make the new sites habitable. The officials seem to have applied the rule of a negative incentive when they forced them to demol-

---

1. *Individual farmers (who had not joined a cooperative).*

ish their houses before building new ones. They must have thought that this would en-sure the establishment of the new village. Moreover they did not give the peasants enough time to prepare themselves psychologically. Of course, the idea of soliciting their views on the how, where and when did not generally arise. Under such circum-stances values are bound to clash. The anger, the criticism, and the traumas of the bro-ken heart are depicted in many oral poems at the time.

Couplet 29
የመንግስቱን መምሪያ እየተቀበልን
እዚህ ጋ ቤት ሠራን እዚህ ጋ አፍርሰን
(Following Mengistu's instructions,
We built a house here
Tearing down another there.)

Couplet 30
ደርጉ በተሾመ በ11 ዓመቱ
ቤት አፍርሱ ይላል እንደ ልጅነቱ
(Eleven years after the Derg came to power,
He says, "Tear down houses!!!"
Just like in his childhood.)

Couplets 29 and 30 constitute a critique of the villagization programme which peas-ants of Rasa portray as childish and ill-planned. Since the new sites did not have any new facilities, services and common resources and since there was hardly any change in locality, they believed the whole exercise defeated its purpose. The only thing it achieved was the grudging obedience of the peasants to the decisions of the cadres and officials. According to couplet 31, it seems that the fact the programme came soon af-ter the 1984/85 catastrophic famine from which the area was just recovering made matters worse. That they find the government's adeptness in concocting devices that torment people a puzzle is suggested in couplet 32.

Couplet 31
ቆላ ደጋ ብዬ አጉርጥን ብወጣ
ደግሞ የተባሰ ቤት አፍርሱ መጣ
(I tackled agurt roaming qolla and däga
Now has come a worse command
The "dismantle your house" bit.)

Couplet 32
እረ ደርጉ ደርጉ ቤት አፍርሱ ማለት አንተም አበዛኸው-ው
የሚጠላውን በምን አገኘኸው?
(Oh Derg! Where did you fetch
This "dismantle your house" business from?
How did you come across an idea the poor abhor?)

It is obvious that a house is not just four walls plus a roof and a floor. There is more to it than that. Memories of good and bad times are associated with the house, its loca-tion, neighbours and the environment at large. The longer one inhabits a dwelling at a certain location and with certain neighbours, the more one gets attached to them. Tear-ing down a house therefore is not a simple undertaking even when one tries to rebuild a house on the same land, in the same location and environment. One does not escape from a similar feeling of guilt as that arising from abandoning ones close friend or a long acquaintance. One can imagine how difficult departing from one's birth place and home is for the peasant who is least prepared psychologically. Couplets 33 and 34 express the utterly inconsiderate and irresponsible attitude of the officials to these psychological predicaments.

Couplet 33

አውራጃውም እውር ወረዳውም እውር
በሊውም እውር ሁሉም እውር ናቸው
የሚቀውን ጎጆ ይፍረስ ማለታቸው::
(ፈቃደ፥1984፤ሙ-ሉ-ጊታ፥1984፥449)

(The awraja is blind, the wäräda is blind,
So is the qäbälé. Blind they all are.
Because they give orders to wreck one's sweet home.)

Couplet 34

ቤት ይፍረስ አሉኑ፥ ልጅ የዳርንበትን፥ ጮጣ ያበላውን
ማፍረስ አልጋውን፥ ትኋን ያፈራውን(ሙ-ሉ-ጊታ፥98)

(They say we should demolish our homes
Homes where we wedded our children
Homes where we had great feasts
We say it is the bed that should be crushed
The bed that breeds bugs.)

There is a hidden meaning in the last line of the Amharic version of couplet 34, rendered here in the last two lines of the English version. The Amharic word "አልጋ" (bed) connotes "the seat of power" and "ትኋን"(bed bug) alludes to the corrupt authorities in power at all levels. Thus the poet longs for the demolition of their authority instead of the destruction of the huts of impoverished peasants.

Couplet 35

መንግስቱ ኃ/ማርያም የወለቴ ልጅ
ብድር አመላለስ እንደዚህ ነው እንጂ(ሙ-ሉ-ጊታ፥ 96)

(Mengistu Haile Mariam, son of a slave
How slick and polished you are in your revenge.)

Villagization is also pictured as an act of revenge committed by the head of government on the people. The poor peasants who dismantle the roofs of their own houses carry the materials to the new site in order to use them for building the new ones. This harrowing experience makes the poet in couplet 35 imagine this to be some vindictive act on the part of Mengistu.

Some of the poems catalogue the hardships the community has been going through year after year instead of simply bemoaning the events of villagization.

Couplet 36

መሬቱም ቢከፈል እችለው ነበር
እዳውም ቢበዛ እችለው ነበር
ጉ ሂዱ ቢሉንም እችለው ነበር
መጣ ሌላ ነገር ቤት አፍርሱ ማለት የሚያደናግር::

(If land were distributed, I could bear it
If debts were plenty, I could bear that too
If I have to go to the war front, I can bear this also
Asking me to tear down my own house
Is definitely the puzzle of puzzles.)

The four lines above perfectly record the injustice most Ethiopian peasants suffered because of the various policies the Derg imposed on them. Each line in the quartet alludes to a major maltreatment endured as a result of one proclamation, directive or another.

Conclusion

By way of summing up, let me mention the following points and reinforce the principal aim of this paper. I have tried to show that historical, political, literary and social science research has not put enough emphasis on oral literature. As pointed out elsewhere (see Fekade, 1997; 1998 and 1999), many researchers are either totally ignorant of the existence of this source of information or are yet unable to appreciate its potential for research. The couplets cited above show that peasants react, through the voice of their oral artists, to almost every important event in their social, political and economic life. My intention in presenting in this article so many poems and jokes is to further reveal to literary and social science researchers the wealth of material "quietly" waiting for them to exploit. Space has not permitted me a detailed analysis of many of the issues they raise.

Another point worth reflecting on concerns the general character of the poems. The poems change with the times and with the events that transpire. If a policy is good they do not hesitate to applaud it, and if they find it destructive they condemn it loudly. The Land Proclamation is a good example. The landless and tenants extol the Proclamation without reserve. On the other hand, the landed class denounces it with bitterness. There are others who speak about it guardedly, balancing (as it were) what they gained and lost. These varied voices are heard in the community. Moreover they are not fixed or stagnant. They change as new guidelines and directives influencing the practical applications of the Proclamation appear. The dialogue between various interest groups is always active and full of life. One needs to be there, at the *tälla, aräqi* and *täjj bét*,[1] at funerals, markets, weddings, *mahber*,[2] and public and religious holidays, to hear and feel these messages.

Drawing a brief analogy with the local media is interesting. When a proclamation comes out, the media generally respond with a chorus of admiration. They bore every person with common sense by telling him/her that the proclamation has been embraced by the people. One sometimes wonders who these people are. Because, as we have seen, the reactions of peasants who daily experience the proclamations and guidelines transmitted over the radio are multifarious. There seems to be more sober portrayal or more democratic dialogue in the oral poetry of peasants than in the image presented to them through government media. They should be laughing their heads off whenever the media tell them how they reacted to a certain proclamation. During the last two decades I have always wondered whether the media officials ever stop and think whom they are addressing. Surely they do not believe in most of what they report on issues pertaining to rural development. Many of them have one or two relatives in the rural areas who tell them their true thoughts and feelings about the state of affairs in the country. Government officials should also know from their private security

---

1. Local drinking places, where people meet—usually in the house of a single woman who prepares talla (local beer), araqi (local brandy) or täjj (honey wine).
2. A social or religious get together and a feasting occasion, usually arranged by a religious organization.

sources and relatives in the rural areas what the true responses of the people in the various regions of the country are. An examination of the collections of oral literature in my possession and those appended to many BA and MA theses reveals an ironic situation. The irony is that the government media, especially the radio, are transmitting biased and linear views untiringly to communities that are very advanced and complex.

When we come to the poems themselves we observe that opposition to a certain policy is often directed at the officials of the lower echelons. Oral poets find these officials partial, discriminating and corrupt in the implementation of policy. Partly, this is because the local officials are more familiar than the policy makers whom they do not see or know. The poems indicate that peasant reactions towards these local officials are often well considered and sober. On the other hand, there are cases where leaders like Haile Sellassie and Mengistu are absolved from blame.

Democratisation Process and Gender

Original Wolde Giorgis

Women in Ethiopia

The poorest of the poor in Ethiopia are women. Not all Ethiopian women may be poor; but among the poorest, the women are worst off. Many women are considered and treated as inferior in the family and mistreated by their husbands and male partners. They suffer injustice and maltreatment by various agents and mechanisms—such as tradition, culture, religion, justice administration bodies, police, prosecutors, judges and family arbitration tribunals.

One important criterion for democracy is participation for all citizens without differences and discrimination. Thus, the Constitution in Art. 25 clearly guarantees equality and makes any discrimination illegal, be it because of race, colour, sex, language, wealth, social status or other differences. This guarantee gives the state a special obligation to protect the vulnerable members of its society, and to guarantee equal access for the weak groups.

Women are a majority in the population. Nevertheless they are among the particularly weak and most vulnerable groups. They depend on men in the family and in traditional society. They suffer discrimination because of traditional attitudes and practices in the society and also in large parts of public opinion. They are disadvantaged in distribution of property even within the family; and they suffer from discrimination in the enforcement of law in judicial institutions.

Discrimination does not affect all women equally harshly. There are women who do not stand behind men in position and influence. But a majority are in no position to enforce their equal rights. And what is more important: discrimination is accepted in practice in public opinion. There is no reaction if women are discriminated, and many people consider it as "natural" that women should be inferior. But there is no justice in nature, nor a "natural" ranking order.

There are still some laws in force in Ethiopia which discriminate against women, though they are in conflict with constitutional guarantees. Nevertheless, Ethiopian women would be far better off today if all the policies and laws already enacted were strictly applied, despite the existence of discriminatory laws. The laws on paper and the reality on the ground, in society and in the law enforcement system, are two different things. Yet some of the abuses that ought to be prohibited by law are not in the law books, while those which are in the law are not applied. Laws that are not discriminatory on paper become discriminatory when applied to women. (For example, Civil Code Art. 645 (1) formally gives both spouses the right to object against the marriage partner practising his/her profession if it is considered detrimental for the family/household. In practice, women will hardly ever invoke this paragraph to prevent their husbands from any job. But it gives husbands a legal base to deny their wives a job and confine them to the household.)

Women are vulnerable in their economic dependence in addition to the burden of oppression imposed on them by culture and tradition. The disparity between the written law and its application has not made women beneficiaries of the democratisation process, whatever the rhetoric.[1]

The Disparity between Law and Life

If the legal situation today is compared to the realities of life, it shows clearly that women suffer multiple discriminations. The ideals as enshrined in the Constitution are far from being realised. Seeing the situation from the point of view of women, gives a gloomy picture of a democratic process which still has a long way to go before it could be considered reasonably established. Democracy is a process which is never finished or achieved once and for all. And a state can never be more democratic than the degree of protection and participation it offers to its weakest members.

Seeing Ethiopian democracy from the viewpoint of Ethiopian women, gives us thus a mirror in which to assess the degree to which democracy has succeeded in transcending and transforming social life. At the same time, it indicates one important dimension as to where the struggle for more democracy has to proceed. Every victory in the women's struggle for equal rights and freedom from discriminatory practice is a step towards more democracy.

We will in the following look at this issue from a very practical angle, describing and analysing a number of typical cases from the experience of the Ethiopian Women Lawyers Association (EWLA). In looking at individual cases which describe individual tragedies, we will face a series of questions of great importance for women today: Are there laws to protect the women? Is there a court system to defend their rights? If courts do not help, what other defence do women have? Is there a public opinion to which they can apply? Is there any organised activity to defend women? Is there room for women to defend their rights themselves? How are women met by society if they try to defend their rights by themselves? What can be done to change discriminatory laws? What can be done to change public awareness and attitudes?

This paper will not be able to answer all of these questions conclusively. But the practice of EWLA can at least contribute to solving some of the problems which are highlighted. In this short paper we will concentrate our focus on the deficiencies in the law from the point of view of protection of the most basic rights of women, and on the problems encountered by women in a court and law enforcement system in which often individual interests and traditional prejudices can win prevalence over legal protection for women.

We will in the following present four cases, to shed some light on these issues. The aim of this article is not to discuss the law in abstract, but its application in everyday life. We will demonstrate that each of these infringements causes a large amount of individual suffering, despair, disillusionment and injustice. Yet discrimination continues every day, because people are more concerned about traditional rules and personal interests, than about the fate of individual women who suffer from it.

---

1. After this paper was written, Proclamation No. 213/2000 (The Revised Family Code) was promulgated. It is a culmination of the efforts of various groups. This law which was issued in December 2000 did away with the power of Family Arbitrators to decide cases and betrothal. It raised the marriage age of boys and girls to 18 years. It abolished the power of the husband as the head of the family and the sole decision maker. It allows a woman who has been cohabiting with a man (without concluding a formal marriage) for more than three years to have a share in the common property. There are also other beneficial provisions which could help to ease the plight of women. However, the new law has so far not proven its efficiency in practice. The real test is the extent of its application. This challenge will be seen in the future.

Case I. Sindu, wife and mother: Divorce

Sindu (EWLA Case No 686) found herself on the streets with her three children in October 1993. Her husband, a high school teacher, kicked her out of the conjugal home built by both of them after their marriage in Harar in 1984. Sindu's husband batters her regularly. Reconciliation is usually effected by elders, but finally she went to court in October 1993. The couple failed to agree to elect a chairperson for the Family Arbitration Tribunal, (hereinafter referred to as the tribunal) which decides divorce-related cases under Ethiopian law (Civil Code articles 668, 674, 676). The court is duty bound to elect one for the parties under the circumstances. It took the court a full year to appoint a chairperson for the tribunal.

In November 1994 the tribunal allowed birr 150 for Sindu from the salary of her husband, to raise 3 children and pay house rent, reasoning that Sindu is employed and earns some money herself. But the chairperson began to create problems for Sindu. He dragged out the hearings and on top of that wanted to date Sindu. She went back to court to have him replaced. The second chairperson was appointed in September 1996. He refused to serve. In the meantime Sindu's husband is living in the common property house and renting out part of it for birr 1,800 per month while Sindu is trying to find a house that is not very far from the school her children were attending. The 150 birr per month from the husband in addition to her salary was not sufficient to pay school fees for three children and other necessities. Hence the children were forced to drop out of a better school and enrol in a poor quality school.

Before appointing the third chairperson for the tribunal, the court ordered Sindu to bring her husband to court one day via an oral message. The husband said: "You are wasting your time believing there is justice. If I kill you now nobody will apprehend me. I won't kill you because you will raise the children while I get married".

Finally the third chairperson was appointed in February 1997. In court the husband claimed to love his wife but always threatened to kill her when they are alone. But for the tribunal he wrote (in June 1997) "I want to be reconciled with my wife, I will try to be a better husband and father, if we separate the children will suffer".

Witnesses were called in: All stated that he regularly drank and then battered his wife; that he gambled and spent a lot of money; that he had tried to burn his wife and children by pouring kerosene on them.

Finally he admitted doing all that, made fun of the tribunal, told them to impose a penalty of a thousand birr if they wished and then walked out on them. Two members of the tribunal elected by him walked out with him.

According to Civil Code art, 678 (1), the tribunal has to decide a divorce within one year from the date of the petition for divorce. In July 1997, the 3 member tribunal reached a verdict: the divorce was decided without attributing fault to any party, and the temporary maintenance of 150 birr allowed in November 1994 was confirmed without any addition for the children for "food, health, education and other things". When the decision was read out aloud there were a birr 800 damages awarded for Sindu, but the final version had no such ruling.

The chairperson deposited the decision of the tribunal in court exactly two months after, in September 1997—for registration (Civil Code art. 729). This move was deliberate for the appeal time from the decision of the tribunal is 60 days. Hence Sindu's right of appeal was denied. She was demanding to see the copy of the decision for two months. The chairperson only gave it to her after depositing it in court and the appeal time had elapsed. Registration by court of the decision of a family arbitration tribunal is routine. But the court gave an adjournment from September 1997 up to June 1998! Sindu was tempted to tell her story to the media and call it a day, but she persisted.

One day in court, the clerks refused her entry to the judge's chambers. She so rocked the compound by crying out loud, so she was detained for a day and then released. Another day there were many people waiting to have their cases posted with a hearing date. She persuaded some of them to stand their ground by shouting "we are not going anywhere, we are not going to leave this compound. We will spend the night here. Nor will we allow the judges to go home" and told the policemen on duty to decide for their lives. The policemen went in and told what had happened to the judges. The judges allowed them to elect representatives to speak for the complainants. Sindu was one of the representatives. She told the story of

171

the people waiting outside. The judges listened. The judges left after 6 p.m. but the cases were posted with dates for hearings within a week. Sindu considered this event a partial victory.

Sindu's divorce was registered in July 1998.

Sindu went in search of the chairperson to ask him why he had not awarded her the 800 birr damages nor decided on proper maintenance for her children, and to ask him to convene the tribunal to decide on the division of the common property.

The chairperson asked Sindu to pay him 200 birr above and beyond the regular fee she was paying him for his services. She did not have the money and told him to give her time. He walked away.

When she finally tracked him down he told her:
— that he had torn two pages of the decision before depositing it in court because she had not paid him well;
— that she earned a salary and could raise her children by herself;
— that women do not need property, as it is women who are lording it over everybody;
— that he did not want to see her case again, and that she should go and have another chairperson appointed;
— that the children would be over 18 when the case was decided.

At that time Sindu decided to give the children to her mother, kill her husband and the chairperson and go to jail. It needed a lot of persuasion to dissuade her.

To date the division of the common property has not been decided upon. Sindu and her three children are fending for themselves. Her ex-husband still retains all the property including Sindu's personal property she left behind when she ran away in the middle of the night when the drunken husband threatened to burn her and the children.

She did not go back to court, though she could have a chairperson appointed again to look at the property issue with other arbitrators. In February 1999 she went to her favourite church outside of Addis and entrusted the case to St. Gabriel by saying "It is up to you to solve it". But she has come back to EWLA since then to seek advice on how to restart her case.

There are many cases dealing with lengthy divorce cases, which deny women the management and administration of their property. Many a woman has given up on her common, and even personal property, due to the impunity of husbands or family arbitration tribunals.

Sindu's case is a combination of various factors. The husband is well aware of the weak or lacking enforcement of laws. The chairperson's claim that Sindu has not paid him well implies that the husband had. Hence bribes, or "better payment" to tribunals, play a vital role in the administration of justice. Women are dependent on their husbands for money and are not in a position to pay well even if they want to. Those women who earn money use it to raise their children or take care of the elderly.

The chairperson not only believes that women should not have property but used his knowledge of the law to deny appeal. In addition he failed to provide final maintenance for the children. There is no requirement by law for the tribunal to be legally trained. This singular issue of allowing non-judges to decide on divorce, custody and maintenance of children and division of property is embodied in the 1960 Civil Code. It has outlived its usefulness, if there ever was any. Hence the law is deficient too. The courts have shared the blame in not deciding even very simple cases with dispatch.

So what should a woman like Sindu do to surmount a combination of factors such as deficiency in the law, an overloaded judiciary, an overbearing husband, backward looking and cunning arbitrators who set out to deny everything that is her due? A three-way campaign should be mounted.

The women themselves should look into their inner selves and decide what to do, bring their sisters together and stand together. Men and women should work together to realise that women are citizens of this world and are here to stay. Hence they should be treated on equal terms with men. This is a very tall order but it has to start somewhere. In fact, it has started.

The government should be pushed to show political will and commitment to change the lives of women in political, social, legal and economic terms. NGOs like EWLA could play a vital role. But much more is needed than the efforts of EWLA to see real change.

Sindu is ready for action, and should tell her story so that her daughters can have a better fate than she was forced to bear.

Case II. Mihret, a school girl: Abduction

Mihret (EWLA Case No 488) used to live in Southern Ethiopia with her mother. On September 14, 1995 she was running an errand when people she knew well offered to give her a ride. In the car was M.A. who told the driver to go to his parents' house about 20 km away. This abduction took place at 3 p.m. in the middle of a busy city road. Mihret was 16 and in grade 12. Mihret tried to shout and struggle, but there were other people in the car ready to manhandle her. When M.A. reached his destination, he raped Mihret, a precondition in all abduction cases (EWLA case nr. 1158, 706,300, BO33, 922, 597, 1408 and many others).

Mihret's parents reported her missing to the police when she failed to show up at home. M.A.'s people told Mihret's family that she was with them; not to worry about her whereabouts. Mihret's mother insisted in having the police investigate the case. M.A.'s relatives went to see Mihret before she was to appear at the police station. They told her to say that she had consented to go with M.A. If she said she was abducted, then they would kill her mother and sisters, burn their house and destroy all their property. Mirhet said she had consented when questioned by the police, the next day.

She stayed at her abductor's house under guard for three months. When Christmas time came she made a Christmas tree, so the abductor thought she was settling down and relieved her of the guards. She ran away and walked for eleven days to reach her aunt. Her aunt brought her to Addis Ababa. She can never go back to her mother because of fear of being re-abducted or other harm.

The police did not want to investigate the case, but there was pressure from various groups. The abductor had powerful friends in high places, and the investigation came to nothing. The public prosecutor dismissed the case as "non-prosecutable". The appeal to high placed prosecutors also failed to bring results. In fact the abductor felt insulted that Mihret had dared to run away.

Mihret is staying with relatives in Addis Ababa. She constantly worries about her younger sister who is still living with her mother and a target for abduction. Mihret is still afraid of her abductor and his family, as they are capable of tracking her down to Addis Ababa. She never feels safe and is wary of strangers. One day in March 1999 she was beaten on the street by hoodlums. They ambushed her, beat her severely and walked away. They did not take any jewellery or touch her bag. So she wondered: "Is it them? What should I do...?"

There are other abducted girls who ran away (EWLA case nr. 922 and 581/92) at the age of 10 and 14 and are condemned to live away from parents. The number of those who could not run away from their abductors is not known.

Mihret is very courageous, rose from her harrowing experience to pick up the pieces and start a new life. But in addition to the trauma of the abduction itself there is always the fear of the abductor's reappearance because it is considered a dent in the pride of the abductor if the "bride" runs away.

Abduction is considered as a tradition by many and is not given the attention it deserves. On the other hand, rape of children as young as four is creating havoc. The connection between rape and abduction is usually overlooked but every abduction has a rape in it. People are more concerned about the issue of rape than divorce or property issues and would willingly raise their voices against it. Every father and mother relates a rape victim to his/her child and reaction is swift and strong. It is possible to create anti-rape and abduction groups to see that those who commit such crimes are shunned by society. Such groups can also help to draw proper attention to the issues and assist in the investigation of the cases.

Some of the Important Legal Provisions—in Theory and Practice

The Legal Documents

Ethiopia has instituted important policies which in theory offer women a protection of their rights and a prominent place in society. There are policies on Women; Population; Health; Education; Environment; Culture and HIV/AIDS. Some of these policies are even enshrined in the law. The spirit behind issuing these policies was certainly beneficial to Ethiopian women. But there are no adequate structures, nor the trained human resources nor the budget to facilitate their implementation. Some critics would add lack of commitment to the list of reasons why laws and policies are not applied.

1. International Human Rights Law

Ethiopia has ratified the major international conventions and instruments and made them part of the laws of the land, in Art. 9 (4) of the Constitution. These laws need to be integrated in the ordinary laws such as the penal and civil codes. How to apply international instruments in Ethiopian courts is still being debated today.

2. The FDRE Constitution

Proclaimed as Proc. 1/1995, the Constitution came into force as of August 21, 1995. It did away with some of the age-old discriminatory laws. It is the supreme law of the land. Any law, customary practice or decision of an organ of the state or a public official which contravenes this constitution is declared invalid, by virtue of Art. 9(1). All citizens, and particularly officials have the duty to observe and obey the constitution (Art. 9(2).

Under the Constitution, human and democratic rights of citizens and peoples are protected (Art. 10). The government and its officials are committed to transparency and accountability (Art. 12). All state legislative, executive and judicial organs at all levels have the responsibility and duty to respect and enforce these provisions (Art. 13). The right to life, to security of person and liberty are guaranteed (Art. 14).

3. Civil and Family law

The Civil and Family laws that govern the capacities of women (and others) are embodied in the 1960 Civil Code. The civil code falls short in many aspects in light of the Constitution and the international instruments.[1] Even those deficient provisions are not fully applied. The process of law enforcement in courts and other organs takes such a long time that it often truly means that justice delayed is justice denied.

4. Penal laws

The current penal code was enacted in 1957. It contains several provisions which are in direct violation of human rights guarantees in the international instruments and the Constitution.

The application of the penal code is today marred with a multitude of problems, the most important ones for the plight of women today occurring in three major groups: a) There are many clear offences violating the rights of women, which are not addressed in the penal code, or, there are only indirect and insufficient provisions. This includes issues like female genital mutilation (FGM); wife battering; domestic violence and sexual harassment. Such violations, practised widely in Ethio-

---

1. People often tend to justify the discriminatory nature of the Civil Code provisions by the conditions at the time of its enactment. However, the Constitution has priority over these provisions, and is binding also for the judges.

pia, are outlawed in the international instruments ratified by Ethiopia, and in the Constitution. But the penal code contains no (or only inadequate) paragraphs for adjudicating them. b) The existing laws are not sufficient, they contain lacuna, and they often do not fulfil international standards. They are often applied by judges in a way that does not take care of women's rights as guaranteed in international instruments and the Constitution. c) The law enforcement bodies often interpret the existing laws in conjunction with cultural traditions or the "public sense of justice". This means in practice that old established practices prevail over the rights of women.

5. Civic laws

The main laws concerning civic rights for women are laws on nationality, pension, employment and land. But there are many other fields of legal security where the equality of women is not taken care of in practice—for example equal opportunities for women in various agencies. The Constitution guarantees in Art. 35 (3) affirmative measures to offset the historical legacy of inequality and discrimination for women. But this is not yet applied widely.

The rule of equality of women is sometimes applied to achieve negative ends. For instance, families may be separated if husband and wife, belonging to different language groups, are assigned to different parts of the country for work. When they apply for an assignment together, the woman may be ridiculed for not living up to her equality.

6. The Sharia laws

The Sharia court system is operational throughout the country side by side with the civil courts. Sharia courts were established in 1944 through Proc.62/1944, which empowers them to settle disputes arising from personal relations such as marriage, child custody, maintenance, succession and similar issues. Formally, a Sharia court can hear disputes if both parties agree.

As citizens of this country, Moslems are entitled to come to the civil courts to settle disputes. This puts the courts in a dilemma. If a husband goes to the Sharia court first, to institute divorce proceedings, then the wife may in practice not have recourse to the civil court. If proof is presented that the case has already been started in the Sharia, the civil courts often refuse to take up a case. On the other hand, if the woman lodges a complaint in the civil courts, the husband's claim that they were married under Moslem law would not budge the civil court judge. She came first to the civil court and has the right to be heard. This has repercussions, as the two court systems follow different practices. The Sharia court will record a divorce if the husband claims to have said three times "I divorce thee". The wife may only be informed about it after the divorce has been legalised. Moslems routinely make property contracts at marriage, called "Nikah". The wife may get nothing but a toothbrush, while the husband is very rich. If the case goes to the civil court, the common property acquired under the marriage is divided equally between the spouses (unless there is a special penalty imposed for being the cause of the divorce or for other serious reasons). Thus, women will tend to go to the civil courts, while men tend to prefer the sharia.

The Constitution provides (Art. 34(5)) that both parties have to agree to settle disputes in the Sharia court; if they do not agree, the civil court will have jurisdiction. This would, in theory, exclude the "first come" practice. However, in practice women are subject to considerable family pressure, sometimes even threats to their life, to make them accept a settlement in the Sharia court.

Some of the Most Common Problems for Women in Civil Law

1. Marriage: Consent and age

Marriage involves the consent of both spouses and entails a minimum age require-ment. Consent should be the corner stone of any marriage. Art. 16 (1 b) of the CEDAW states that women should have "the same right freely to choose a spouse and to enter into marriage only with their free and full endorsement". Also Art. 34(2) of the Constitution provides that marriage should be based on the free and full consent of both spouses.

Art. 586(1) of the Civil Code specifically requires the personal consent of both spouses at the time of marriage. But Art. 560 provides for a betrothal agreement be-tween the two families, and Art. 562 authorises parents or guardians to oppose the marriage even if the spouses already have consented.

In practice we see today many children's lives wrecked by forced early marriages, and radio and television refer frequently to marriages that lack the age and consent required.

The right to freely enter marriage and choose a spouse is directly related to the age at marriage. Early marriage restricts freedom of choice. It also limits the right to education, the right to work, to health, and the right to decide on the number and spacing of children.

2. Legal Capacity of Married Women

The Constitution guarantees the equal rights of spouses at the conclusion of mar-riage, during marriage and at its dissolution (Art. 34(1)). A married woman has the right to carry out the occupation of her choice. But Civil Code Art. 645 (1) allows the spouse to object where such occupation is considered against the interest of the household.[1] The wife can receive her salary and administer her personal property, but the domain of common property is in the husband's authority, as is parental au-thority (Art. 637, 644, 656). The legal capacities of man and woman are equal on paper, but the legal capacity of a married woman is not equal with her husband's in the civil code. This clearly contravenes CEDAW and the Constitution.

Registration of marriage is very essential to women. Without it, problems arise in proving marriage, for pensions, child paternity and many other rights including the curbing of early marriage. Art. 118 of the civil code makes registration of mar-riages compulsory. But the registers were not established and registration was sus-pended. The registers still have not become operational except for civil marriages at the Municipalities.

3. Bigamy and Polygamy

Under the Civil Code Art. 585, bigamy is prohibited. Non-conformity entails crim-inal liability for the authorities who consented and witnessed the marriage which can be dissolved at the request of either spouse of the bigamous person or by the public prosecutor.

However, the Constitution allows the use of customary and religious laws in marriage disputes, if both parties agree, and the establishment of customary and re-ligious courts (Art. 34(5) and 78 (5). Their practice differs from the civil courts also in matters of polygamy.

---

1. See Hillima Taddesse: "Discriminatory Norms and Application against Women in the Ethiopian Family Law", EWLA Sponsored Research Report, Nov. 1996.

Polygamy is a violation of the human dignity of women. International instruments do not specifically address the issue of polygamy, but it violates the principle of equal rights of men and women in marriage. It is imposed on women on the basis of sex. Bigamy has created problems for women in the allocation of pensions, common property, and the rights of children.

4. Divorce and common property
Despite constitutional guarantees and provisions in international instruments, women are not equal with men during marriage and its dissolution according to the civil code. Sharia courts exist side by side with the civil courts, and decide according to religious traditions and principles. The daily practice often does not conform to the civil code, especially where family arbitration tribunals decide, which consist of people who do not have sufficient legal knowledge.

In marriage, the husband has authority over common property. Under Art. 651 of the civil code, the administration of personal property may also be entrusted to the other spouse—a clause almost exclusively used to give the husband control over the wife's property.

Wife battering and other domestic violence are not considered serious grounds for divorce. A wife who is persistently battered and runs away to save her life or health, may lose all the property she has worked for.

Practice in family arbitration tribunals often does not follow the civil code, as members of these tribunals are not required to have intimate knowledge of the law. Even when there is no discrimination in the written laws, the tribunals have often with their prejudiced decisions and through corrupt practices wrecked the lives of women and children.[1]

5. Personal relations
The husband is the head of the family, the wife owes him obedience in all lawful things which he orders (civil code art. 635). The common residence is chosen by the husband. He owes protection to his wife and watches her relations and guides her in her conduct (Art. 641, 644). If he cannot afford servants, the wife is bound to stay at home and take care of household duties (Art. 646). A married woman takes the domicile of her husband. Paternal authority also lies with the husband (Art. 637, 641).

These discriminatory provisions have given predominance to the husband and made slaves out of wives. Needless to say these provisions violate the regulations laid down in the CEDAW and other instruments and in the Constitution.

6. Child custody and provisional measures
In the case of divorce, the family arbitration tribunals are supposed to provide maintenance and shelter to the wife and the children while divorce is pending. But in practice, the wife is kicked out of the home with her children, or she escapes the husband's violence. The family arbitrators rarely provide shelter even if divorce proceedings take years. This contravenes the provisions on maintenance in the Civil Code. Alimony does not exist in Ethiopia, but Art. 821 (a) makes the husband the primary person to provide maintenance to his wife.

---

1. See Original Woldegiorgis: "The Functions of Family Arbitrators under the Ethiopian Civil Code", EWLA sponsored Research Report, May 1997.

7. Irregular unions

A woman living with a man in a lasting relationship which is not formalised as marriage, may consider herself his wife, but may be disowned when the relationship breaks up. The man living with her is considered the father of her children but he will be required only to give her three months maintenance, according to art. 717(2) (six months according to the English version of the code).

This state of affairs is very prejudicial to women. In other countries, where both partners enter into such a relationship knowingly, women get some share of common property and maintenance after the relationship has continued for some time.

8. Inheritance

According to the civil code, unlike in many other African countries, the capacity to inherit does not depend on sex or age or nationality of the heir (Art. 837). There are no provisions in the code limiting the capacity of women to make testaments. But in reality, due to tradition or custom, women and girl children are often excluded from inheriting. In Muslim families the boy gets two thirds of the estate, while the girl gets only one third. Legitimate and illegitimate children are equal in inheritance (Art. 872(A).

Though the law is not discriminatory, the overall practice is in many ways continuing to disadvantage women as regards inheritance.

The Most Common Problems for Women in Penal Law

Today the world has recognised that women's rights are human rights and that violence against women constitutes a violation of human rights. Violence against women takes place mainly in three spheres: in the family, in the community, and by the state.

Violence perpetrated or condoned by the state encompasses acts done by public officials or other agents of the state, including the police, security forces, prison guards etc. The failure of the state to effectively investigate and prosecute violations of women—for example, cases of sexual abuse or rape in prison—can be considered as condoning violence by the state.

Violence in the community includes rape, incest, sexual abuse, abduction, sexual harassment and intimidation at work, educational institutions and elsewhere, traficking in women and forced prostitution.

Violence in the family includes battering, sexual abuse of female children in the household, dowry related violence, marital rape, female genital mutilation and others. This category also includes verbal abuse, which can in some cases be worse than physical battering. One may distinguish four categories of abuses of women: physical, emotional, sexual and economic abuse.[1]

1. Rape

Rape has according to penal code art. 589[2] a maximum penalty of ten years rigorous imprisonment. A minimum penalty is not provided. The proof of rape is difficult to establish, and many consider rape not to be a serious offence, at least if it concerns an adult woman. In light of the prevalence of HIV/AIDS, there is a growing argument that marital rape should also be penalised by law. The UN Declaration on the

---

1. See Hillima Taddesse: "The Rights of Women under Ethiopian Penal Law", EWLA Sponsored Research Report, Feb. 1997.
2. The Penal Code of 1957 is now under revision.

Elimination of Violence against Women (DEVAW) and the 1995 Beijing Platform for Action consider it as a form of violence against women.

2. Abduction

Abduction is common in Ethiopia, as a means of concluding marriage. A girl is carried off by force, and first she would be raped. Every abduction has a rape in it. But the law does not take account of this aspect. Art. 558 sets a maximum of 3 years rigorous imprisonment for abduction. If a woman is responsible and freely contracts a marriage with her abductor, proceedings will not be instituted unless the marriage is annulled by law (Art. 558 (2)).

How could a woman carried off through violence make a free contract of marriage? Free consent must be given by both spouses before marriage, not after the woman is forcefully dragged off and raped. Girls under the age limit are doubly injured because the age requirement of the civil law is violated in addition to the abduction. Children cannot give consent.

3. Prostitution and trafficking

Trafficking in women and the exploitation of prostitution are violence against women. Ethiopia has ratified the UN Convention to deal with it. The international "Convention for the Suppression of the Traffic in Persons and of the Exploitation of the Prostitution of Others" considers prostitutes as victims and is very severe on procurers and traffickers.

The Ethiopian penal code does not punish prostitutes. Those who make a profession of, or live, by procuring through the prostitution of others are punishable. Trafficking is punishable under penal code art. 605. But in practice this offence is seldom punished, except recently for some few cases of traffickers being apprehended for cheating women into recruitment to work in foreign countries.

4. Domestic violence

A wide field of problems for women in Ethiopia is domestic violence, not only committed by the husband on his wife, but also by men belonging to the household on domestic servants etc. Women are often abused by men near them, and it may be much more difficult both to resist and to prove in court such violations. Many countries do not provide laws against domestic violence. Ethiopia has no specific legal provision against domestic violence.

5. Sexual harassment

There are abundant cases of sexual harassment in Ethiopia, but the law does not specifically penalise it. It occurs at workplaces, on the streets and in educational institutions. The position of power and authority, which the man who harasses a woman has over her, is extremely relevant. The labour proclamation of 1993 (No. 42/93) does not mention sexual harassment. The penal code deals with it only indirectly. Art. 592 and 593 penalise sexual abuses of inmates of educational institutions by those in positions of authority. There is no provision at all covering sexual harassment between students themselves or co-workers.

6. Female genital mutilation (FGM)

This traditional practice dates back many centuries. It involves cutting and removing parts or all of the female genitalia. There are various types of FGM. It is a very painful operation that deprives a woman of a vital part of her sexual organs. After-effects range from infections to serious problems during intercourse and child delivery, not to mention the psychological trauma.

The penal code does not make any reference to FGM. The only indirect provision to use against FGM could be Art. 538 (b) of the Penal Code against intentionally maiming, disabling or disfiguring another person. The Constitution protects women against harmful traditional practices (Art. 35(4). But there are no adequate penalties embodied in the penal law.

7. Abortion

Induced abortion is punishable under Ethiopian law, even after incest, rape- or abduction- induced pregnancies. There is no time limit, and even assistance to abortion is punished. The only exception (Art. 534) is abortion done to prevent serious danger for the mother's life. But the exception is dependent on such difficult procedures that it is hardly ever applicable. Doctors performing abortions without observing the legal steps are liable to punishment.[1]

8. Polygamy, enslavement and adultery

Adultery is very common in Ethiopia. Under the civil code it is a serious cause for divorce and entails the loss of common property for the adulterous spouse. Adultery is punishable only on demand of the offended spouse. Polygamy or bigamy is punishable under art. 616 of the Penal Code. Yet, bigamy and polygamy are very common in parts of the country, and are tolerated under traditional or religious laws.

Enslavement is embodied under art. 565 of the penal code, and is punishable by from 5 to 20 years rigorous imprisonment plus a fine not exceeding 20,000 birr. For organisations, the fine is in Art. 567 increased to 50,000 birr. However, this paragraph is seldom invoked against travel agencies who send young girls to Arab countries to be exploited as "domestic servants".

Civic Laws

The main laws to be seen under this section concern nationality, pension, employment and access to land for women. But there are other areas like equal opportunities for women in various contexts. The Constitution promises women affirmative measures to offset the historical legacy of inequality and discrimination (Art. 35 (3)). But this policy is reflected neither in the electoral laws nor in the Federal Lands Administration Proclamation (proc 89/97). The practice of *kebele* administrations often discriminates women in spite of legal and constitutional provisions and guarantees. For instance, if the husband, as the head of household, dies, the widow and her children are very often deprived of their house and of services which they are entitled to. This is so because in the traditional understanding of *kebele* leaders a woman is not always accepted as an independent household head.

1. Employment

The labour proclamation (Proc.42/93) has a separate section on "working conditions for women". It prohibits the dismissal of a woman during her pregnancy and for four months following childbirth. If a company has to reduce the work force, expectant mothers are to be the last ones to be dismissed among workers with equal skills (art. 29(3) and 87(5)).

Art. 42(1 d) of the Constitution provides that "women workers have the right to equal pay for equal work". Maternity leave and affirmative action are provided for

---

1.   Doctors who perform abortions without following the legal procedures could in addition be barred from practising their profession under Penal Code Art. 535.

in Art. 35. The CEDAW has a series of provisions to protect the rights and particular needs of women, and especially expecting mothers. Ethiopian law does take care of the most essential rights but much is left wanting when it comes to the everyday application.

2. Pension laws

The Public Servants Pension Decree of 1961 (No 46/61), with amendments in 1963 (No. 209/63) and 1974 (No. 5/1974) provides for a pension for old age at 55 years and for a disabled person, after a minimum employment of 10 years. Children, parents, widows and widowers get pension entitlements in the case that an employee dies. A widow is entitled to 50 per cent of the husband's pension.

A widower, however, is only entitled to a pension after his wife's death,[1] if he was wholly or mainly supported by his wife at the time of her death. The law here seems to be discriminating against men; however, upon closer viewing it does not appear so. A woman has paid as much in contributions to the pension fund as a man. It is discrimination that she should leave less security and entitlements to her closest family if she dies, than her husband would. It is the children who suffer for this discriminatory practice of Ethiopian legal practice. Another flaw in the legal practice is that a divorced women does not get a pension. Though she has contributed four per cent of his salary—which is "common property"—the law does not even mention any right on pension for her or for the children.

3. Land

Art. 35 (7) of the Constitution gives women the right to acquire, administer, control, use and transfer property. In particular, they have equal rights with men to the use, transfer, administration and control of land.

The civil code does not discriminate on the basis of gender with regard to ownership and inheritance of land. The 1975 proclamation of "land to the tiller" envisaged allocation of land to heads of families irrespective of sex. But in the practice of land redistributions women did not fare well, especially married ones.

Today, except for Amhara and Tigray Regional States, the regions have not enacted laws regarding land. In those two regions women have acquired the right to land. But it remains to be seen how this will work in practice. Women have benefited from Art. 40 (4) of the Constitution which states that Ethiopian peasants have the right to obtain land without payment and provides protection against eviction from their land.

Women living in other regions have not attained this constitutional right. Many a woman works long hours every day in the fields of her husband, without remuneration, nor benefit or the right to the produce. When the husband dies or they are divorced, she is evicted by the relatives of the husband from the land she has worked for all her life, or she may stay on by marrying the brother of the deceased husband.[2]

4. Nationality

The Ethiopian law on nationality was enacted in 1930 and amended in 1933. The Constitution provides (Art. 6(1) that any person of either sex shall be an Ethiopian national if one parent is Ethiopian. Art. 33(1) states that marriage to a foreign national shall not annul Ethiopian nationality. However, the law of 1933 continues to be practised. It deprives a woman who marries a foreign national of her Ethiopian

---

1. This law has now been corrected by Proclamation 190/1999. A husband gets his wife's pension without any condition as a matter of right as of December 28, 1999.
2. Women being evicted from land is common in Oromia, Gambella and Benishangul-Gumuz regional states.

nationality, provided she acquires the nationality of her husband, while an Ethiopian man does not lose his nationality when marrying a foreigner. Likewise, children of an Ethiopian man married to a foreign women are considered Ethiopian, while children of an Ethiopian woman married to a foreigner get the father's nationality and lose their right to Ethiopian citizenship.

Justice Administration Bodies

Laws cannot act on their own. They need people to put life into them. In legal provisions, we cannot just see the written laws and be satisfied, if the proper application is inadequate or lacking. One thing is the fact that some provisions provided for in the Constitution and in the international legal instruments are not contained in Ethiopian law. An even more depressing observation is the fact that the law is applied in discriminatory ways, or not applied at all. This is in particular difficult to handle as such practice may vary widely from one region to another and from one court to the next.

The cases told above give examples of arbitrary and unpredictable decisions in courts and in arbitration tribunals. The problem with such differences is not only that the system denies women their legal rights, but even more, that it creates a feeling of legal insecurity. Women cannot trust the rights they have got on paper, particularly if practice varies and the outcome of a legal suit can not be predicted. And the fact that different court systems—the traditional and sharia courts and the state courts—exist side by side and compete against one another, makes legal security entirely unpredictable and renders the human rights dependent on luck and the goodwill of those who administer the different jurisdictive institutions. The following two cases will give further examples of such unpredictability.

Women are often victims of prostitution, trafficking, domestic violence and sexual harassment. Many of them are denied access to justice due to distance, family responsibility and/or poverty. If a woman cannot afford to leave her daily duties to go to court, much less to pay for transport, she has little chance even to claim her rights she may not even know of.

In addition the application of the laws depends on the kebele, the police, the family arbitration tribunals, the public prosecutors, and the courts. This complicates matters for women even more at various stages of a law suit.

The two following cases will give some further examples of how women experience their helplessness faced with problems which, by law, they should be protected against.

Case III. Meskerem, a girl child: Rape

Meskerem (EWLA Case No 510) was only 6 when she was raped by her 19 year old neighbour (T.T.). Her father was bedridden and her mother collect fuelwood for the family's livelihood. T.T. and Meskerem used to live in the same compound and use the same toilet. On Sept. 6, 1994 all the neighbours were gathered at a house where somebody had died. T.T. went into Meskerem's house, woke her up, offered to buy her bread and carried her to his house and raped her.

When the case was reported to the police, T.T.'s parents claimed that he was 14 years old; though his school principal produced written evidence that T.T. was 19. Births are not registered properly in Ethiopia. When girls are abducted or raped parents tend to lower the ages of boy-children to have them classified as young offenders where they get away with a reprimand or a sojourn in a reformatory (Penal Code, articles 161–182). On the other hand a girl child's age is always raised, especially in abduction cases, usually beyond 15, to claim

---

that she had given her consent—because under civil law a girl is capable of marriage at age 15 (Civil Code art. 581).

Hence T.T.'s case was forwarded to the juvenile court. When the public prosecutor asked T.T why he had raped Meskerem, he responded "... she is always asking me to buy her bread, I was fed up with her and I wanted to shut up her bread request for ever".

In the meantime Meskerem's mother was able to get some help from NGOs and other groups, and could move to another part of the city. But Meskerem became very ill. The Black Lion Hospital operated on her, gave her some medicine but there was lots of smelly discharge and the wounds failed to heal. To add to her problems, an STD (Sexually Transmitted Disease) was diagnosed.

Meskerem had to discontinue school. She then went to the Fistula Clinic in Addis Ababa where there were specialists. They also gave her some medicine and requested that she stay in bed during the medication. But she did not get better. Finally the Ethiopian Women Lawyers Association cited her case as an example at a certain meeting. The Ethiopian Herald wrote about her, and the response was good. A woman offered money for medication, and she was taken to a private clinic. The doctor went over and above his duty to help her. EWLA volunteers went along to the clinic to see that the doctor's instructions were carried out properly.

Now Meskerem is recovering and doing well in school but she still wakes in the middle of the night and wets her bed. She has nightmares too. And an abiding fear of young boys.

How would you react if you were Meskerem's mother or father?

Case IV. Senait, a would-be employee: Labour contract

Senait (EWLA case No 695) was only 20 years old, had completed 12th grade and had no job when she contacted a Travel Agency with a beautiful office in Addis Ababa. She paid 7,000 birr (equivalent of USD 875) to go to Bahrain employed as a nanny for $210 a month. Nothing was written down. All the transactions were done orally. She borrowed the 7,000 birr to pay back from her salary when she reached Bahrain. On Nov. 19, 1994 she was taken to a house in Bahrain where the job was to wash clothes and do all cleaning jobs. The salary promised ($210) was reduced to $100. The job was too heavy for Senait to handle. She had to be up by 5 a.m. and work until midnight. So she requested to be returned home, after working for 9 months. She was paid only $200 for nine months. Senait's employers had painted her bedroom and bought her hair oil; so they claimed to have deducted these items from her salary. She insisted on going back and was taken to the agency in Bahrain that transacted the employment from the Bahrain side. She was told "Do as you are told, do not ask to go to your country as if you had one, you have no country". In the heat of the argument she was slapped and manhandled, then she does not remember a thing.

She woke up in a hospital. She was told that she was thrown from a window on the third floor and brought to the hospital by a passer-by. Her back was broken and had been bound to iron. The police came along and made her sign a document written in Arabic and told her to leave the country. The doctors told them that she was in no condition to travel, but the police insisted. So the nurses and doctors raised the transport money. While this was being done, Senait stayed in the doctor's office for two days. Then she came home. The travel agency responsible was closed and the whereabouts of the people in the agency was unknown. Senait, so hopeful of employment and so young, came back crushed with a broken back and with no money for medication or her livelihood. Some travel agencies work illegally without undue worries about sending unsuspecting victims to all types of hardships and even death. Poverty plays a major role in these cases.

Democracy and Public Awareness about Discrimination against Women

Democracy demands that all citizens are equal. It depends on an active involvement of the state in protecting the rights of women and offering them equal chances for participation in public life.

The above-mentioned stories of women are taken as examples only. EWLA has many other cases where women have been the defenseless victims of discrimination in society, in the courts, and in the law. For instance, Moslem women do not have an equal share of the common property during divorce even by law (EWLA cases nr. 294, 231). Many women complain of unequal treatment in employment, promotion and dismissal in general and maternity and sick leaves in particular (EWLA cases nr. 443, 454, 287, 191, 197). The absence of registration of marriages has led to many bigamous marriages, and has complicated pension payments to widows.

Women are also victims of prostitution, trafficking, domestic violence and sexual harassment. Because of their family responsibilities, distance to courts, and/or poverty they are in practice denied access to justice. In addition, the application of the laws depends on the kebele, the police, the family arbitration tribunals, the public prosecutors and the courts. Each of these can complicate matters even more for women, as they may demand bribes, or sexual favours, or for other reasons refuse or delay or distort the services expected of them.

The burdens and injustices have to be borne by women as long as society accepts that women are treated as inferior. What can women do to change such attitudes and reclaim their proper place in society, free of anxieties and violence, as equal and free citizens?

Women have to speak out against violations and injustices. Publicity has resulted in remarkable effects in recent years, especially in cases of abduction and rape. Some women are ready to take action and go public. What is needed now is the organising of women and networking, so that women's voices are heard loud and clear and can make an impact on public awareness. To enlist the support of men is of paramount importance. A viable strategy is needed. For example, stories of violations should be told publicly and relayed on radio and television. They can touch the hearts of people and move them to react.

Many women in decision-making positions can add force to such campaigns. But equally important is to organise grass roots women to meet decision-making women half way, to complement them and form a powerful movement to improve the lives of all women.

It cannot be overlooked that poverty is one of the major reasons reinforcing the evils women want to overcome. Poverty makes people both reluctant to take any risks, and unable to join such a wide movement. Overbearing poverty has caused many a husband or male partner to lash out at their female partners, just to vent their fury. EWLA summons husbands and male partners to its offices when needed, to sit down and discuss issues in order to settle cases out of court. We cannot help noticing that most men actually understand the dismal position their wives are in, but when poverty creates a disparate situation, they vent their fury against their nearest and dearest.

NGOs can play a vital role in bringing issues in focus. But the political will and commitment of the government is central to the issue of equal democratic rights and freedoms for women.

Yet, it is not a question that can be left to women alone. If democracy is the rule of the people, then it can never be better than the protection and inclusion it offers its own population. The issue of minorities aside, a state cannot have more democracy than it offers the majority of its own population. Therefore, the issue of rights for women is an issue for both men and women: they cannot achieve more democratic conditions of life unless they achieve them together, and unless women are included together with men, both in building democracy and in enjoying its fruits.

References

EWLA cases numbers BO33, 191, 197, 231, 287, 294, 300, 443, 454, 488, 510, 597, 686, 695, 706, 922, 1158, 1408, 184/92, 581/92.

Oral interviews with Sindu, Mehret, Meskerem, and Senait.

The State of the Private Press in Ethiopia

Shimelis Bonsa

Introduction

The Legal Framework

> Everyone has the right to freedom of opinion and expression; this right includes freedom to hold opinions without interference and to seek, receive, and impart information and ideas through any media and regardless of frontiers (Article 19, Universal Declaration of Human Rights (UDHR), 1948).

Pursuant to its ratification of the 1948 Universal Declaration of Human Rights (UDHR), the Transitional Government of Ethiopia (TGE) has agreed to respect individual human rights including the freedom of expression fully and without any limitations. Taking advantage of such government declaration of intent, a large number of newspapers and magazines began to appear in Addis Ababa. This proliferation of periodicals was a dramatic demonstration of the people's long-standing dissatisfaction with the government-controlled media and their hunger for an alternative source of information (EHRCO, 1995: 67).

Magazines were the first to appear on the market in 1990/91:'*Tsedey*' (December), '*Hibir*' (January), '*Ifoyta*' (February), '*Tobiya*' and '*Ruh*' (April). This was followed by the publication of private newspapers, the earliest of which was reportedly '*Eyita*' (May, 1984 E.C.), followed by '*Addis Dimts*' and '*Addis Tribune*' (the latter being the first private English Weekly) (Tedbabe, 1990 E.C.: 24). The proliferation of private newspapers operating on the basis of the TGE charter and without any license and censorship continued unabated even after the promulgation of the Freedom of the Press Act in 1992.

The legislation (A Proclamation to Provide for the Freedom of the Press No. 34/ 1992) issued on 21 October was, indeed, a positive step forward. Unlike the previous two regimes, which had guaranteed the freedom of speech and press in their constitutions (Article 41 of the Revised Constitution of 1955 and Article 47 of the 1987 constitution of the Peoples' Democratic Republic of Ethiopia (PDRE)), but never implemented it, the press law of the TGE legitimized the existence of a private press.

The legislation has freed the incipient press from the long-standing captivity to pre-print censorship (Article 3, sub-title 2). Any Ethiopian national was allowed to run a press business (Article 4, sub-title 1) after fulfilling a number of requirements (Article 7, sub-title 1). The law also gave the press the right of access to and dissemination of information (Article 8, sub-title 1–2). In addition, it provided for the right of reply (Article 9) and delineated the responsibilities of the press (Articles 10–14) as well as the taking of legal measures (Articles 15–16), including the penalty (Article 20) in the event of an illegal press product or a breach of the regulations. These ranged from one to three years imprisonment or from Birr 10,000 to Birr 50,000 in fines, or both.

Subsequently, an incredibly large number of licenses were issued to private publishers of newspapers and magazines. About 200 newspapers and 87 magazines came into existence in a matter of five years (1992–97). An important element of this process was the rise of the Islamic press dealing, apart from religious topics, with economic, social and political issues affecting the Muslim community both locally and at the international level (Hussein, 1994: 792–794).

This development was indicative of the fact that the emerging private papers possessed a great potential to give expression to the hitherto unheard "voices from below". However, the number of active private newspapers has inevitably fallen, owing principally to market stabilisation and government pressure.[1]

Operation of the Private Press

Origin

> Any person who is an Ethiopian national may, singly or jointly with other persons having Ethiopian nationality, carry on any press activity (Article 5, sub-title 1, Press Law: 34/ 1992).

This concession and the fact that there was no restrictive ceiling on such issues as financial standing or professional competence facilitated the entry of almost anyone into the profession of journalism.[2] There are multiple motivations for becoming a journalist or starting a newspaper enterprise. These range from professional ("attraction to journalism") and political ("love of the motherland") to economic ("as a livelihood" or "for profit making"). Of the three, political motivations appear to be predominant and this is partly attributable to the circumstances in which most of the papers evolved.[3]

Other important prerequisites for founding a newspaper enterprise are the qualification of entrants and the availability of capital. It is difficult to agree on the order of importance of such qualities or on what exactly the qualifications for a career in journalism are. Despite enormous variations from one individual to another, there are universally shared important attributes that make up a good journalist: non-partisanship, open-mindedness, an inquiring mind, and the ability to write in a fairly clear, simple and direct language and preferably in short sentences. These qualities can be acquired and/or developed further through pre-service training in a school of journalism and/or on-the-job training (Barton, 1966:14–17). An examination of the pre-service educational and professional profile of most journalists indicates that a majority of them are high school graduates and had little or no previous experience or training whatsoever in journalism.[4]

Two phases can be broadly identified in the progress of the independent press with regard to the professional and educational qualifications of its members. The first period, covering the years in the immediate aftermath of EPRDF's assumption of power, was bedecked with periodicals of high professional standing produced by people with many years of journalistic experience. The private press of this period was characterized by a relatively high level of professionalism in terms both of the individuals involved and the quality of publications they produced. In the second

---

1. ODA (1996:33) in a survey it conducted in 1996 claims that 336 licenses have been granted. This may possibly include periodicals owned by the government and/or government and non-government organizations.
2. Interviews: Sisay Agena and Zegeye Haile. The latter, proprietor and publisher of a newspaper, started his business with an initial capital of only Birr 255.0, the amount required for registration. See also Tedbabe Tilahun, 1990 E.C.: p. 63.
3. Interviews: Sisay, Befekadu Moroda, Biruk Kebede and Tedbabe.
4. Interviews: thirty-one editors and reporters selected from ten newspapers.

phase, a larger proportion of the journalists tended not to have any sound experience and/or training for venturing into and working in the private press enterprise.[1]

Turning to capital investment, there was considerable disparity in this. Generally speaking, most of the private publishers entered the press with a comparatively weak financial and technical base.[2] The following table, which should be considered with caution, lists the registered capital of some selected papers and could help in illustrating the resource diversity outlined above.

Table 1. Registered Capital of Ten Private Newspapers

No	Name of newspaper	Year of establishment in E.C.	Registered capital in Eth. Birr
1	Tobiya	Oct. 1986	50,000
2	Reporter (Amharic)	Aug. 1987	15,000
3	Beza	Oct. 1986	8,000
4	Ma'ebel	Dec. 1987	7,000
5	Mebruk	Sept. 1988	5,000
6	Seyfe Nebelbal	Aug. 1986	5,000
7	Tomar	Feb. 1985	5,000
8	Eth'op	Oct. 1986	5,000
9	Genanaw	Nov. 1987	5,000
10	Tarik	Mar. 1986	3,000

Source: Mass Media License Registration and Control Department, 1990 E.C.

Finally, when we come to the question of newspaper ownership. Private newspapers in Ethiopia are owned, run and controlled by people for whom the newspaper enterprise is a livelihood, a profit-generating venture and/or a political instrument. The prevalent situation is one of exclusive individual ownership. This tends to limit the possibility of a merger and consequently of a much better chance of survival and growth. Nevertheless, joint newspaper ownership, dictated as much by the need for efficiency as by scarcity of resources, is also fairly represented. In fact, in most cases, the comparatively more efficient and successful papers happen to be communally owned.[3]

Organizational Structure

In a modestly developed press, duties are not only defined and shared out, they are also highly specialized. True, there are instances of functional mobility between different organs of a newspaper establishment as, for example, in the case of an editor being responsible for non-editorial roles such as advertising. But, in general, there are two distinct and demarcated areas of operation: the managerial and the editorial (Barton, 1966: 41–42, 60–61).

In the Ethiopian case, such a well-structured system of operating a newspaper establishment is novel and is limited to only a few papers. Most papers are run by a comparatively small staff ranging from three (the lowest) to eight (the highest).[4] This would mean that a person, usually male, is expected to handle several and different responsibilities at one and the same time. This pattern of functional duplication is

1. Interviews: Befekadu, Goshu Moges, Netsanet Tesfaye, Yohannes Abebe, Wole Gurmu.
2. Interviews: Alemtsehay, Abebe, Befekadu, Sisay, Yohannes. See also Tedbabe (1990 E.C.: 60–61).
3. Interviews: Eskindir Nega, Ephrem Endale, Goshu, Sisay, Wole.
4. Interviews: Yonas Fikre, Yohannes. There was even a widespread rumor that attributed the ownership and running of a certain newspaper to a single individual.

indicative of the financial and organizational limitations of most papers. However, it may also be argued that such a structure could be, and indeed is, realistic in view of the level at which an independent press enterprise finds itself at present.[1]

Table 2. Functional Duplication in Eight Newspapers

No	Job title	NP1	NP2	NP3	Publisher NP4	NP5	NP6	NP7	NP8
1	Manager	x	x	x	x	x	x	x	x
2	Editor-in-chief	x		x	x	x	x	x	x
3	Deputy editor-in-chief		x						
4	Editor		x						
5	Reporter	x	x	x	x	x	x	x	x
6	Advertising agent	x			x	x		x	x
7	Feature writer	x	x		x			x	
8	Managing editor		x						

NP.: Newspaper, as listed in Table 1.

Process of Newspaper Production

> Any press and its agents shall, without prejudice to rights confirmed by other laws, have the right to seek, obtain and report news and information from any government source of news and information. (Article 8, Sub-title 1, Press Law: 34/1992)

The right enshrined in the article is a response to a fundamental human right—the right to know, and one of the basic functions of a purposeful press. The provision of access to knowledge and events far beyond the boundaries of an individual's own observation and experience could rightly be seen as the initial step in creating an informed public, which in its turn is the beginning of a democratic society (Sommerlad, 1966: 55, 57). The situation in Ethiopia has been strongly influenced by the infancy of the private press and the unique circumstances in which it evolved. Despite some basic similarities, the extent to which information is obtained and the way it eventually is published differ considerably from paper to paper.

News and information are obtained from a myriad of sources as well as through different methods of local, national and international character (Teel and Taylor, 1992:119). Locally, interviewing is the principal medium of information gathering. Accordingly, reporters go out to various areas in and, occasionally, outside of Addis Ababa, employing different methods including friendship networks or other useful connections, and even bribes. Papers with a relatively stronger financial base send their reporters to the provinces and employ the services of associate reporters and freelancers stationed in the provinces.[2] Individuals as well as groups (armed and political), inside and outside Ethiopia, also provide out of public or private interest information, at times vital, to the private press. This could be rendered with or without payment, orally or in writing, through personal appearance, telephone, post or fax.[3]

The possibility of getting information from officials is dependent, among other things, on the degree of one's proximity to the government in power. This in turn depends on such factors as friendship (created and/or cemented by political or other

1. Interviews: Alemtsehay, Biruk, Befekadu, Eskindir, Ephrem, Sisay, Tedbabe, Yohannes, Qidist Belachew. Female representation in the private press enterprise is so negligible that it tends to make the press an almost completely male dominated area.
2. Interviews: Alemtsehay, Goshu, Tedbabe, Wole.
3. Interviews: Alemtsehay, Befekadu, Biruk, Dawit Kebede, Ephrem, Goshu, Yonas, Yohannes.

motivations) and the attitude of the officials themselves. A broad distinction can accordingly be made:

1. those with a smooth relationship with and hence comparatively easier access to the government;
2. those with an 'attitude' of head-on collision with the government and consequently remote from its sources of information; and
3. those with a history of a 'love-hate' relationship with and fluctuating access to the government.

Another source of news and information is the state-owned electronic and print media. News and information which are reported on one of the media reappear in private newspapers with certain modifications and alterations (a practice known in the private press as maschoh—"magnify"). In addition to press releases from resident local and international bodies, there are cases of "sale" of news and information by several journalists working for the government but having a dubious relationship with the private press.[1]

With regard to external sources, the use of associate reporters, freelance contributors including "well-wishers" or "friends of the private press", foreign periodicals, fax and Internet facilities as well as radio and television monitoring have become an established practice in the private press. For most papers which do not possess such information technology access is provided in return for payment.[2]

In this connection, one can make the observation that a national news agency could contribute to the growth and efficiency of the private press. Unfortunately, the prevailing antipathy between the government and the private press and the weak financial standing of the latter has limited such a possibility.

Speaking of newspaper output, the government press, for example, tends to present a picture of homogeneity and shows very little evidence of "investigative, critical or even mildly original journalistic activity" (ODA, 1996: 36). When it comes to the private press, two broad categories can be identified. On the one hand, there is a small core of newspapers that tend to concentrate on what might be referred to as "safe" topics, and with occasional and guarded discussion of political issues. In addition to these "apolitical papers", there are those with a generally more favorable (or "critically supportive", as they would prefer it to be called) attitude towards the government.

On the other hand, there are a large number of papers (including some with down-market tabloid titles such as Godanaw,) which are "...short on facts... with unsourced stories and rumors..." (ODA, 1996: 37) with, at times, serious security implications. Quite apart from those sensational and irresponsible papers, there are newspapers (such as Tobiya) that, through their strong, substantiated critique of issues of national concern, have commanded respect and secured a sizeable readership.

Economics of Newspaper Production

We have so far seen the professional side of newspaper production, which requires skilled work, character and educational qualifications. However, as a commercial undertaking newspapers have to make a profit to survive. The very production of a

---

1. Interviews: Abebe Tadesse, Tedbabe, Yonas, Yohannis.
2. Interviews: Alemayehu Fanta, Befekadu, Dawit, Ephrem, Tedbabe.

single paper as well as its success in an increasingly competitive market is premised upon a wide range of variables. The multiplicity of the challenges faced tends to make the running of a newspaper enterprise an uphill struggle.

With the exception, perhaps, of printing and newsprint costs there is a significant cost differentiation among private newspapers that is attributable, among other things, to the financial position of each paper at the time of or immediately after its establishment. A sizeable number of the private papers and all the state papers are printed at the government owned Berhanena Selam Printing Enterprise (BSPE). There is, however, at present a new trend towards using alternative (that is, comparatively cheaper) private printers, the Bole Printing Press (BPP) being the one generally preferred. This shift should, nevertheless, be seen more as a pragmatic and therefore temporary move dictated principally by price fluctuation, not as something leading to a permanent attachment to one of them. In fact, the printing cost decreases with an increase in the number of copies. However, this inducement for increased newspaper publication is counterbalanced by the small size of the readership with a stable purchasing power and reading habits (ODA, 1996: 37).

The printing cost is covered in two major ways. Financially strong newspapers like 'Reporter' and 'Tobiya' themselves provide the money needed for publication. Most private papers, on the other hand, suffering as they do from an unstable financial base, have to depend on wholesale distributors, losing in the process a significant portion of their cover price.[1]

Table 3. Rise in Printing and Newsprint Costs in the BSPE between 1993 and 1997

No.	Date of Price rise in E.C.	Weekly Issue	No. of pages	Printing & news print cost in Birr	Difference in Birr	Price Increase in %	Difference from previous price in %
1	21-04-85	10,000	8	2085.76			
2	02-05-85	"	"	4174.80	2089.04	100.16	
3	30-06-85	"	"	4635.72	2549.96	122	21.84
4	28-08-85	"	"	4715.72	2629.96	126.1	4.1
5	15-10-85	"	"	2946.10	860.34	41	-85.1
6	06-11-85	"	"	3547.49	1461.73	70.1	-15
7	28-12-85	"	"	3325.77	1240.01	59.5	44.5
8	05-13-85	30,000	"	9250.69	2802.89	43.5	-16
9	02-01-86	10,000	"	4750.00	2664.24	127.7	84.2
10	25-05-86	5,000	"	6193.42	605.17	10.8	-116.9
11	07-08-86	10,000	"	4305.22	2219.64	106.4	95.6
12	19-09-86	"	"	3662.05	1576.29	76.6	-30.8
13	26-08-87	5,000	"	2557.38	1514.15	145.1	68.6
14	22-10-87	10,000	"	4675.23	2589.47	124.1	-21
15	29-11-87	5,000	"	2037.10	994.22	95.3	-28
16	13-06-88	"	"	3006.80	1963.92	188.3	-93
17	27-09-89	"	"	1925.60	882.72	84.6	-103.6
18	26-10-89	"	"	1964.65	921.77	88.4	3.8

Source: BSPE Finance Department: 1990 E.C.; Tedbabe, p. 49.

Newsprint is an acutely scarce and expensive imported item and poor countries do not have the necessary foreign currency for imports. In Ethiopia, the proliferation of private newspapers has inevitably increased the demand for newsprint production and imports. Table 3 is illustrative of the enormous rise in printing and newsprint costs in the BSPE between 1993 and 1997.

---

1. Interviews: Befekadu, Fekade Mahtemeworq, Zelalem Hailu.

With regard to place of work, a large majority of newspapers (nine out of the ten interviewed) rented offices, mostly in groups of two or more and located in shabby quarters of the city. A small section of the private papers use the residences of their publishers (for instance, 'Beza') or rent a whole compound for a fairly large sum of money (for example, 'Reporter', 'The Sun', and 'Tobiya').[1] The quality of the offices owned or rented is extremely variable, ranging from the least furnished ones lacking even the basic equipment needed for such a commercial undertaking to ones equipped with the necessary Information and Communication Technologies (ICTs). Those papers belonging to the first category would have to hire such services and consequently incur additional expenses.[2]

Table 4. Condition of Places of Work of Some Selected Newspapers

No	Type of Renting	Size of Rented Office	Rent in Birr	Per cent
1	Alone	One Room	250-300	20
2	Alone/Two to Three	Two to Three Rooms	450 and above	50
3	Alone/Four and Above	Five Rooms and More	1,500 and above	30

Source: Information Gathered from Interviews with Selected Newspapers.

Advertising is a decisive element in determining the status of a newspaper enterprise. Its paucity, or even absence, in most private papers has limited the possibility of overcoming an array of difficulties. The position of advertising differs from paper to paper. There is a group of financially stable and influential newspapers (such as Reporter and Tobiya) enjoying mass circulation, where the advertisement space exceeds 40 per cent of the newspaper size and where advertisement revenue accounts for 50 per cent or more of their total income. At the other end of the advertising scale are found a large number of underequipped and understaffed papers, which fail to attract advertisements.[3] Success or failure to attract advertising is bound to impact on a newspaper's capacity to maintain a large staff with a reasonable salary, or to subscribe to or buy news. That in turn affects the paper's quality, its sales price and eventually its financial viability. Table 5 shows the financial status of a private newspaper, *Eth'op,* in the month of April 1998. It has a weekly circulation of about 5,000 copies (Tedbabe, 1990 E.C.: 68).

The survival of a paper under such extreme conditions has been made possible through reducing costs in such areas as salaries and payments for services, and financial assistance (as well as credit) from family members, relatives, wholesalers, and 'sources' based in foreign countries, and by working in low cost areas and maintaining a comparatively small staff. Some papers, in fact, have found the solution in sensational or irresponsible journalism, which has tended to attract a wide readership.

1. Interviews: Abebe, Alemtsehay, Befekadu, Biruk, Dawit, Eskindir, Ephrem, Sisay, Yohannes, Wole.
2. Tedbabe (1990 E.C.; 64-65) has found out in his survey of 20 papers that 80 per cent of them did not own computers.
3. Interview: Alemayehu, Alemtsehay, Goshu, Sisay, Wole.

Table 5. Financial Performance of *Eth'op* in the Month of April 1998

| | Income | | | Expenditure | |
No	Title	Amount in Birr	No	Title	Amount in Birr
1	Sale Price	13,200	1	Newsprint and printing costs	7848.0
2	Total	13,200	2	Office rent	200.0
			3	Posting	200.0
			4	Salary (Editor-in-chief)	600.0
			5	" (Deputy editor)	500.0
			6	" (Reporter)	400.0
			7	Freelancer (4x155)	620.0
			8	News purchased (4x75)	300.0
			9	Telephone	150.0
			10	Fax	150.0
			11	Entertainment (guests)	150.0
			12	Transport	300.0
			13	Computer service	680.0
			14	Commission (wholesaler)	800.0
			15	Subscription	160.0
			16	Purchase of perishable goods	150.0
				Total	13,208.0

Total Income	13,200
Total Expenses	13,208
Difference	-8

Source: *Eth'op.*

Process of Newspaper Distribution

> Any press and its agents shall have the right to disseminate news, information and other products of press in their possession (Article 8, Sub-title 2, Press Law: 34/1992).

It is no use having a first class newspaper only to find that it is late in reaching its target or, even worse, as it happens at times, it fails altogether to be delivered to many potential readers. Newspaper circulation in Ethiopia is an arduous struggle in view, particularly, of the absence of a good network of transport and communication facilities. A system of newspaper distribution has evolved in the course of the last eight years during which the private press enterprise has been in existence. At the beginning, publication of newspapers, which were few in number (three in 1992 and twenty-nine in 1993), was handled by the proprietors themselves. Acquisition of newspapers for distribution was possible only on payment in cash to the publishers. However, with a significant increase in the number of new titles as of 1994 (sixty-four in total) the importance of credit and of distributors grew correspondingly. In the process a new network of newspaper distribution came into being, consisting of two different groups of newspapers and a channel of distribution made up of whole-sale distributors, retail distributors, and vendors.[1]

The first part of the network refers to a select few papers (classified here as Category 1, such as Reporter and Tobiya) which have a wide circulation and readership and are, therefore, influential and financially stable. They handle publication and circulation themselves, the latter through full time employees, the circulation managers. To the second category belong a considerable number of newspapers (Category 2, such as Goh, Mebruk, and Ma'ebel) which are, in most cases, financially

---

1. Interviews: Fekade, Sisay, Zelalem.

shaky and whose publication and circulation are entrusted to a few established wholesalers.[1] With respect to the channel of distribution there is an evolving pattern which reflects the distinction outlined above.

A brief exposition of the roles of two of the most important operatives involved in the distribution system, vendors and wholesalers, is essential. A significant proportion of the newspaper vendors are young, male, and have a poor social and educational background. The Gurage vendors, in particular, use a pre-existing traditional Gurage trading network and experience in small-scale business. This has emerged as an outstanding phenomenon in the private press enterprise.[2]

The rise of wholesale distributors is equally inextricably linked with the history of the private press. These come from backgrounds as varied socially as booksellers, newspaper vendors and unemployed youth. Educationally, they include elementary and high school graduates and dropouts. Their initial capital has been obtained partly through their own occupational skills and endeavors and partly by the skillful manipulation of a variety of networks such as partnership and patronage. Within a period of a few years, the more successful ones have managed to create an effective distribution network.[3]

Many of the wholesalers work independently. But sometimes they join up in a group of two or three. They have offices that they use alone, in groups or in partnership with publishers. In the case of "Category 1" papers, their role is limited to wholesale acquisition of papers on credit or on payment in full or in part and their distribution in return for a commission of 40 per cent. Concerning "Category 2" papers, some wholesalers control distribution as well as circulation of a significant number of newspapers.[4]

The money which wholesalers need for newspaper publication and distribution is acquired in at least two main ways: money taken from their own personal accounts and that which is collected, in a retrospective way, from retail distributors and vendors. The latter is a common practice whereby retailers and vendors who have received newspapers from wholesalers- publishers on credit are expected to pay after the sale of the papers is completed and a day or two before publication begins.[5]

Newspaper distribution follows a network that has evolved in the course of the development of the private press. The wholesaler–publisher is entrusted with the task of apportioning newspapers the number of which is proportionate to the financial strength of the receivers (retailers and vendors) and the size of readership of the area they come from. Non-publishing wholesalers representing different sectors of the capital and important provincial towns receive from the wholesaler-publisher their share on the basis of the request they tabled prior to publication. Areas like Mercato receive the largest number of newspapers owing partly to the larger size of readership there and partly to the existence of wholesalers responsible for distributing newspapers to provincial towns.[6]

The transaction is conducted in two major ways: through prior payment by those whose credit is not yet firmly established and on credit, which is the dominant medium of transaction. Business operation on credit applies only to those who live in Addis Ababa and who are well known. Its extension to provincial distributors is a

1. Interviews: Alemtsehay, Alemayehu, Biruk, Befekadu, Fekade, Goshu, Wole. See also Tedbabe (1990 E.C.: 76).
2. Interviews: Alemtsehay, Yonas.
3. Interviews: Fekade, Tedbabe, Zelalem.
4. Interviews: Alemtsehay, Fekade, Goshu, Mekonnen Desalegn, Tesfa, Zekarias.
5. Interviews: Shafi, Negash.
6. Interviews: Fekade, Mekonnen, Zekarias, Zelalem.

rarity in view of experiences of absconding. Transaction on credit goes down to the level of vendors who after having received the newspapers on credit are expected to pay the following day from their sales.

The price of a newspaper increases progressively depending on the level of acquisition. For instance, a wholesaler–publisher sells a single copy of a weekly (5,000 copies, eight pages, single colour paper) for a unit price of 0.66 cents (with, however, a fluctuating unit cost of production) to a retail distributor with four cents profit (00.4x5,000=200). A retailer sells the same paper to a newspaper vendor for 0.75 cents earning nine cents (00.9x5,000=450). The vendors eventually dispose of the paper to the readers for one Birr with a profit of 0.25 Birr (0.25x5,000=1,250). (This price description does not apply to papers like Addis Tribune, Reporter, and Tobiya, for which the reader pays Birr 1.50.)[1]

Accordingly, the weekly income of the proprietor is Birr 1,138.80 which is obtained by deducting printing and newsprint costs (Birr 1,962) and the profits of wholesaler–publisher (200), retailer (450) and vendor (1,250). The margin of profit of the proprietor, retailer and vendor is insignificant in view of the high weekly cost of production sustained by the former and the large number of operatives represented in the latter two. The greatest beneficiary is, therefore, the wholesaler-publisher who would earn Birr 200 as a 4 per cent commission on every weekly paper of 5,000 copies. If he were publishing four papers a week his weekly income would be Birr 800 and his monthly earning, Birr 3,200. There is now a pattern evolving as a reaction to this diminishing margin of profit, particularly for the proprietors. It is a network of circulation that establishes a direct link between the proprietor–publisher > wholesaler (or proprietor > wholesaler–publisher) and the vendor by removing the retailers.[2]

The catchment area of most private newspapers is confined to the capital and a few provincial towns. Newspaper delivery to the reader follows a pattern which may be defined as stepped—distribution, beginning from a publisher's office to a station in Addis Ababa and then to a major provincial town and finally to smaller towns. In Addis Ababa, a number of quarters are selected as major distribution stations. Such stations also serve as distribution centers for provincial towns located near and far. A typical example in this respect is Mercato, the largest receiver of private newspapers and the biggest distribution center with the longest hours of distribution to areas in the capital and most provincial towns.[3] Most newspapers are delivered to the readership by vendors selling at newsstands located at important meeting points. English language newspapers are sold in supermarkets, restaurants and areas frequented by the rich and the educated, Ethiopians and foreigners alike, through either subscription or direct purchase.

Circulation of a newspaper is a whole day undertaking. Newspapers are distributed to vendors between 6:00 am (at times 5:30 am) and 7:00 a.m. Heavy circulation begins from the time of acquisition to10:00 a.m. in the morning and from 5:00 to 6:00 p.m. in the afternoon, the latter coinciding with the end of working day for most employees. The lowest level of newspaper circulation and discount sale price belong to the period between 6:00 and 9:00 p.m. There are areas (like Arat Kilo) where evening circulation at a reduced price is common. There are, in fact, groups of individuals who usually come to such areas from 5:00 to 6:00 p.m. to buy unsold

---

1. Interviews: Befekadu, Tedbabe. Obtaining financial information was a problem of considerable magnitude. When such information was given, it was as much incomplete as it was embellished.
2. Interviews: Befekadu, Tedbabe.
3. Interviews: Fekade, Shafi, Mekonnen Zerihun.

papers in bulk for about 0.35 cents each which they dispose of later for 0.50 cents. On the surface a vendor who sells a paper at a discount for resale might appear to lose. This is, however, offset by hiring papers out to readers for temporary reading for a certain fee.[1]

Contrary to the earlier years, multiple readership is now becoming a common practice. At present newspapers might change hands a dozen times on a single day. This is done as hawkers hire them out by the hour at a charge to each client of about one-tenth of the full price; that is a minimum of ten cents for a one Birr paper and twenty cents for one that costs a Birr and fifty cents. Under such circumstances, a newspaper vendor prefers to engage in hiring papers out to readers for a flexible fee for much of the day and then disposing of them later at a discount ranging from 35 to 50 cents.[2]

Problems of Establishment, Growth and Survival

The existence of some kind of understanding between the private press and the government is fundamental to the status of the press. In countries like Ethiopia where democracy is at an experimental stage and the concept of professional communication is novel, the journalist is suspect. The private press is, in fact, continually walking a tightrope and destined to offend the authorities, irrespective of whether it is careful and tactful or otherwise. In addition to this reciprocal suspicion the growth of the independent press is retarded by such practical problems as low literacy rate and shortage of qualified personnel, high poverty level, and financial difficulties. In the following section some outstanding problems of the private press will be outlined.

The Press Law: Proclamation No. 34/1992

The press law of the Transitional Government of Ethiopia (Proc. No. 34/1992) could be taken as a significant achievement in the process of political liberalisation. However, in practice, rather than regulating the activities of the private press the law has been stifling its growth through an array of punitive and prohibitive articles. In fact, many people are led to believe that this contradictory legal document was promulgated less by the desire to promote press freedom than by political expediency (Ethiopia, 1994:136). To begin with, some of the provisions in the press law were drafted on the basis of articles enshrined in the Penal Code of 1955 and the Civil Code of 1957. Thus, relevant articles of both codes cited in the press law would have the same binding power as those of the press law. The result is multiplication as well as duplication of legal provisions which, complex and confusing as they are, can be and often are invoked against journalists critical of the government.

The press law itself is full of restrictive provisions and has been declared "most undemocratic" (Ethiopia, 1994: 136), with heavy-handed penalties for offences or breaches that are considered petty by other laws of the country. Article 8, sub-title 3 which introduces a distinction between news and information is like an "odious and inexcusable tax upon political knowledge" (Harrison, 1974: 75) denying the press an important source of hard news (in contradistinction to Article 8, sub-title 1). In Article 10, sub-title 2 (A-D), restrictions against circulation of certain news

---

1. Interviews: Abebe, Fekade, Shafi.
2. Interviews: Fekade, Shafi.

items are so broadly stated that they are always open to abuse and that many journalists find them difficult to understand and act accordingly. Beside the inherent problems lying with the law itself, its provisions were (and still are) ignored by officials of the government. These include forced closure of sources of information in violation of Article 8 sub-title 4, A and B, and uncooperativeness of officials denying transparency and accountability contrary to the provision in Article 19.[1]

The penalties for violation, say, of any of the obligations under Article 10 are both multiple and exorbitant, ranging from one to three years imprisonment or a fine of Birr ten thousand to fifty thousand, or both. This provision for inordinate penalty is destined to increase as the government uses its powers to charge and punish journalists and publishers for a variety of contraventions and through the application of stipulations of the Penal Code. The inherent limitations of the press law, its lack of detailed provisions, the multiplication of repressive legislations and the absence of a genuinely independent and experienced judiciary are all impediments to the rise of a journalism of high professional standards. The importance of the press law as a legal guarantee of freedom of expression is thus seriously compromised by a restrictive legal machinery (Nigatu, 1986 E.C.: 19).

Consequently, many journalists and publishers have been harassed, intimidated, detained, imprisoned and/or fined, often in violation of the laws of the country including the constitution. Besides this, harassment and beating of newspaper vendors have been common, particularly in the early days of the press, thereby causing a reduction in the sale of newspapers. There have been arbitrary (with no formal court warrant) and extended (from 48 hours up to several months) detentions, in violation of Article 17, sub-title 2 and Article 19, sub-title 3 of the constitution of the Federal Democratic Republic of Ethiopia. The situation is further complicated by the practice of collective charging and detention and demand of exorbitant bail money. For instance, with regard to bail the lowest demanded of a journalist on a single charge until 1998 was Birr 2,000 and the highest Birr 50,000. In multiple charges the range is said to be between Birr 5,000 and Birr 280,000. In addition to money, residential houses, cars and licenses were used to bail journalists out. This has been partially responsible for the closure of several periodicals and the flight of a good number of the more professional and qualified members of the private press.[2] This, however, does not mean that government actions always lack legal justification. Many members of the private press have been prosecuted and penalized for committing crimes such as publishing false news and for inaccurate and irresponsible reporting.[3]

Economic Constraints

In developing countries like Ethiopia, newspaper publishing is not an attractive business proposition given the multiplicity of problems such as: shortage of capital for investment, ever increasing printing and newsprint costs under conditions of scarcity and foreign exchange control, the paucity of advertising and sales, and absence of trained and experienced staff for technical and editorial production and management. Newspaper circulation is hindered by low literacy rate, high poverty level, lack of motivation and established channels of distribution. Many people have, thus, been turning to businesses that are safer, more profitable and do not incur political complications and the considerable risk of running a newspaper. In Ethiopia, the in-

1. Interviews: Befekadu, Dawit, Sisay.
2. Interviews: Goshu, Sisay, Wole. See also Tedbabe (1990 E.C.: 42, 47–48).
3. Interviews: Biruk, Yonas. See also Tedbabe (1990 E.C.: 48).

cipient private press has been struggling to survive and be profitable in the face of such formidable problems. With few exceptions, private papers operate with only a slight margin of profit.

The high cost of newsprint, induced by the sharp increase on newsprint prices in the world market, coupled with a high printing cost, rendered a number of private papers financially weak and unstable. The tremendous increase in printing and newsprint costs (89.4 per cent between 1993 and 1997) and in the sales price of a newspaper (314 per cent, from 0.35 cents in 1992 to 1.10 cents in 1997 for an eight page, single colour paper) is illustrative of the difficulties facing the emerging independent press enterprise in Ethiopia (ODA, 1996; 35; Tedbabe, 1990 E.C.: 49-50). The procurement of equipment such as computers, printers, fax, e-mail and internet facilities is seriously hampered by the poor financial standing of most newspapers. Poor conditions of work (such as working in low quality, heavily congested and inadequately provided premises) are additional indicators of the scarcity of resources in the private press.[1]

The situation is made even worse by the underdevelopment of advertising in Ethiopia. One of the peculiar characteristics of the newspaper business is that the cost of production is almost invariably higher than sales price. Discrepancy between revenue and expenditure (due to reduced total sales) would usually exist even in times when a newspaper is properly costed and sold at a profitable price. For the paper to survive, the gap has to be bridged by other means ranging from the common to the unethical: commercial advertising, subsidy by government, organisations or individuals, and blackmail.[2] While subsidy and unethical practices are less common in the Ethiopian situation, commercial advertising, a fundamental factor behind the success or failure of a newspaper business, is very limited. This could be ascribed to the comparatively low level of business and commercial activity and the novelty of sales promotion. Under such circumstances, the financial capacity or the inclination to advertise is confined to a few manufacturers or traders. These hard, inescapable economic facts are principal reasons for the low circulation and poor quality of many papers and the bankruptcy and closure of others.[3]

Only a few newspapers benefit from positive changes in advertising. In only a handful of private newspapers (like Addis Tribune, Reporter, and Tobiya) is advertising claimed to have accounted for, on average, 40 per cent of their total space, providing something between one-third and two-thirds of their total revenue. A slightly larger number of papers (such as The Sun) claim that they have a ratio of news to advertising reaching 80:20. In a vast majority of the papers (for instance, Goh), the ratio is 90:10, or they have no advertising at all.[4] This situation is as much an outcome of their limited circulation as it is of the poor economic standing of the readership. The perception that these papers are of low quality, antagonistic to the government in power, and full of political scandal and "purient or salacious stories" (Ethiopia: 1994: 138) and the consequent fear of association with such "libelious" papers have discouraged the flow of advertising from private or government sources.

Stepping up circulation to increase revenue from sales and to build the basis on which advertising rates can be established and space sold is a problem as formidable as that of venturing into a newspaper enterprise in the first place. In addition to the low literacy rate, prevalent poverty (which is partly responsible for multiple reader-

1. Interviews: Befekadu, Sisay, Zegeye.
2. Interviews: Sisay, Yonas, Yohannes. See also Sommerlad (1966: 72-73).
3. Interviews: Sisay, Yonas.
4. Interviews: Abebe, Alemtsehay, Ephrem, Wole.

ship of papers), and poor reading culture (or motivation), there is an underdeveloped system of newspaper distribution in the capital and in the provinces. In the latter, in fact, the problem of distribution increases progressively as one moves further from the center. In relatively remote areas, for instance, papers are never to be seen and when they are they are frequently several days old on arrival and might be sold for twice their original price (ODA,1996:39; Sommerlad, 1966: 74–75).

Newspaper distribution is also seriously constrained by government measures to stop or limit newspaper accessibility to areas outside the capital. This act emanates from the official characterization of most private newspapers as anti-government. This has been diligently pursued, particularly in 1994 and 1995, by relevant organs of the government, in flagrant violation of the press law (see, for instance, Article 8, sub-title 2). There were even cases where newspapers sent to the provinces were confiscated and burnt. Newspaper distributors based in provincial towns were also detained. Newspaper vendors in the capital and other major provincial towns were harassed and beaten.[1]

Except for an occasional explosion in newspaper production and circulation, such as in the early days of the Ethio-Eritrean conflict in 1998, the general trend nowadays is for distribution to decrease. This is due, among other things, to what may be referred to as "communal reading" of papers and "newspaper hiring", practices which are becoming increasingly appealing to both readers and vendors. Both practices have tended to discourage readers from buying papers to read or vendors from acquiring a large number of papers for sale.[2] Hiring and communal reading are, in fact, a reflection partly of poverty and partly of the low captivating power of several newspapers. This practice, though beneficial to the toiling vendors, could be inimical to the growth of a viable free press.

Professional-Ethical Problems

One major obstacle to newspaper development is the problem of staff, a key factor in the successful launching of a newspaper. People with the knowledge and skills required to design a newspaper, provide an attractive editorial content and deal with such vital issues as supplies, finance, advertising and circulation, are in short supply. Pathetically poor conditions of work and rates of pay combined with the low status of the profession have made it an uphill struggle for Ethiopian journalism to attract talent. The problem is particularly acute with regard to editorial staff. The number of qualified and experienced journalists is incommensurate with that of the private newspapers under circulation. Concentration of the few qualified journalists in a small number of newspapers (like 'Reporter' and 'Tobiya') has limited the possibility of disseminating journalistic knowledge and experience. Many newspapers are run by underqualified individuals with little or no experience, let alone training.[3]

An increasing number of journalists have attended short-term ("crash") training workshops and seminars organized in the capital by several foreign organizations, alone or in collaboration with local counterparts, focussing on such areas as basic journalism, news gathering and reporting, feature and editorial writing, newspaper management and handling of technical issues. Notwithstanding their positive contribution, the utility of these workshops and seminars has been seriously limited by

---

1. Interviews: Abebe, Alemtsehay, Ephrem, Wole.
2. Publishers and EFPJA have tried hard, but in vain, to put an end to this chronic tendency towards undermining the progress of an independent press enterprise.
3. Interviews: Alemtsehay, Befekadu, Ephrem, Goshu, Yonas.

the fact that they were conducted, in most cases, in a language few of the trainees understood, that is English. Moreover these courses have been short and intermittent and too technical to comprehend and to apply to current Ethiopian realities. Besides this, most private newspapers were too understaffed to spare people for the workshops. Representation of the private press in the training programmes and workshops of the Ethiopian Mass Media Training Institute (founded in 1995 with the aim of training journalists working in the government media) has so far been negligible. The closure after one and half years of a privately owned school for training in basic journalistic skills has worsened the problem.[1]

All this is reflected in low journalistic standards and ethics in many papers. This is clearly seen in the rampancy of misquoting, misinterpreting, and plagiarism, the focus on trivial issues, poor layout, subjectivity, sensationalism, fixation on most sordid and volatile issues, obscenity and outright lies. Many papers could, in fact, safely be described as collections of opinions and all the above rather than as sources of information (ODA, 1996: 36; Tedbabe, 1990 E.C.: 69, 72).

The use of what has come to be known as tapela is a typical index of this downward slide of many papers. Tapela (a term originally used to denote the travel directions of taxis in Addis Ababa) refers here to unemployed or underemployed, literate or semi-literate individuals who are recruited for a small fee by newspaper publishers as pro forma "editors". The tapela have no real influence on editing the newspaper, but are in practice hired to represent a paper in court, and to be prosecuted and bear the consequences of its decisions instead of the one who really edits the paper.[2] In most cases such unqualified tapela are used in low quality papers where the driving force is not standard or ethics but profit.[3] Thus, for instance, lies are made into news. The person who is penalized for publication of such news is the editor, according to the press law (Article 10, sub-title 3(1)). In repeated cases the tapela have been in prison in his place. Some of these tapela know that what they are paid for is a punishable undertaking, but nonetheless carry on in order to survive. But there are several tapela who, illiterate as they are, are completely unaware of what is written in the papers for which they serve as "editors".[4]

Conclusion

The private press in Ethiopia, as in other developing countries under similar circumstances, could be said to be reminiscent of the press in more developed areas a century ago. This applies to its multiplicity, urban concentration, economic insecurity, limited advertising, comparatively small circulation, relatively untrained staff and, frequently, modest equipment.

Another important distinctive feature of the private press in Ethiopia is polarization. The private press in Ethiopia has begun life not as an instrument of government but as a rebel. Accordingly, the story it presents, interlocked as it is at every point with the political and social changes in the country, is a saga of valor in the defence and, to a large extent, the fostering of the democratization process.

---

1. Interviews: Biruk, Dawit, Qidist, Netsanet, Sisay.
2. Interviews: Bekefaku, Dawit, Goshu, Tedbabe, Yohannes. Editors were used as fronts and were also subject to frequent reshuffling. This was in response to fear of loss of qualified editors and subsequent suspension or closure of newspapers. The problem with such an arrangement is that the employee might not be as much committed to the paper as was his/her predecessor.
3. Interviews: Biruk, Ephrem, Yonas. See also Ethiopia (1994:132–134).
4. Interviews: Ephrem, Biruk.

The independent press has, despite its infancy, been informative, daring and remarkably outspoken. It has vigorously and audaciously reported on topics of national concern and of absorbing interest to readers. At the same time, the private press has been libellous, uninvesitigative, gullible, irresponsible and highly sensational. For some papers, the boundary between news reporting and news making is, in fact, blurred.

In the process of evolution, full of trials and tribulations, the private press has come to assume an outspokenly partisan character. This intense feeling which is partly due to the exclusionary policies and practices of the government in power as well as to the urban origin of most private journalists, has indeed become a mark of identification of a large number of private newspapers. The mutual antipathy and war of words between the Ethiopian Journalists' Association and the Ethiopian Free Press Journalists' Association is demonstrative of this polarization. It may be argued that this is also an acute manifestation of a tradition of political intolerance as witnessed in the infighting and consequent fratricide (sororicide too) between various political groupings in the country's recent history. Instead of a pluralistic press representing a wide spectrum of opinions there is, therefore, now a partisan press serving as the mouthpiece of a polarized population. The term "polarization" should not suggest, however, that the private press has had a monolithic stand vis-à-vis the government.

The private press in Ethiopia has a great potential to give voice to the interests of the "grass roots". The existence of a viable and vibrant press is one of the foundations of democracy. The experience of many countries, such as those in Latin America, reveals the importance to democracy of a state tempered by "a pluralistic, autonomously organized civil society to check the power of the state and give expression to popular interests" (Smith, 1996: 166; Diamond and Linz, 1989: 27–39; Dessalegn, 1991: 1–22). The private press, as an integral part of civil society, can thus be an important force, a "fourth estate", empowering the poor, listening to the "voices from below", fostering a responsive and accountable government and contributing to the vitality of democracy in Ethiopia.

Informants (interviewed in Addis Ababa, August–December 1999)

No.	Name	Job Description
1	Abebe Tadesse	Editor-in-chief (*Capital*)
2	Alemayehu Fanta	Reporter (*Addis Tribune*)
3	Alemtsehay Mengistu	Editor (*Reporter*)
4	Befekadu Moreda	Editor-in-chief, proprietor (*Tomar*)
5	Biruk Kebede	Managing Editor (*Beza*) Finance Department BSPEI
6	Danie	Editor-in-chief, proprietor (*Fiameta*)
7	Dawit Kebede	Editor-in-chief (*The Sun*)
8	Ephrem Endale	Editor-in-chief, proprietor (*Menelik*)
9	Eskindir Nega	Wholesaler, publisher
10	Fekade Mahetemeworq	Senior editor (*Tobiya*)
11	Goshu Moges	Newspaper vendor
12	Hailu	Wholesaler, publisher
13	Mekonnen Desalegn	Wholesaler, publisher
14	Mekonnen Zerihu	Retail distributor
15	Negash	Ex editor-in-chief and director of Mahider (*A'Emro*)
16	Netsant Tesfaye	Deputy editor-in-chief
17	Qidist Belachew	Newspaper vendor
18	Shaf	Proprietor (*Eth'op*)
19	Sisay Agena	Reporter (*Reporter*)
20	Tedbabe Tilahun	Veteran journalist
21	Teferi Wosen	Manager *(Tobiya)*
22	Wole Gurmu	Proprietor *Goh* and *Moresh*
23	Yohannis Abebe	Has a lot of experience in the private press
24	Yonas Fikre	Editor-in-Chief (*Genanaw*)
25	Zegeye Haile	Proprietor
26	Zekarias Tesfa	Wholesaler, publisher
27	Zelalem Hailu	Wholesaler, publisher

References

Aalen, Lovise and Siegfried Pausewang, 2001: *Withering Democracy: Local Elections in Ethiopia.* February/March 2001. Oslo: Norwegian Institute of Human Rights, Working Paper 2001:07.

Aalen, Lovise and Siegfried Pausewang, 2002: *Ethiopia 2001: Local Elections in the Southern Region.* Oslo: Norwegian Institute of Human Rights, NORDEM Report 03/2002.

Abebe Zegeye and Siegfried Pausewang (eds), 1994: *Ethiopia in Change: Peasantry, Nationalism and Democracy.* London and New York: British Academic Press.

Abélès, Marc, 1981: "In Search of the Monarch: Introduction of the State among the Gamo of Ethiopia", in Donald Crummey and C.C. Stewart, *Modes of Production in Africa: The Precolonial Era.* Beverley Hills & London: Sage Publications.

Abraham Hussein and Habtamu Wondimu, n.d.: *BaSelteñña Qwanqwa Tanagari Hezb Ya'Azarenat Barbare Hebratasab Bahel-na Tarik.* Addis Ababa.

Agri-Service Ethiopia, 2000: *Proceedings of the Panel Discussion on the Role and Contribution of NGOs in Rural Development in Ethiopia.* Addis Ababa: Agri-Service Ethiopia.

Ake, C., 1995: "The democratisation of disempowerment", in J. Hippler (ed.) *The Democratisation of Disempowerment.* London: Pluto Press.

Alamayahu Nari Wergaso, 1985 EC: *Ässat YaGurage Bahel-na YaItyopya Masaratawi Tarik.* Vol. I. Addis Ababa.

Amoako, K.Y., 2000: *Perspectives on Africa's Development. Selected Speeches.* New York: United Nations.

Andargatchew Tiruneh, 1993: *The Ethiopian Revolution 1974–1987: A Transformation from an Aristocratic to a Totalitarian Autocracy.* Cambridge: Cambridge University Press.

Andreassen, Bård-Anders, 1995: "Menneskerettigheter og bistanden", in Nils Chr. Stenseth, Kjetil Paulsen and Rolf Karlsen (eds), *Afrika—natur, samfunn og bistand.* Oslo: Ad Notam Gyldendal.

Ansah, P.A.V., 1991: "The Legal and Political Framework of Free and Pluralistic Press in Africa." *Working Document Prepared for the United Nations and UNESCO Seminar on Promoting an Independent and Pluralistic African Press,* 29 April to 3 May, 1991. Windhoek, Namibia.

Aspen, Harald, 1989: "Aspects of the distribution and utilization of land, labour, and capital in a rural community: The case of one Peasant Association in Northern Shäwa, Ethiopia". Paper presented at the *Workshop on Problems and Prospects of Rural Development in Ethiopia,* arranged by Institute of Development Research, Addis Ababa University, Nazareth 1–2 December 1989.

Aspen, Harald, 1993: *Competition and Co-operation. North Ethiopian Peasant Households and Their Resource Base.* Working Papers on Ethiopian Development, No. 7. Centre for Environment and Development, University of Trondheim.

Aspen, Harald, 1994: "Spirits, Mediums and Human Worlds. The Amhara Peasants of the North Ethiopian Highlands and their Traditions of Knowledge." Dr.art. dissertation, Department of Social Anthropology, University of Trondheim.

Aspen, Harald, 1995: *The 1995 National and Regional Elections in Ethiopia: Local Perspectives.* Working Papers on Ethiopian Development, No. 10. Centre for Environment and Development, University of Trondheim.

Aspen, Harald, 1997: "What Is Culture? Amhara Creativity as a Case in Point", in Katsuyoshi et al., (eds) *Ethiopia in Broader Perspective. Papers of the XIIIth International Conference on Ethiopian Studies, Kyoto, 12–17 December 1997.* Kyoto: Shokado Booksellers.

Atkinson, Paul and Martyn Hammersley, 1993: Ethnography. Principles in Practice. Second Edition. London and New York: Tavistock

Babbie, Earl, 1992: *The Practice of Social Research.* Belmont, Cal.: Wadsworth Publishing Company.

Bahru Zewde, 1984: "Economic Origins of the Absolutist State in Ethiopia (1916–1935)", in *Journal of Ethiopian Studies,* XVII.

Bahru Zewde, 1991: *A history of modern Ethiopia.* Addis Ababa: Addis Ababa University Press.

Bahru Zewde, 1999: "The Burden of History. The Constraints and Challenges of the Democratization Process in Ethiopia", in Hyslop (ed.) .

Baldwin, G., 1988: "Non-Governmental Organisations and African Development: An Inquiry", (mimeo).

Barkan, Joel D., et al., 1998: *Decentralization and Democratization in Sub-Saharan Africa.* Occasional Papers 45 through 49, International Programs, University of Iowa.

Barth, Fredrik, 1993: "A Personal View of Present Tasks and Priorities in Cultural and Social Anthropology", in Robert Borofsky (ed.) *Assessing Cultural Anthropology.* Columbus: McGraw-Hill.

Barton, Frank, 1966: *The Press in Africa. Nairobi:* East African Publishing House.

Bayleyegn Tasew, 2000: "An Anyuaa (Anuak) Myth and Its Implication in 'Kwor'". Paper presented at the National Workshop of the Ethiopian chapter of OSSREA, February 2000.

Bazaara, Nyangabyaki, 2000: *Contemporary Civil Society and the Democratization Process in Uganda: A Preliminary Exploration.* Kampala: Centre for Basic Research.

Beebe, James, 2001: *Rapid Assessment Process. An Introduction.* Walnut Creek, New York, Oxford: Altamira.

Beets, N. et al., 1988: "Big and Still Beautiful: Enquiry on the Efficiency of Three INGOs in South Asia", Programme Evaluation, 32.

Bekalu Mola,1997. "Collaboration for Development between Non-Governmental Organisations and Community Based Organisations: An Analysis of Case Studies in Ethiopia". Unpublished report prepared for SPADE, Addis Ababa.

Blair, Harry, 1997: "Donors, Democratisation and Civil Society", in Hume and Edwards (eds), pp. 23–42.

Boafo, S.T. Kwame, 1992: "Mass Media in Africa: Constraints and Possible Solutions", in *Media Development,* vol. 39, no. 1.

Bratton, Michael, 1989: "The Politics of Government-NGO Relations in Africa", in *World Development,* vol. 17, no. 4, pp. 569–587.

Bratton, Michael, 1989b: "Beyond the State: Civil Society and Associational Life in Africa", in *World Politics,* vol. XLI, no. 3, pp. 407-30.

Braukämper, Ulrich, 1983: *Die Kambata. Geschichte und Gesellschaft eines südäthiopischen Bauernvolkes.* Wiesbaden: Steiner.

Brodhead, T., 1987: "NGOs: In One Year, Out the Other?" in *World Development,* supplement, 15, pp. 1–6.

Brosio, Giorgio and Sanjeev Gupta, 1997: "Fiscal Federalism in Ethiopia", in IMF, *Fiscal Federalism in Theory and Practice,* Washington D.C.

Brøgger, Jan, 1986: *Belief and experience among the Sidamo: A case study towards an anthropology of knowledge.* Oslo/Oxford: Norwegian University Press/ Oxford University Press.

Calvert, S. and P. Calvert, 1996: *Politics and Society in the Third World: An Introduction.* Hertfordshire: Prentice Hall.

Campbell, Will, 1996: *The Potential for Donor Mediation in NGO-State Relations: An Ethiopian Case Study.* IDS Working Paper 33. Brighton: Institute of Development Studies.

CEDAW, 1979: *Convention on the Elimination of all Forms of Discrimination against Women.* United Nations.

Cernea, M., 1988: "Non-Governmental Organisations and Local Development", in *World Bank Discussion Paper,* 40.

Chernetsov, Sevir B., 1993: "On the Origin of the Amhara", in *St. Petersburg Journal of African Studies,* 1, 97–103.

Civil Code, The Ethiopian, 1960, Addis Ababa: *Negarit Gazeta,* procl. no. 165, year 19, no.2.

Clapham, Christopher, 1988: *Transformation and Continuity in Revolutionary Ethiopia.* Cambridge: Cambridge University Press.

Clapham, C., 1992. "Haile Selassie's government revisited", in *The Sixth MSU Conference on Northeast Africa:* Michigan State University Conference Compendium. East Lansing: Michigan State University Press.

Clark, Jeffrey, 1991: *Democratising Development: The Role of Voluntary Organisations.* London: Earthscan Publishers.

Clark, J., 2000: *Civil Society, NGOs, and Development in Ethiopia. A Snapshot View.* Washington, D.C.: World Bank.

Clayton, Andrew, P. Oakley and J. Taylor, 2000: *Civil Society Organizations and Service Provision.* Civil Society and Social Movements Paper No. 2. Geneva: UNRISD.

Cohen, J.M., 1974: *Local Government Reform in Ethiopia: An Analysis of the Problems and Prospects of the* Awraja *Self-Government Proposal with Particular Emphasis on Rural Change.* Washington, D.C.: USAID.

Constitution of the Federal Democratic Republic of Ethiopia, Addis Ababa, 8 December 1994, English translation; Amharic original version published in *Negarit Gazeta* in 1995.

Costantinos Berhe, 1993: "Enhancing Dialogue, Cooperation and Interface between Governments and Development Organisations", unpublished report to the UN-ECA, Addis Ababa.

CRDA (Christian Relief and Development Association), 1995: *Directory of Members.* Addis Ababa

CRDA, 1997: *Principles and Laws Regulating NGOs.* Addis Ababa, March.

CRDA, 1998–2000: *CRDA News.* Addis Ababa.

CRDA, 1998: 25 *Years of Service to the People of Ethiopia.* Silver Jubilee Anniversary Issue. Addis Ababa, May.

CRDA, 1999 *Directories of Members and Associate Members.* Various Years.

CRDA, Addis Ababa. *Code of Conduct for NGOs in Ethiopia.* Addis Ababa.

Crook, R. and J. Manor, 1991: *Enhancing Participation and Institutional Performance: Democratic Decentralization in South Asia and West Africa.* A Report to ESCOR, the Overseas Development Administration.

CSA, (Central Statistical Authority), 1990: *Population and housing census 1984: Analytical report on Sidamo region.* Addis Ababa: Office of the Population and Housing Census Commission.

CSO, (Central Statistical Office), 1984: *Population and Housing Census, Preliminary Report.* Addis Ababa, Ethiopia

Davey, Kenneth, et.al., 1996: *Urban Management: The Challenge of Growth.* Hong Kong: Avebury.

Davidson, Basil, 1992: *The Black Man's Burden. Africa and the Curse of the Nation-State.* London: James Currey.

De Waal, Alex, 1997: *Famine Crimes: Politics and the Disaster Relief Industry in Africa.* London/ Bloomington: James Currey/Indiana University Press.

Dejene Aredo, 1993: *The Informal and Semi-Formal Financial Sector in Ethiopia.* AERC Research Paper 21. African Economic Research Consortium, Nairobi.

Denbaru Alamu et al., 1987 EC. *Gogot: YaGurage Beheresab Tarik, Bahel-na Qwanqwa.* Walqite.

Dessalegn Rahmato, 1984: *Agrarian Reform in Ethiopia.* Uppsala: Scandinavian Institute of African Studies.

Dessalegn Rahmato, 1991: *Famine and Survival Strategies: A Case Study from Northeast Ethiopia.* Uppsala: The Scandinavian Institute of African Studies.

Dessalegn Rahmato, 1991: "Investing in Tradition. Peasants and Rural Institutions in Post-Revolution Ethiopia", in *Sociologia Ruralis,* 2/3, pp. 169–83.

Dessalegn Rahmato, 1992:. "The land question and reform policy: Issues for debate", in *Dialogue,* Journal of Addis Ababa Teachers' Association, 3rd series, 7(1), 43–47.

Dessalegn Rahmato, 1993: "Agrarian Change and Agrarian Crisis: State and Peasantry in Ethiopia", in *Africa,* vol. 62, no.1, pp. 36-55.

Dessalegn Rahmato, 1994: "The Unquiet Countryside. The Collapse of 'Socialism' and Rural Agitations, 1990–1991", in Abebe Zegeye and S. Pausewang (eds), pp. 242–79.

Dessalegn Rahmato, 1994: "Land policy in Ethiopia at the crossroads", in Dessalegn Rahmato (ed.), *Land tenure and land policy in Ethiopia after the Derg.* Trondheim: Center for Environment and Development, University of Trondheim.

Desta Kassa, 1993: Desta Kassa, *Content Analysis of Protest Oral Poems Composed against the Därg regime.* BA Thesis. Department of Ethiopian Languages & Literature, AAU.

Desta Lorenso, 1982: *Yekambata Hebretasab Balaejotchinna Sinekalachew.* Addis Ababa: Addis Ababa University (B.A. thesis).

DEVAW, (Declaration on the Elimination of Violence against Women), 1994: United Nations.

Devereux, Stephen and John Hoddinott, 1993: *Fieldwork in Developing Countries.* Boulder, Col.: Lynne Rienner.

Diamond, L. and Linz, J.J., 1989: "Introduction: Politics, Society and Democracy in Latin America", in Diamond, L., Linz, J.J. and Lipset, S.M. (eds), *Democracy in Developing Countries,* Vol. 4, Boulder: Lyme Rienner.

Donham, James, D. and W. (eds), 1986: *The Southern Marches of Imperial Ethiopia. Essays in History and Social Anthropology.* Cambridge University Press.

DPPC, (Disaster Prevention and Preparedness Commission) 2000: (Unpublished data sources). No other details.

Duchrow, Ulrich and Franz Josef Hinkelammert, 2002: *Leben ist mehr als Kapital. Alternativen zur globalen Diktatur des Eigentums.* Oberursel: Publik-Forum.

Duffield, Mark and John Prendergast, 1994: *Without Troops and Tanks: Humanitarian Intervention in Ethiopia and Eritrea*. Lawrenceville, NJ: Red Sea Press.

EEA, (Ethiopian Economic Association), 1992–1996: *Ethiopian Journal of Economics*. Biannual journal.

EEA, 1992–1998. *Annual Conference Proceedings*. Addis Ababa: EEA.

EEA, 1997–1999. *Economic Focus*. Bimonthly bulletin.

Ege, Svein, 1997: *The Promised Land: The Amhara Land Redistribution of 1997*. Working Papers on Ethiopian Development No. 12. Norwegian University of Science and Technology, Centre for Environment and Development.

EHRCO, (Ethiopian Human Rights Council) 1995: *Democracy, Rule of Law and Human Rights in Ethiopia: Rhetoric and Practice*. Addis Ababa.

EHRCO, 1996: Compiled Reports of EHRCO (December 12, 1991 to May 6, 1996). Addis Ababa.

EHRCO, 1998–1999. Special Report Nos. 12–26 (Amharic). Addis Ababa.

Elliot, C., 1987: "Some Aspects of Relations between the North and the South in the NGO Sector", in *World Development*, 15, supplement.

ESSWA, (Ethiopian Society of Sociologists, Social Workers and Anthropologists), 1998: *The Role of Indigenous Associations and Institutions in Development. Abstracts*. Workshop organized by ESSWA, Addis Ababa, 25–26 June.

ESTC, (Ethiopian Science and Technology Commission) 1998: *Profile of Science and Technology Professional Associations in Ethiopia*. Addis Ababa.

Ethiopia—Transition to Democracy, 1994: Proceedings of a Workshop. Washington D.C.: National Academy Press.

EWLA, (Ethiopian Women Lawyers Association), 1997–1998: *Dimtsachen*. Newsletter.

EWLA, 1999: *EWLA Activity Report* (Jan. 1996–Oct. 1999). Addis Ababa.

EWLA, 2000: *Berchi*. The Journal of Ethiopian Women Lawyers Association, 1,1, Summer 2000.

EWLA, Various years. Research Documents.

Fantu Cheru and Ole Zethner, 1989: "Report on the Evaluation of UNSO Fuelwood Projects in Nazareth and Debre Birhan, Washington". Unpublished MS.

Fasil Gebrekiros, 1990: "An Assessment of the Economic Consequences of Drought, Crop Failure and Famine in Ethiopia, 1973/74–1985/86", in *Ethiopian Journal of Development Research*, IDR Monograph Series, 1, pp. 1–57.

FDRE, (Federal Democratic Republic of Ethiopia), 1995: "A Proclamation of the Constitution of the Federal Democratic Republic of Ethiopia", in *Negarit Gazetta*, 1st year, No.1, Addis Ababa.

Fecadu Gadamu, 1972: *Ethnic Associations in Ethiopia and the Maintenance of Urban Rural Relationships with Special Reference to the Alemgana-Wolamo Road Construction Association*. PhD thesis. University of London.

Fecadu Gadamu, 1986. "Traditional Social Setting of the Kistane (Soddo) in Central Ethiopia", in *Paideuma*, 32.

Fekade Azeze, 1997: "Bibliography of BA Theses on Oral Literature". Submitted to the Department of Ethiopian Languages & Literature at Addis Ababa University, 1966–1997. Unpublished. In Amharic and English.

Fekade Azeze, 1998: *Unheard Voices. Drought, Famine and God in Ethiopian Oral Poetry*. Addis Ababa: Addis Ababa University Press and Norwegian University of Science and Technology.

Fekade Azeze, 1999: "Major Contents of Oral Literatures Told in Amharic", in Habtamu Wondimu et al., *Non-Formal Education in Ethiopia: An Overview of the Current Situation*. Proceedings of the National Conference on the Situation of Non-Formal Education in Ethiopia, 12–13 March 1999. Addis Ababa: University Printing Press.

Fenta Mandefro, 1998: "Decentralization in Post-Derg Ethiopia: Aspects of Federal-Regional Relations". Unpublished M.A. Thesis. Regional and Local Development Studies, Addis Ababa University.

Fowler, A., 1990: *The Political Dimension of NGO Expansion in Eastern and Southern Africa and the Role of International Aid*. Nairobi: The Ford Foundation.

Fowler, A., 1991: "The Role of NGOs in Changing State-Society Relations: Perspectives from Eastern and Southern Africa", in *Development Policy Review*, 9, pp. 53–84.

Freire, Paulo, 1970: *Pedagogy of the Oppressed*. New York: Salisbury Press.

Friedman, John, 1992: *Empowerment: The Politics of Alternative Development*. Cambridge, MA: Blackwell Publishers.

Gebreyesus Hailemariam, 1991: *The Guragué and Their Culture*. New York: Vantage Press.

Gebru Tareke, 1991: *Ethiopia. Power and Protest. Peasants in the Twentieth Century*. Cambridge University Press.

Getachew Demeke, 1990: "Potentials and Limitations of Local NGOs: Lessons from Eastern and Southern Africa". Unpublished.

Getahun Asres, 1992: *A Study of Oral Poetry on Peasant Producers' Cooperatives in Däbrä Marqös District*. BA Thesis. Department of Ethiopian Languages & Literature, Addis Ababa University.

Getie Gelaye, 1994: *The Social Life of Yetnora Agricultural Producers' Cooperative and Its Reflections in Amharic Oral Poetry*. MA Thesis. School of Graduate Studies, Addis Ababa University.

Getie Gelaye, 1999: "Peasant Poetics and State Discourse in Ethiopia: Amharic Oral Poetry as a Response to the 1996–97 Land Redistribution Policy", in *Northeast African Studies*, vol. 6, no. 1–2, pp. 171–206.

Gramsci, A., 1971: *Selections from the Prison Notebooks*. Edited and translated by Q. Hoare and G.N. Smith. New York: International Publishers.

Gran, G., 1983: *Development by People: Citizen Construction of a Just World*. New York: Praeger.

Gurage People's Self-Help Development Organization, 1991 EC: *Ägurage Qicha* (Kitcha: The Gurage Customary Law). Addis Ababa.

Habteselassie Hagos, 1998: *The Role of Professional and Trade Associations in the Development of Managerial Capacity*. Proceedings of the Third Annual Conference on Management in Ethiopia, pp. 215–56. Ethiopian Management Professionals Association, Addis Ababa.

Halliday, F. and M. Molyneux, 1981: *The Ethiopian Revolution*. London: Verso.

Hamer, J., 1970: "Sidamo generational class cycles: A political gerontocracy", in *Africa*, vol. 40, no. 1, pp. 50–70.

Hamer, J., 1976: "Myth, ritual and authority of elders in an Ethiopian society", in *Africa*, vol. 46, no. 4, pp. 327–339.

Hamer, J., 1987: *Humane Development. Participation and change among the Sidama of Ethiopia*. Tuscaloosa, AL: The University of Alabama Press.

Hamer, J., 1998: "The Sidama of Ethiopia and Rational Communication Action in Policy and Dispute Settlement", in Anthropos, vol. 93, pp. 137–153.

Hancock, G., 1985: *Ethiopia: The Challenge of Hunger*. London: Victor Gollancz.

Harrison, Stanley, 1974: *Poor Men's Guardians: A Record of the Struggles for Democratic Newspaper Press, 1763–1973*. London: Lawrence and Wishart.

Hawthorn, Geoffry, 1993: "Sub-Saharan Africa" in David Held (ed.) 1993, *Prospects for Democracy*, pp. 330–354. Cambridge: Polity Press.

Hearn, Julie, 1999: *Foreign Aid, Democratization and Civil Society in Africa: A Study of South Africa, Ghana and Uganda*. Discussion Paper No. 368, Institute of Development Studies, University of Sussex, Brighton.

Hellinger, D., 1987: "NGOs and the Large Aid Donors", in *World Development*, vol. 15, pp. 135–143.

Hillima Taddesse, 1996: *Discriminatory Norms and Application against Women in the Ethiopian Family Law*. EWLA sponsored Research Report, Nov. 1996.

Hillima Taddesse, 1997: *The Rights of Women under Ethiopian Penal Law*. EWLA sponsored Research Report, Feb. 1997.

Hovde, R. L., 1992: "NGOs in Ethiopia: The Role of the CRDA". A Paper prepared for the Third International Conference of Research on Voluntary and Non-Profit Organisations", Indianapolis.

Hume, David and M. Edwards (eds), 1997: *NGOs, States and Donors. Too Close for Comfort? London*: Macmillan Press.

Hussein Ahmed, 1994: *Islam and Islamic Discourse in Ethiopia (1973–1993)*. Papers of the 12th International Conference of Ethiopian Studies. Michigan State University, 5–10 September 1994. New Jersey: The Red Sea Press.

Hyden, Goran, and Michael Bratton (eds), 1992: *Governance and Politics in Africa*. Boulder/London: Lynne Rienner.

Hyslop, Jonathan (ed.), 1999: *African Democracy in the Era of Globalization*. Johannesburg: Witwatersrand University Press.

IEG, (Imperial Government of Ethiopia), 1960: *The Civil Code of the Empire of Ethiopia*. Addis Ababa: Berhanena Selam Printing Press.

International Panel, 2000: *Rwanda: The Preventable Genocide.* The Report of (the) International Panel of Eminent Personalities to Investigate the 1994 Genocide in Rwanda and the Surrounding Events. Addis Ababa: IPEP (OAU).

Jacobsen, Knut Dahl, 1964: *Teknisk hjelp og politisk struktur.* Oslo: Universitetsforlaget.

Kajese, K. T., 1990: "African NGO Decolonisation: A Critical Choice for the 1990s", in *Critical Choices for the NGO Community: African Development in the 1990s,* Seminar Proceedings, 30, Proceedings of A Conference held at the African Studies Centre, University of Edinburgh, 24–25 May.

Kasate-Berhan Tasama, 1951 EC: *Ya'Amareñña Mazgaba Qalat.* Addis Ababa.

Kasfir, Nelson (ed.) 1998: *Civil Society and Democracy in Africa.* London: Frank Cass.

Kassahun Berhanu, 1994a: "Philanthropic Giving in Traditional Ethiopia". Paper Presented at the *Second East African Workshop on Fund Raising by Voluntary Organisations,* Nairobi, 25–29 April.

Kassahun Berhanu, 1994b: *An Overview of Selected Ethiopian NGOs: A Baseline Situational Survey.* A Report to the Swedish Save the Children, Addis Ababa.

Keesing, R. M., 1981: *Cultural Anthropology: A Contemporary Perspective,* second edition. New York: Holt Rinehart and Winston.

Keesing, R. M., 1987: "Anthropology as Interpretive Quest", in *Current Anthropology,* vol. 38, no. 2.

Kellas, James G., 1991: *The Politics of Nationalism and Ethnicity.* London: MacMillan.

Keller, Edmond J., 1988: *Revolutionary Ethiopia: From Empire to People's Republic.* Bloomington: University of Indiana Press.

Kerina, Kakuna, 1996: *Clampdown in Addis : Ethiopia's Journalists at Risk.* New York: Committee to Protect Journalists.

Lakoff, G., 1987: *Women, fire, and dangerous things.* Chicago: University of Chicago Press.

Lapiso G. Dilebo, 1982: *Ye Etiopia Rejjim Ye mengistinna Ye hizb Tarik.* Addis Ababa: Addis Ababa University (B.A. thesis).

Leemans, A.F., 1970: *Changing Patterns of Local Government.* The Hague: International Union of Local Authorities.

Lefort, René, 1983: Ethiopia: *An Heretical Revoultion.* London: Zed Press.

Levine, D. N., 1974: *Greater Ethiopia.* Chicago: The University of Chicago Press.

Lewis, I. M., 1970: "Wealth, influence and prestige among Shoa Galla", in E. Tuden, & L. Plotnikov (eds), *Social stratification in Africa.* New York: The Free Press.

Litvack, J., J. Ahmad and R. Bird, 1998: *Rethinking Decentralization in Developing Countries.* World Bank Sector Series. Washington, D.C.

Lowe, Chris, 1999: "Civil Society, the Domestic Realm, History and Democracy in South Africa", in Jonathan Hyslop (1999).

Makumbe, John M., 1998: "Decentralization, Democracy and Development in Zimbabwe", in Barkan, Joel D., et al., (eds), *Decentralization and Democratization in Sub-Saharan Africa.* Occasional Papers 45 through 49, International Programs, University of Iowa.

Mamdani, Mahmood, 1996: *Citizen and Subject. Contemporary Africa and the Legacy of Late Colonialism.* Princeton: Princeton University Press.

Markakis, John, (1974): *Ethiopia: Anatomy of a traditional polity.* Oxford: Clarendon Press.

Markakis, John and Nega Ayele, 1978: *Class and Revolution in Ethiopia.* Nottingham: Spokesman.

Mazrui, Ali A., 2001: "Who Killed Democracy in Africa? Clues of the Past, Concerns of the Future". Keynote address, Conference on *Democracy, Sustainable Development and Poverty: Are They Compatible?* 4–6 December 2001, Addis Ababa.

MEDAC, (Ministry of Development and Cooperation), 1998: *Regional Development in Ethiopia: An Overview.* Department of Regional Planning and Development, Addis Ababa.

Meheret Ayenew, 1998: *Some Preliminary Observations on Institutional and Administrative Gaps in Ethiopia's Decentralization Process.* Working Paper No. 1, Regional and Local Development Studies, Addis Ababa University, September, 1998.

Mesfin Woldemariam, 1984: *Rural Vulnerability to Famine in Ethiopia, 1958–1977.* New Delhi: Vikas.

MoA (Ministry of Agriculture) / Hans Hurni, 1995: *Guidelines for Development Agents on Soil Conservation in Ethiopia.* Bern/Addis Ababa, 1986, 1995 (reprint, unchanged).

Molla Makonnen, 1993: *Content Analysis of Political Oral Poems Told in Qobbo Wäräda.* BA Thesis. Department of Ethiopian Languages & Literature, Addis Ababa University.

Mulugeta Dejenu, Amare Lemma, Solomon Tekle Mariam and Siegfried Pausewang, 1987/1991: *Achefer-Shebadino-Study*, Bergen/Rome/Addis Ababa: FAO / CMI.

Mulugeta Mesganaw, 1992: *Content Analysis of Protest Poetry (oral) Collected from Semada Wäräda*. BA Thesis. Department of Ethiopian Languages & Literature, Addis Ababa University.

Ng'ethe, Njuguna, 1998: "The Politics of Democratization through Decentralization in Kenya: Policy and Practice with Emphasis on the District Focus for Rural Development", in Barkan, Joel et al., (eds).

Nigatu Tesfaye, 1986 E.C.: "Ye Press Netsanet Hig Weyis ye Gazetegna Mekicha Awaj". *Guramayle*.

NIHR, (Norwegian Institute of Human Rights), 1992: *Local and Regional Elections in Ethiopia 21 Jume 1992*. Report of the Norwegian Observer Group. (Human Rights Report No.1.) Oslo: Norwegian Institute of Human Rights.

OAU, 2000: *The Preventable Genocide. Report of the International Panel of Eminent Personalities to Investigate the 1994 Genocide in Rwanda and the Surrounding Events*. Addis Ababa: OAU-IPEP.

ODA, (Overseas Development Administration), 1996: *Ethiopian Media Review*.

OECD, 1998: *Voluntary Aid for Development: The Role of NGOs*. Paris.

Ogden, C. K. and I. A. Richards, 1946: *The meaning of meaning: A study of the influence of language upon thought and of the science of symbolism* (8th ed.). New York: Harcout, Brace & World.

Olowu, Dele, 1993: *African Local Governments as Instruments of Economic and Social Development*. The Hague: The International Union of Local Authorities.

Original Woldegiorgis, 1997: *The Functions of Family Arbitrators Under the Ethiopian Civil Code*. EWLA sponsored Research Report, May 1997.

Ottaway, M. and D., 1978: *Ethiopia: Empire in Revolution*. New York: Africana.

Ottaway, Marina, 1990: "The crisis of the Ethiopian state and economy", in Marina Ottaway (ed.), *The political economy of Ethiopia*. New York: Praeger.

Padron, M., 1987: "Non-Governmental Development Organisations: From Develop-ment Aid to Development Cooperation", in *World Development*, vol. 15, pp. 69–77.

Pankhurst, Alula, 1992: *Resettlement and Famine in Ethiopia: The Villagers' Experience*. Manchester/New York: Manchester University Press.

Pankhurst, Richard, 1958: "Self-Help in Ethiopia", in *Ethiopian Observer*, vol. 11, no. 11.

Pankhurst, Richard, 1966: "The Great Ethiopian Famine of 1888–1892. A New Assessment", in *Journal of the History of Medicine and Allied Sciences*, vol. 21, pp. 95–134.

Pausewang, Siegfried, 1983: *Peasants, Land and Society: A Social History of Land Reform in Ethiopia*. München: Weltforum Verlag.

Pausewang, Siegfried, Fantu Cheru, Stefan Bruene, Eshetu Chole (eds) 1990: *Ethiopia: Rural Development Options*. London: ZED Books

Pausewang, Siegfried, 1992: "Regional and Woreda elections, Ethiopia, June 21, 1992". Unpublished report.

Pausewang, Siegfried, 1994: *The 1994 Election and Democracy in Ethiopia*, Oslo: Norwegian Institute of Human Rights, (Human Rights Report No. 4).

Pausewang, Siegfried, 1994a: "Local Democracy and Central Control" in Abebe Zegeye and Siegfried Pausewang (eds), *Ethiopia in Change. Peasantry, Nationalism and Democracy*, pp. 207–230. London & New York: British Academic Press.

Pausewang, Siegfried, 1996: "Ethiopia", in *Human Rights in Developing Countries Yearbook 1996*, pp. 195–247. The Hague: Kluwer .

Pausewang, Siegfried, 1996a: *ENWEYAY (Let's Discuss)*. Report from a training programme for democracy in rural Ethiopia (Working Paper WP 1996:8). Bergen: CMI.

Pausewang, Siegfried, 2001: *Ethiopia 2001: In-between Elections in Southern Region* (Working Paper 2001:14). Oslo: Norwegian Institute of Human Rights.

Pausewang, Siegfried, Kjetil Tronvoll and Lovise Aalen (eds) 2002: *Ethiopia since the Derg: A Decade of Democratic Pretension and Performance*. London: ZED Books.

PDRE, (Peoples' Democratic Republic of Ethiopia), 1987: "A Proclamation to Establish Autonomous and Administrative Regions of the Peoples' Democratic Republic of Ethiopia", in *Negarit Gazetta*, 47th year, No. 14, Addis Ababa. Penal Code, The Ethiopian, 1958, Addis Ababa: Negarit Gazeta, procl. no. 158, year 16 no.1.

PMAC (Preliminary Military Administrative Council) 1975: *Public Ownership of Rural Lands Proclamation.* 34 Year/No. 26. Proclamation No. 31 of 1975, pp.93–101, Made on 29 April 1975. Came into force as of 4 March 1975.

PMAC, 1978: *A Proclamation to Provide for the Establishment of Cooperative Societies.* Proclamation No. 138 of 1978, pp.41–48. Made on 3rd March 1978.

Poluha, Eva, 1993: "'Democracy' in Africa—interpretations of priorities". Paper presented at the session of the Pan African Association of Social Anthropologists entitled "African Anthropology: Past, Present and Future Perspectives", during the *13th International Congress of Anthropological and Ethnological Sciences,* Mexico.

Poluha, Eva, 1994: "Publicity and the Wielding of Power—A Case from Gojjam, Ethiopia", in Harold G. Marcus (ed.) *New Trends in Ethiopian Studies: Papers of the 12th International Conference of Ethiopian Studies,* vol. 2, pp. 954–965. *Lawrenceville, NJ:* Red Sea Press.

Poluha, Eva, 1995: *The 1995 Ethiopian Elections Viewed from the Grassroots. A Report to Sida.* Stockholm: SIDA.

Publik-Forum, 2002: Globalisierung. Die Welt zerstören oder gestalten", Dossier in the periodical *Publik-Forum,* Oberursel, Feb. 2002.

Ritchald and Chazan (eds) 1988: *The precarious balance.* Boulder, CO: Westview Press.

Rogers, E. M., 1983: *Diffusion of innovations.* New York: The Free Press.

Rondinelli, D.A. et al., 1989: "Analyzing Decentralization Policies in Developing Countries: A Political Economy Framework", in *Development and Change,* vol.20.

Rondinelli, D.A., John R. Nellis and G. S. Cheema, 1983: *Decentralization in Developing Countries.* Washington, D.C.: The World Bank.

Schneider, Wolfgang, 1990: *Leipziger Demontagebuch.* Leipzig and Weimar: Kiepenheuer.

Sen, Amarthya, 1981: *Poverty and Famines: An Essay on Entitlement and Deprivation.* Clarendon Press, Oxford.

Sen, Amarthya, 1992: *Inequality Reexamined.* Cambridge, Mass.: Harvard University Press.

Sen, Amarthya, 1999: *Development as Freedom.* London: Oxford University Press.

Sen, Amarthya, 1999: "The Value of Democracy", in *Development Outreach,* vol.1, no. 1, Washington DC: The World Bank Institute,.

Seyoum Gebregziabher, 1969: "The Development of Some Institutions Concerned with Labour Relations in Ethiopia". Mimeo. Haile Selassie University, Department of Public Administration, Addis Ababa.

Shack, William, 1966. *The Gurage. A People of the Ensete Culture.* London: Oxford University Press.

Shack, William, 1968: "On Gurage Judicial Structure and African Political Theory", in *Journal of Ethiopian Studies,* vol. 2.

Shimelis, Bonsa, "A History of Kistane Migration to 1974". (Forthcoming.)

Sida, 1999: *ANRS/Sida Co-operation in Rural Development. Programme Report of the 1999 Sida Technical Supervision Team.* Prepared by Alemayehu Mengistu, Ian Christoplos, Dessalegn Rahmato and Nils-Ivar Isaksson. Stockholm: Sida.

Sidama Zone Planning and Economic Development Department, 1995: *Socio-Economic Profile of Sidama Administrative Zone.* Awassa, Ethiopia

Sileshi Sisaye, 1979: "Urban Migration and the Labor Movement in Ethiopia", in *Proceedings of the Fifth International Conference of Ethiopian Studies,* April 13–16, 1978. Chicago Circle: University of Illinois.

Sklar, Richard, 1999: "The Significance of Mixed Government in Southern African Studies", in Jonathan Hyslop (ed.).

Slater, David, 1989: "Territorial Power and the Peripheral State: The Issue of Decentralization", in *Development and Change,* vol. 20, London: Sage.

Smillie, I., 1995: *The Alms Bazaar: Altruism under Fire—Non-Profit Organisations and International Development.* London: Intermediate Technology Publications.

Smith, B. C., 1980: "Measuring Decentralization", in Jones, G.W. (ed.), *New Approaches to the Study of Central-Local Government Relationships.* London: GOWER, SSRC.

Smith, B.C., 1985: *Decentralization: The Territorial Dimension of the State.* London: George Allen & Unwin.

Smith, B.L., 1996: "Sustainable Local Democracy", in *Public Administration and Development,* vol.16.

Soddo Gordanna Sababa Dimokrasiyawi Taklalocha, 1986 EC: *YaKestane Gurage Emat (Hezb) Tarik.* Addis Ababa.

Sommerlad, E. Lloyd, 1966: *The Press in Developing Countries.* Sydney: Sydney University Press.

Spradley, James P., 1980: *Participant Observation.* Chicago: Holt, Reinhart and Winston.

Stanley, S., and D. Karsten, 1968: *The luwa system of the Garbiccho sub-tribe of the Sidamo (Southern Ethiopia) as a special case of an age-set system.* Stuttgart, Germany: Paiduma.

Tecle Haimanot Gebre Selassie, 2000: *A Historical Survey of the Fuga Low-Caste Occupational Communities of South-Central Ethiopia.* PhD thesis. History, Addis Abeba University.

Tedbabe Tilahun, 1990 E.C: *Be Ethiyopia Ye Gil Pres Edgetina Chigroch.* B.A. Thesis, Ethiopian Languages and Literature, Addis Ababa University.

Teel, Leonard Ray and Ron Taylor, 1992: *An Introduction to Journalism: Into the Newsroom.* New Delhi: Prentice-Hall of India.

Teferi Abate, 1997a: "Land Redistribution and the Micro-Dynamics of Land Access and Use in Amhara: The Case of Two Communities in South Wollo" in Katsuyoshi Fukui, Eisei Kurimoto, and Masayoshi Shegeta (eds) *Ethiopia in Broader Perspective: Papers of the 13th International Conference of Ethiopian Studies,* vol. 2, pp. 768–797. Kyoto: Shokado Booksellers.

Teferi Abate, 1997b: "Struggle over Policy Loose-Ends: Idioms of Livelihood and the Many Ways of Obtaining and Losing Land in South Wollo, Amhara", paper presented at the Fourth Workshop of the Land Tenure Project, IDR, Addis Ababa 28–29 November 1997.

Teferi Abate, 2000: *Government Intervention and Socioeconomic Change in a Northeast Ethiopian Community: An Anthropological Study.* Ph.D. dissertation in social anthropology, Boston University.

Tegegne Teka, 1994: *International NGOs in Rural Development in Ethiopia: The Case of Wolaita Province,*Ph.D. Dissertation, University of Cambridge.

Tegegne Teka, 2000: *Internatonal Non-Governmental Organisations in Rural Development in Ethiopia.* Frankfurt am Main: Peter Lang.

Tesfaye Habiso, 1983: *Kambatanna Hadiyya Yeastedader Akababinna Yebiherasabotch Tarik Be-Etiopia Yetarik Gatsita.* Monograph in Amharic, Addis Ababa.

Tesfaye Tafesse, 1995: *Villagization in Northern Shewa, Ethiopia: Impact Assessment.* Münster: Politikwissenschaft Bd. 32. Zugh: Osnabrück, Univ., Diss. Lit Verlag.

Teshale Teshome, 1994: *The making of modern Ethiopia 1896–1974.* Lawrenceville, NJ: Red Sea Press.

TGE, (Transitional Government of Ethiopia), 1992: "A Proclamation to Provide for the Establishment of National/Regional Self-Governments", in *Negarit Gazetta,* 51st year, No, 7, Addis Ababa, Ethiopia.

TGE, 1994: *The Constitution of the Federal Democratic Republic of Ethiopia* (Unofficial English translation of the Amharic original), Addis Ababa, 8 December.

TGE, 1995, Proclamation No. 111/1995: "A Proclamation to Ensure the Conformity of the Electoral Law of Ethiopia Proclamation with the Constitution of the Federal Democratic Republic of Ethiopia" in *Negarit Gazeta* no. 9, 23 February 1995, pp. 148–165.

Tronvoll, Kjetil and Øyvind Aadland, 1995: *The process of democratisation in Ethiopia: An expression of popular participation or political resistance?* (Human Rights Report nr. 5). Oslo: Norwegian Institute of Human Rights.

Tronvoll, Kjetil and Siegfried Pausewang (eds), 2000: *The Ethiopian 2000 Elections: Democracy Advanced or Restricted?* Oslo: Norwegian Institute of Human Rights.

Tucker, S.P., 1998: *Ethiopia in Transition.* Writenet.

UNECA, (United Nations Economic Commission for Africa), n.d.: *Documenting Successful NGOs' Experience. A Case Study of Ethiopia.* Public Administration, Human Resources and Social Development Division, UNECA, Addis Ababa.

UNRISD, (United Nations Research Institute for Social Development), 2000: *Visible Hands: Taking Responsibility for Social Development.* Geneva: UNRISD.

Van Diesen, Arthur and Karen Walker, 1999: *The Changing Face of Aid to Ethiopia.* Christian Aid, London, January.

Van Rooy, A., 1998: *Civil Society and the Aid Industry.* London: Earthscan.

Vecchiato, N. L., 1985: *Culture, health, and socialism in Ethiopia: The Sidamo case.* Los Angeles: University of California.

Vestal, Theodore M., 1999: Ethiopia: *A Post Cold War African State.* Vestport/London: Praeger.

Warqu Tasfa (ed.), 1987 EC: *Aymallal.* Addis Ababa.

Webb, Patrick, J.v. Braun, Yisehac Yohannes, 1992: *Famine in Ethiopia: Policy Implications of Coping with Failure at National and Household Levels.* Research Report 92. Washington: IFPRI

Weston, A., 1994: "Reflections on NGOs, Sustainable Livelihoods, and Promoting an Enabling Environment".The North South Institute (unpublished).

Weston, W. W., and J.B. Brown, 1989: "The importance of patients' beliefs", in M. Stewart and D. Robes (eds), *Communication with medical patients* (pp. 77–85). Newbury Park, CA: Sage.

WFP, 1997: *Interim Evaluation of Project Ethiopia 2488.* Dok. WFP/EB.2R/97/2/Add.2.

WFP, 1998: *Policy Issues: WFP and the Environment.* Dok. WFP/EB.3/98/3.

WFP/CMI, 1994: *Canada/Norway/Netherlands: Evaluation of the World Food Programme.* ("Tripartite Evaluation"), Bergen/Quebec/Oslo/Amsterdam.

Worku Nida, 1983 EC: *Jabdu. YaGurage Bahel-na Tarik.* Addis Ababa.

World Bank, 1995: *World Development Report 1995.* New York: Oxford University Press.

World Bank, 1998: *Nurturing Civil Society at the World Bank.* Social Development Paper No. 24.Washington, D.C.: World Bank.

World Bank, 2000: Can Africa Claim the 21st Century? Washington: IBRD/ World Bank.

Wunsch, J. and D. Olowu, 1993: The Failure of the Centralized State. San Fransciso, California: ICS Press.

YaGordanna Shango Wogatge, 1986 EC: *YaGordanna Shango.* Addis Ababa.

YaGordanna Shango Wogatge, 1992 EC: *YaKestane Gurage Hezb YaGordanna Shango Bahlawi Matadadarya Danb.* Addis Ababa.

YaGurage Bet-na Nuro Azagaj Committee, 1948 EC: *Gurage-na Nurow.* Addis Ababa.

Yeraswork Admassie, 1988: *Impact and Sustainability Study of WFP—Assisted Project ETH 2488/ II Rehabilitation of Forest, Grazing and Agricultural Lands.* Addis Ababa: WFP.

Yersaswork Admassie, 1995: *Twenty Years to Nowhere. Property Rights, Land Management and Conservation in Ethiopia.* Ph.D. dissertation. Uppsala: Department of Sociology, Uppsala Univ.

Yigremew Adal, 1997a: "Rural Land Holding Readjustment and Rural Organizations in West Gojjam, Amhara Region: A Summary Report", Paper presented at the Fourth Workshop of the Land Tenure Project, Institute of Development Research, 28–29 November 1997.

Yigremew Adal, 1997b: "Rural Land Holding Readjustment in West Gojjam, Amhara Region", in *Ethiopian Journal of Development Research,* vol. 19, no. 2, pp. 57–89.

Yigremew Adal, 2000: "Preliminary Assessment of the Impacts of the Post-Derg Land Policy on Agricultural Production: A Case Study of Land Redistribution in Two Communities in Northwest Ethiopia", in Workneh Negatu et al. (eds), *Proceedings of the 4th Annual Conference of the Agricultural Economics Society of Ethiopia.* Addis Ababa: Agricultural Economics Society.

Yigremew Adal, 2001: *Land Redistribution and Female-Headed Households. A Study in Two Rural Communities in Northwest Ethiopia.* FSS Discussion Paper No. 5, November. Addis Ababa: Forum for Social Studies: .

Yä-märét kefefel plan, 1989: (Document in Amharic, Amhara Kelel Executive Committee, T'er 1989 EC).

Zawdu Nahusannay, 1993: *Content Analysis of Oral Poems Composed around Däbrä Tabor by Opposing or Supporting the Därg and EPRDF.* BA Thesis. Department of Ethiopian Languages & Literature, Addis Ababa University.

Zegeye Asfaw, 2000: "General Overview of NGOs in Ethiopia", in *Agri-Service Ethiopia,* 2000, pp.1–15.

Contributors

Øyvind Aadland is associate professor and director of the Extension and Consultancy Department of Gimlekollen School of Journalism and Communication in Kristiansand, Norway, and senior research affiliate at the Norwegian Institute of Human Rights at the University of Oslo. He has a masters degree from the Theological Faculty of Oslo University and M.A. and Ph.D in Crosscultural Communic ation from Northwestern University in Evanston, Illinois. He grew up in Ethiopia and has served as a priest in Mekane Yesus Church. He has had research experience in Ethiopia for the last six years.

Harald Aspen is associate professor in social anthropology at the Norwegian University of Science and Technology in Trondheim, Norway. He obtained his M.A. 1986 (with fieldwork in Gambia), and Ph.D. (dr. art.) in 1994 (fieldwork in Ethiopia). He has been working with Ethiopian issues since 1988, with several periods of fieldwork in Shäwa and south Wälo. His Ph.D. thesis is *Amhara Traditions of Knowledge. Spirit Mediums and Their Clients* (2001). He has published several articles and reports, among others *Competition and Co-operation. North Ethiopian Peasant Households and Their Resource Base* (1993); The 1995 National and Regional Elections in Ethiopia: Local Perspectives (1995); Poverty and Resources. Ethiopian Rural Realities (edited with Abdulhamid B. Kello (1999).

Bahru Zewde is professor of history at the University of Addis Ababa, specialising in modern Ethiopian history and intellectual history. He has a Ph.D. from London University. He is chairman of the Board of Advisers of the Forum for Social Studies and Resident Vice President of the Organisation for Social Science Research in Eastern and Southern Africa (OSSREA). Bahru is the author of a number of books and articles, including *A History and Modern Ethiopia* (1991) and *Pioneers of Change in Ethiopia: The Reform of the Early Twentieth Century* (forthcoming).

Dessalegn Rahmato is the manager of the Forum for Social Studies, an independent policy research institute established in 1998. He was for many years a senior research fellow at the Institute of Development Reserarch at Addis Ababa University. His research interest lies in agrarian change, land tenure food security, and environmental policy. He has published extensively on these topics. He is currently working on a manuscript on the process of agrarian change in Ethiopia over the last fifty years.

Svein Ege is senior researcher at the Department of Social Anthropology, Norwegian University of Technology and Science (NTNU). He is a historian and has published a book and several articles in Ethiopian history. He has worked extensively on development issues, in particular those related to land tenure and land use. He launched and was the first coordinator of the "Peasant Production and Development in Ethiopia" programme, a joint venture of NTNU and the Institute of Development Research, Addis Ababa University. In addition to his historical work he has edited anthologies and published several articles and a book on Ethiopian development issues. He is the author of *Class, State and Power in Africa: A Case Study of the Kingdom of Shäwa (Ethiopia) about 1840* (Wiesbaden 1996) and *The Promised Land: The Amhara Land Redistribution of 1997* (Trondheim 1997).

Fekade Azeze did his BA at Haile Selassie University (Addis Ababa) in Ethiopian Languages and Literature, his M.A. and Ph.D. in Literature at the University of Sheffied in England. He is now Associate Professor of Ethiopian and African Languages at the Institute of Lanugage Studies, Addis Ababa University. He is the author of four volumes of poems, three of which have already been published. He is keenly interested in oral literature. In 1988 he published a book entitled *Unheard Voices: Drought, Famine and God in Ethiopian Oral Poetry.*

Kassahun Berhanu is assistant professor at the Department of Political Science and International Relations of Addis Ababa University. Born in 1953, his education was interrupted by more than five years of political imprisonment under the military dictatorship of Mengistu. Released in 1982, Kassahun obtained his M.A. in the Hague in 1991 and his Ph.D. in Amsterdam in 2000. He is the author of several publications on elections, land allocation in resettlements, decentralisation and on democracy, state building and nationalities, His Ph.D. thesis was on Returnees, Resettlement and Power Relations. The Making of a Political Constituency in Humera, Ethiopia (Amsterdam 2000).

Meheret Ayenew is assistant professor of Public Management and Policy, Faculty of Business and Economics, Addis Ababa University. He received his B.A. degree from the same university and his Masters and Ph.D. degrees from the University of Pittsburgh and State University of New York–Albany in the United States, respectively. His interests include development management, governance and decentralisation.

Original Wolde Giorgis is a lawyer and an activist. She worked for the Ethiopian Women Lawyers Association (EWLA), as a defence lawyer and a councillor for women in legal and social difficulties. She has collected substantial material on the legal problems for women in Ethiopia and on individual cases. Original is a member of the Board of Advisers of the Forum of Social Studies. She has also written several articles on women, land and the law.

Siegfried Pausewang is a rural sociologist and a senior research fellow at the Chr. Michelsen Institute for Development and Human Rights in Bergen, Norway. He obtained his Ph.D. in sociology and political science in 1967 in Marburg, Germany. He has had research experience in Ethiopia since 1967 and was assistant professor in sociology at Addis Ababa University from 1967 to 1971. Since 1991 he has been following the democratisation process in Ethiopia, particularly in rural areas; he has produced studies on elections since 1991. His publications include among others *Land Reform in Ethiopia* (1977), *Land Tenure and Rural Society in Ethiopia* (1983), *Rural Development Options* (1989), *Ethiopia in Change* (1991), *Human Rights in Ethiopia* (1996), *Elections and Democratisation* (1992, 1993, 1994, 2000, 2001, and 2002).

Shimelis Bonsa is a lecturer and junior member of faculty in the History Department of Addis Ababa University, teaching Ethiopian and African history. He received his B.A. in 1990 and M.A. in 1997. His research interest is in class and ethnicity; urban economy; gender relations. He has produced research reports on the history of Gurage voluntary urban migration; Kistane Gurage voluntary associations; Kistane women market traders; Gurage shoe-shiners in the urban informal economy of Addis Ababa. His publications are *The History of Migration, Urbanisation and*

Urban Labour Undertakings of the Kistane Gurage (1997); *Survey of the Private Press 1991–1999* (2000); *A History of Kistane Migration to 1974* (forthcoming).

Yacob Arsano is assistant professor of political science and international relations at Addis Ababa University and a research associate at the Eidgenossische Technische Hochschule (Swiss Federal Institute of Technology in Zürich). He has taught courses in the areas of Hydropolitics and Comparative Politics. Yacob has produced numerous research reports on traditional institutions and resource conflict mitigation. His published contributions include: *Sharing Water Resources for Economic Co-operation in the Horn of Africa* (1996) and *Shrinking Resources of Ethiopian Pastoralists* (1998). At present Yacob is a Ph.D. candidate at the University of Zürich.